1918

1918
THE YEAR OF VICTORIES

MARTIN MARIX EVANS

This edition published in 2017 by Arcturus Publishing Limited
26/27 Bickels Yard, 151–153 Bermondsey Street,
London SE1 3HA

AD000001UK

Book design by Alex Ingr
Cover design by Dani Leigh
Maps by Alex Ingr and Simon Towey

Printed in the UK

CONTENTS

INTRODUCTION   7

PART ONE: **LESSONS OF WAR**

1 THE GERMAN EXPERIENCE   11

2 THE ALLIED EXPERIENCE   21

PART TWO: **THE GERMAN OFFENSIVES**

3 OPERATION MICHAEL   43

4 OPERATION GEORGETTE   71

5 OPERATION BLÜCHER-YORCK   87

6 THE FINAL OFFENSIVES   107

PART THREE: **THE GERMAN ARMY DESTROYED**

7 THE SOISSONS SALIENT   129

8 THE SOMME FRONT   155

9 THE AMERICANS ACT ALONE   177

10 WITH THE FRENCH IN CHAMPAGNE   197

11 THE DEFEAT OF THE GERMAN ARMY   207

FURTHER READING & SOURCES   238

BIBLIOGRAPHY   238

INDEX OF ARMIES, BATTLES & COMMANDERS   239

INTRODUCTION

THE FINAL MONTHS of the First World War were the ultimate test of two very different concepts of how the war should be fought. The Germans gambled in 1917 when they resumed unrestricted submarine warfare in an effort to impose a blockade on imports to Europe. They knew their decision was bound to bring the USA into the war, but decided that they would be able to defeat the Allies on the Western Front before significant American influence was felt. They hoped to achieve this by sophisticated use of artillery and new tactics developed for the infantry. The relevance of air power and tank warfare was not taken into account, and the expenditure of their soldiers' lives was accepted at comparatively high levels.

The political and practical consequences of heavy casualties were clear to the Allies. Their approach to winning the war was to develop what Professor Gary Sheffield has characterised as weapon systems, the balanced combination of infantry, artillery, armoured fighting vehicles and aircraft to overcome both fixed defence line and less structured, open warfare styles of resistance.

The efforts of both sides were dogged by error, misunderstanding, uncertainty and mistrust. They were made distressingly glorious by the valour and steadfastness of the fighting men. The search by the leaders for understanding, and thus victory, was an undertaking that it is both moving and rewarding to study; even more so if it is possible to avoid hindsight and manage genuinely to recreate the point of view of those who bore the terrible responsibility of command. Much remains to be done by scholars to achieve that end. This, therefore, is an account of the start of that process.

PART ONE
LESSONS OF WAR

1

THE GERMAN EXPERIENCE

BY NOVEMBER 1917, it was clear that Germany's chances of winning the war were becoming slimmer as time passed. If they could not defeat the Allies, or persuade one of them to make a separate peace in 1918, they would face certain defeat in 1919. The Allied blockade was preventing Germany's sea-borne imports from being shipped in, while the Allied convoy system denied the German U-boat blockade similar success. The Americans had entered the war in April 1917, with the consequence of putting victory in the war of industrial production beyond German reach. What was more, the build-up of American forces in Europe was now becoming significant and by the end of 1918 could be foreseen as being overwhelming. Of their adversaries the Germans thought that the French were highly professional and strongly motivated while the British were stubborn and tough, but lacking in operational sophistication and flexibility. Given that the French army had mutinied that year, unknown to the Germans, and being unable to foresee the events of the coming July and August, the inaccuracy of these assessments is understandable but was to prove a fatal error.

The German experience on the Western Front had been mainly of success in defence. Only two major offensive campaigns had been attempted so far: the initial invasion of France and Belgium in 1914 and the assault on Verdun. The first outran both their command and control capability and their supply lines, a lesson that went unheeded. The second was planned as a device to tempt France into suicidal counter-attacks, but a failure by the Germans to adhere to their strategy, allowing themselves to be drawn into the attack, counter-attack, counter-to-the-counter-attack sequence that is war of attrition, led to their failure. On the Eastern Front, however, they had enjoyed success in aggression and particularly in the weeks immediately prior to their late

1917 cogitations. On 3 September they had taken the Baltic port of Riga after a stunning artillery bombardment.

THE INVENTION OF THE FIREWALTZ

The nature of artillery had been transformed during the late nineteenth and early twentieth centuries, and the First World War is rightly seen as a conflict in which the gunners were supreme. The experience of the South African War between the British and the Boers (1899–1902) had shown the potential of the quick-firing field gun, a gun that used shells in cartridge cases, and guns that absorbed the recoil and did not need to be re-aimed with every firing. The war between Japan and Russia (1904–5) had demonstrated that artillery was best used from a distance, delivering indirect fire, as the gunners were too vulnerable to the new invention, the machine-gun. It also showed how effective heavy guns could be in destroying fortified positions. At the start of the First World War the hardware was available in the form of guns, but the ammunition was still fairly primitive and the way in which soldiers thought the guns could be used was quite simple.

The Germans in particular had developed heavy guns for use against fortifications; they were, after all, the people who planned to strike against the Belgian and French forts in what they foresaw as the most likely war to come. They had started the war with 5,086 field guns and 2,280 howitzers and heavier guns. By 1918 the field guns had only increased in numbers to 6,764 but the heavy guns had gone up to 12,286, indicating the importance they attached to counter-battery work, shooting at the enemy guns from afar, and an outlook influenced by the experience of static warfare. Heavy guns are not easily moved and re-deployed, but if you are operating in a trench war environment, and using guns with a range of tens of miles, that is acceptable. Such guns are obviously suited to the destruction of enemy fortifications and by 1917 were used in this way by both sides. However, as the British learned to their cost before Passchendaele, the destruction is not limited to the fortifications alone; the whole environment is smashed into fragments which, mixed with rain, creates a barrier to the advance as formidable as the defence it replaces.

The object of the exercise is not mere destruction. To succeed, the enemy's ability to resist and respond has to be neutralised. The man who transformed German artillery tactics was a reserve Lieutenant-Colonel, Georg Bruchmüller. He was born in Berlin on 11 December 1863 and served as a gunner both in heavy fortress artillery units, and as an instructor until he was invalided out of the army in 1913. When war broke out he was recalled to active duty on the Eastern Front and proved himself so effective that he was awarded the Blue Max, the Pour le Merite, the highest Prussian decoration, in May 1917. The key to this success was his recognition of the importance of neutralisation and the fact that it could be achieved more quickly and economically with what became known as the *Feuerwalze*, the Firewaltz. The name came from the orchestration of a number of elements in a sequence in time. Its objective was to break enemy morale, pin him in position and open the way to overcoming him with a massive assault.

To do this, Bruchmüller planned his bombardments with great precision. He used a mix of shells – gas of various types, high explosive and shrapnel. Fire was brought down at different times on different, precisely-defined targets. Instead of the days of shelling that preceded attacks in 1916 and 1917, he needed only hours. In its most simple form the bombardment went through three phases: first, a short attack on the enemy's command quarters and communications systems; second, fire on their artillery positions and, third, shelling of the infantry defences.

Bruchmüller organised his artillery into groupings with specific tasks to perform. The AKA (*Artillerie-Kampf-Artillerie*) was charged with the destruction of enemy artillery and used field guns because of their high rates of fire and the availability of ammunition in great quantity. The IKA (*Infanterie-Kampf-Artillerie*) was principally concerned with action against enemy infantry and were under the command of divisions. At corps level were the AKA and the long-range artillery, FEKA (*Fern-Kampf-Artillerie*), responsible for the attacks on deep-battle targets such as reserves. Finally, at field army level, were the heavy artillery groups known as SCHWEFLA (*Schwere Flachbahn*), heavy flat-trajectory, with responsibility for the destruction of major installations such as concrete shelters and railway bridges. Each of these might be required to act alone on in concert with another.

The selection of the appropriate gas or mix of gasses for a particular purpose was another of Bruchmüller's specialities. Mustard gas immobilises by causing blisters on skin and in the lungs and is long lasting, so was useful for shielding the flanks of an operation and for putting enemy gunners out of action. Gas-masks were proof against poison gas such as chlorine, but not against the non-lethal arsine which made the victim vomit. A mix of these therefore worked very well, the latter forcing the removal of the gas-mask in order to expose the target to the former and kill him. Arsine shells were marked with a blue cross, chlorine with green and the cocktail was called *Buntkreuz*, multi-coloured. The cold-blooded horror of the technique was not a characteristic of the Germans alone; this was becoming a highly technical war on all sides.

The final contribution to the effectiveness of Bruchmüller's bombardments was the element of surprise. In order to overcome the vagaries of weapon performance and atmospheric conditions it had been the custom to carry out test-firings. A shot would be directed at a target, the extent to which it missed taken into account, adjustments made and another one tried. Eventually the adjustments needed for the given gun, its ammunition, the wind and the weather would be determined and the process called registration would be complete. By this time the people on the receiving end would be well aware of what was going on. The problem was, of course, shared by the Allies and both sides devised methods of overcoming it. Captain Erich Pulkowski produced the German solution which involved test firing each gun at a location removed from the combat zone and establishing its performance as an individual weapon in a range of atmospheric conditions. It could then be fired on a target identified by map reference alone.

The effectiveness of Bruchmüller's methods was demonstrated at Riga in September 1917, and the colonel was moved to the Western Front in 1918 to organise the artillery for the German offensives.

THE INFANTRY

The German tank, the A7V as it was designated after the department responsible for its development, was a failure both in its performance and in the trivial number built. The tactical concepts that were to inform infantry training excluded the tank and the aircraft as well. While aircraft, reconnaissance, fighter and bomber, were significant, the possibility of domination of a land battle by command of the air was an idea that far outran the technical development of the flying machines of the time. Close support by *Schlachtstaffeln*, battle squadrons, was a requirement of the tactical plan, and no doubt seemed impressive at the time, but was not sufficiently formidable to make a great difference. The achievements of the German army in the forthcoming attacks were thus to depend on the abilities of the gunners and foot-soldiers alone.

In January 1918 General Erich Ludendorff had published *The Attack in Positional Warfare*, the work of Captain Hermann Geyer, which was the blueprint for the training of troops in readiness for the battles of that year. The German battalion, of which there were three to a regiment, consisted of four rifle companies with five light machine-guns and two mortars, a machine-gun company with twelve Maxims and a mortar platoon with four *Minenwerfer*. The tactics for Ludendorff's offensive grew out of this. Special training was to be given to all infantrymen to turn them into *Stosstruppen*, shock-troops, whose task was to punch a hole in the adversary's line and push on through, leaving it to following troops to clean up strongpoints by-passed by the initial attackers. The approach derived to an extent from the failure of German pillboxes and barbed wire to prevent British advances at Ypres in August and September of 1917, before the weather turned the field to a mud-bath. The shock-troops would be accompanied by a creeping barrage rather than following one, and would depend on grenades and light machine-guns, the new Bergmanns where available. Flares would be used to request a speeding-up of the barrage's progress and bugle calls would provide communication at the early stage, before telephone lines could be deployed.

The reduction of the strongpoints by the next wave was made possible by bringing forward man-hauled trench mortars, *Minenwerfer*, and field artillery with four horse-drawn guns to each regiment. By this means the Germans intended to breach the Allied line. Ludendorff was not inclined to worry much about what would happen next. He pointed out that they had broken through at Riga and all had followed from that satisfactorily and the October smashing of the Italian line at Caporetto using similar tactics in a more primitive form reinforced his confidence.

In a memorandum issued on 1 May 1918, based on the experience of the 28th Division in the March/April offensive, the German author, Captain Schmidt of the General Staff, discussed what he termed 'the battle in the intermediate zone' which he defined as the battle against an adversary who no longer has a continuous line of defence. This memo was acquired by the French who published it in their Fourth Army Bulletin of 23 July and GHQ, American Expeditionary Force issued it in English on 19 August 1918. The author's comments were, it seems, respected by his foes. He starts by speaking of another aspect of the new tactics, the 'battle of position' or the prepared attack for abolishing trench warfare. In this phase, after a prepared artillery attack, large masses of infantry, organised in depth, are launched at the same, pre-determined time and overcome the enemy by the act of advancing. It is with the next stage, the battle in the intermediate zone, that troubles begin. Here Captain Schmidt is recounting experience, not the pre-offensive theory of January 1918:

> *Once the barrage has ceased the attackers are exposed to machine-gun fire from the flanks, defensive artillery, tank attacks and infantry fire. The nature of the battle changes continually and the divisional command can do nothing to influence the fight in detail. It must concern itself with the supply of reserves to exploit areas of lesser resistance, and with artillery fire to secure flanks while the conduct of the fighting devolves on the junior commanders. A clear tactical insight, knowledge of other branches of the service, the faculty for*

rapid decision and high personal merit are the qualities which char-
acterise the victorious subordinate commander in the battle in the
intermediate zone.

Schmidt points out the long-term problem here; it depends on the quality of the field commanders, the captains, lieutenants and non-
commissioned officers on the battlefield itself. It also depends, he says,
on the support of other arms for the infantry's enterprise:

The battalion thus becomes a mixed body of troops composed of
companies of infantry and machine-guns, light trench mortars and
accompanying artillery... It permits the battalion commander to ful-
fil the duties which fall to his lot in the intermediate zone without
outside aid [my emphasis].

It is clear that the German tactical concept was a very powerful one and
that this combination of sophisticated artillery work and supplemented infantry operation presented a new, very real threat to the Allies. It
is also clear that the risks associated with it in practice are great, both
in terms of the losses likely to be sustained at the front and the difficulty of communication with, and control of, the fighting force.

THE FORMULATION OF PLANS

The signature of the Treaty of Brest-Litovsk on 3 March 1918 brought
the war between Russia and Germany to an end. It had been the
inevitable outcome of the revolution the previous autumn and the ces-
sation of hostilities on the Eastern front was assumed in German
planning. In November 1917 there were 150 German divisions on the
Western Front; by February there were 180 and by the end of March
another twelve would have arrived. Furthermore the forces that
Ludendorff could place in the forefront of the battle were to include
seven Guards units, three Bavarian regular divisions and a Marine division: all troops of the highest quality.

What to do with the men they knew were becoming available was considered at a meeting in Mons held on 11 November 1917, exactly a year before the last shot of the war was to be fired at this same location. Two schools of thought became evident, one for hitting the British in Flanders and forcing them back to the Channel ports to extract their submission, and the other for pinching out the Verdun salient and bringing the French to the point of surrender. The Flanders plan ran the risk of bogging down, while the Verdun plan might well provoke a British attack which they would be hard pressed to resist while busy on the Meuse. Ludendorff himself offered a third idea, favouring Artois or Picardy as the scene for the offensive they all knew they had to undertake. The meeting came to no conclusions, but plans were to be examined for a number of possible operations in the coming weeks; *Saint George* south of Ypres, *Mars* at Arras, *Michael* against the southern end of the British line on the Somme, and two hooks either side of Verdun, and *Castor* and *Pollux*.

What had changed after the November meeting was the British attack at Cambrai on 20 November 1917 in which a surprise artillery bombardment coupled with a tank attack had smashed the German line, but which had failed when exploitation was unsuccessful and counterattacks drove them back. British capacity to launch a fresh offensive before late spring or early summer 1918 was thus lacking and the reallocation of British reserves reduced the attraction of a German offensive in Flanders. Ludendorff toured the front on 20 December and decided on Michael, but after another top-level meeting at Bad Kreuznach on 27 December no fewer than twelve plans for operations at different locations all along the front from the North Sea to Switzerland were on the table. The discussions and modifications to possible plans went on into January. Ludendorff travelled from one army to another, weighing up the evidence and arguing the possible outcomes.

General Hermann von Kuhl, chief of staff to Crown Prince Rupprecht, had considerable misgivings about Michael, which he was largely expected to arrange. The plan to drive through the British between Péronne and Arras in a bid to divide them from the French by reaching the sea appeared to him too vague, with no solid objective, while to have his southern flank covered by an army reporting to a different Army Group commander, the Crown Prince, son of Wilhelm II, suggested politics had over-ridden military wisdom. Further, without the British reserves being distracted by an attack to the north in the shape of Saint George, he gave the whole enterprise little chance of success. He met Ludendorff at Mons on 3 February to have his hopes of the Flanders operation dashed. Meanwhile Colonel Georg Wetzell, Ludendorff's chief of the operations division of his general staff, was advocating a series of attacks to be made successively at various places up and down the front, what he called a hammer-blow strategy. It is clear that it took a long time and much discussion before the series of attacks that were to become known as the *Kaiserschlacht*, the Kaiser's Battle, were defined and ordered, and the attacks themselves were much-modified ideas by the time they came into effect.

Field Marshal Paul von Hindenburg, Chief of the General Staff, issued the final orders on 10 March. The attack was to take place on 21 March with, in simplified terms, the taking of the Cambrai salient, a breakout towards Péronne and, while the left flank was held against any French intervention from the south, the attack would wheel northwards to roll up the British. The whole operation was, in fact, a good deal more complicated with numerous provisions for change and vague objectives.

THE GERMAN FORCES

Against the British the Germans arrayed their Seventeenth Army, with eighteen divisions and 2,236 guns under General Otto von Below, in the north facing Arras. The Second Army, comprising twenty divisions and 1,789 guns under General Georg von der Marwitz, was north of St Quentin and the Eighteenth Army, twenty-seven divisions, 2,448 guns and nine tanks under General Oskar von Hutier faced the River Oise. The German guns outnumbered the British by a ratio of five to two and included 1,000 weapons transferred from the Russian front. As far as possible the troops and artillery were moved under cover of darkness to conceal the point of attack from the British. They were ready.

2

THE ALLIED EXPERIENCE

The problem endemic to the alliance was just that: it was an alliance, a cooperative venture; coalition warmaking, as a leading scholar has put it. This was felt both at the overall command level and in the relationships between units of different nations attempting to work together in the field. Field Marshal Sir Douglas Haig did not report to the French commander-in-chief of the armies of the north, General Henri Pétain, but maintained his attitude of treating his requests as if they were orders, just as he had those of Pétain's predecessors. With the entry of the United States of America into the war, General John J. Pershing arrived on the scene, expressly charged by his chief, Secretary of War Newton D. Baker, with maintaining 'the underlying idea... that the forces of the United States are a separate and distinct component of the combined forces, the identity of which must be preserved.' So here was another country's commander-in-chief, not under French orders and not willing to split up his army to shore up the sagging strength of his allies. The potential for confusion in opposing a unified enemy force is clear, and it was fortunate for the Allies that, in the planning of Operation Michael, Ludendorff had muddied the waters of his own stream by having two army groups involved.

RELATIONS BETWEEN THE MEN

At lower levels of the hierarchy relations between British and French were rarely of crucial importance as, for the most part, each unit fought alongside its own countrymen and took orders from its own officers. The Americans, however, were parcelled out for training and their first fighting experience was with the French and British until the formation of the American First Army in August 1918. They found the experience stimulating in some respects, unpleasant in others and, sometimes, plain baffling. Lieutenant-Colonel Calvin H. Goddard, making preparations in June 1942 for working with allies in a later war, made a study of their experiences. He took the precaution of suggesting that, to avoid offending their foreign friends, his conclusions should not be given general circulation!

The American officers found their British opposite numbers difficult to get to know, but soon realised they acted no differently between themselves. The Australians were much more to their liking – relaxed, friendly and easy-going. There was a good deal of adverse comment on the fighting ability of British troops, but the report points out that there were underlying reasons such as battle fatigue or the inexperience and, indeed, the inadequacy of conscripted men as Britain neared the bottom of the barrel in manpower. Colonel Goddard went on to say, 'Under all other conditions, the British proved excellent team-mates, and American admiration for their courage and tenacity was not wanting, though the AEF in general rated itself equal, if not superior, to the English in fighting ability.'

The French were, they felt, more experienced and more efficient in their approach to fighting, suffering fewer casualties for an objective gained, even though they were slower. Although the Americans made faster progress, they became exhausted more quickly and were sooner in need of relief and replacement. In administration the Americans considered themselves quite as efficient as their Allies and more so than the French, whom they found to be hampered by paperwork. 'French meticulousness of method, infinite care for detail, slowness in accomplishing a stint of work were incomprehensible to the more rough and ready Yankee...' They found the British had done away with bureaucracy to a remarkable degree. 'There were times when the British could and did, accomplish by the employment of simple verbal orders, results which would have required, under AEF practice, the preparation of elaborate series of written instructions.' In one respect the French approach was very satisfactory, the maintenance of the dossier. This was 'a neat little packet of papers which each commander inherited from his French predecessor. These dossiers had been kept up with the neatness and precision of a business ledger, and contained complete maps of the position held, detailed accounts of its organisation, the general system of defence and attack, and itemised lists of all trench stores... much valuable information...'

Language did give problems. Between British and Americans it was largely in the realm of vocabulary. An officer of the AEF needed motor trucks, for example, by which the British quartermaster understood he meant conveyances that ran on rails rather than 'lorries'. With the French a sufficient supply of interpreters or of officers able to speak the other's language was vital. Where they were lacking, as in the instance reported of part of 109th U. S. Infantry, which '...did not understand the zero hour, nor when the artillery barrage would be laid down. They therefore did not secure the benefit of this barrage, and suffered casualties in consequence.'

The most severe shocks for the Americans came from the British where rations were concerned and hygiene in the case of the French. Goddard wrote:

Stated briefly, British rations were terrible from the American soldier's standpoint, no matter where encountered. Especially disliked was the substitution of tea for coffee, and the lack of good red meat in the diet. The Britisher's jam and cheese, on which he appeared to thrive, were anathema to the American.

In the matter of accommodation:

American soldiers, unlike the French, were not used to sharing stables and lofts in common with barnyard fowl and domestic animals of assorted varieties... Just as the American soldier never quite came to realise that the insanitary French billets offered to him were the best the country afforded, so he never ceased to complain over the uncomfortable French box cars which he customarily occupied when on a journey by rail.

The Americans were shocked by the conditions in which the French lived village life. Manure heaps appeared to be symbols of prosperity and success, and American attempts to clean up were vigorously resisted! The 37th Division reported, 'The French soldier has lost a great deal of his romance to the American soldier. Part of this is possibly due to the conditions found to exist in billets and barracks wherever French units have been succeeded by American units...

As comrades on the field of battle, the Americans respected the French but felt that they were content to let the Americans shoulder the greater burden of fighting. The doughboys' view of the British was that they were good fellows, worth risking one's life for. Goddard went on:

> He was often of low morale after his four years of pounding by forces almost always superior to his own, but unless physically below par, quite able to snap back into a first-class fighting man once the odds were half-way even... the Englishman knew how to handle himself in battle, and to reach his objective with a minimum of casualties. He acted with deliberation rather than dash, but this was an indication of sound good sense rather than lack of courage, of which he possessed full measure. He did not equal the American in initiative or intelligence.

Goddard's observations on the Australians are interesting:

> We do know that not all elements of the British Army got along harmoniously, as witness the fact that the English fraternised less with the Australian than did the American. This was not remarkable, however, since the dislike of the Australian for the Englishman was traditional; for an Australian soldier to salute a British officer was a phenomenon almost unheard of. In the matter of observing discipline he was more than casual, though conceding its vital importance in time of battle. But he was a fighting man to be reckoned with under any and all conditions, and even if he did pause to conduct private 'salvage' operations, this mattered little compared with the fact that

he gained his objectives and gained them handsomely. Further, he took to the Americans, and they to him, with simple spontaneity.

THE ALLIED ARTILLERY

The French and British experience up to the close of 1917 had been, for the most part, of attack. Their losses had been grievous, but their learning great. The Battle of the Somme had opened on 1 July 1916 with the largest losses ever suffered by a British army in a single day and the army was not commanded by people so idiotic as to be careless of the fact. Working out what had gone wrong and how to achieve a better performance took some time, but the British generals were determined to win the war and knew perfectly well that wanton destruction of their own troops was not the way to victory.

In December 1916 the British manual *Instructions for the Training of Divisions for Offensive Action* (SS 135) was published, to be followed in February 1917 by *Instructions for the Training of Platoons for Offensive Action* (SS 143), growing out of studies and reports made as early as July 1916. The former established clearly that the creeping barrage was the key to attacking fortified positions. A lifting barrage was used on the first day of the Somme, that is, the shellfire fell on the front line of trenches for a given time and then lifted on to the next line of fortifications, in theory to shield the attackers from reinforcements. The creeping barrage moved forward steadily at a suitable pace with the attackers close behind it. Indeed, it was held preferable to suffer 'friendly fire' casualties in a modest number from such a procedure than risk the far greater damage that leaving too large a space between shellfall and advancing men brought on one's own troops. The manual was also written assuming that meticulous staff-work and detailed preparation was vital to success – far from the improvisation of the dashing cavalryman of popular imagination. The Allies, like the Germans, had increased the proportion of heavy guns to field artillery significantly since 1914. There was, crucially, a great refinement of shells and their detonation devices. In July 1916 the high explosive shells had been using fuses that, if they detonated at all, were so sluggish that the missile exploded when well dug into the ground. The introduction of the sensitive and reliable .106 percussion fuse gave instant detonation and the consequent lateral fragmentation of the shellcase was a much more effective destroyer of barbed wire than the shrapnel of the field guns. In addition to the developments in high explosive shells were those in smoke and gas shells which, from 1917 onwards, constituted an increasing part of an offensive bombardment.

While Bruchmüller was perfecting his firewaltz, British artillery-men, among them Lieutenant-General Sir Nöel Birch, Major-General Sir Herbert Uniacke and Brigadier-General H. H. Tudor, were building the sophistication and expertise of their approach. At the Battle of Cambrai, when the tank was first used in massed formations, complete surprise was achieved with an artillery barrage undertaken without preliminary registration of the guns, very like the achievement of Captain Pulkowski on his side. The British had also given a good deal of attention to counter-battery work, that is, to locating and destroying enemy guns. The first method, the 'flash-buzz' system, became redundant as German explosives were improved and it was the use of microphones introduced late in 1916 that made sound ranging effective, not only locating the source of the sound but the nature of the gun that uttered it.

An American Engineer, Walter Roberts, later wrote a memoir for his family and explained how this worked:

After March 26 I was assigned to Sound Ranging and since this service is not much heard of nowadays it may be worthwhile to describe it sufficiently to make its purpose and method clear. Briefly, its object was to locate a source of sound, particularly the big boom of a gun or explosion of a shell, by means of sound alone. Thus the method worked equally well at night or in fog, and could not be fooled by putting camouflage over a gun. The Germans understood the possibility of doing this and even tried it in a crude way with stop watches, but the British and French had developed highly sophisticated equipment which made results accurate and fast. Their equipment could be used simply to locate on a map the spot where an enemy gun was located, or where one of our shells landed. But its best trick was to combine the two so as to help our gunners knock out an enemy gun. This was called 'Counter Battery' work. It was possible to tell our gunners very accurately whether their shells were going over or short, right or left, and how much, even when vagaries of wind or temperature prevented accurate location of the enemy gun itself, since these vagaries affected the locations of shell and gun equally.

Sound Ranging was perhaps the most highly secret innovation in the first world war and each outfit at the front included some dynamite and orders to blow it up if in danger of capture. We were not even supposed to mention our service by name, but only by initials (SRS). The 'security' was however hardly comparable to that surrounding radar and the atom bomb in the Second World War.

Anyway, I can now explain SRS in detail if the reader can concentrate for the rest of this paragraph. First imagine yourself in the central station dug-out of one of our sound ranging sections. On one side there is a table with a detailed map of the territory extending several miles around glued to the top. On this map there are six spots marked at intervals of about one kilometer along or close behind our front line trenches. Each spot represents a microphone designed to be responsive to big booms of sound but not very sensitive to the lighter and sharper sounds of rifle fire. Each microphone is connected to the central station by wires laid along the ground or sometimes strung on little posts. When an enemy gun fires, the sound reaching the nearest microphone causes a pulse of current to flow to the central station along its connecting wire line. A little later the sound reaches the next nearest microphone and similarly produces a little pulse of current over its particular line. In this way, each big bang reaches the central station in the form of six current pulses, one in each of the six lines. These pulses are photographed on moving film or paper as little jogs in six otherwise fairly straight lines running the length of the film. In addition to these lines there are cross lines produced by a rotating wheel with a thin slit in it to expose the film once every one hundredth of a second. The film reader can determine the time difference of arrival of the sound at any pair of microphones by counting the number of cross lines between the jogs produced by the two microphones.

Roberts goes on to describe how sophisticated calculations could be made to interpret the results, but also tells of a more simple method the person who did the mathematics, a man they called the computer, could use:

If the foregoing sounds complicated, you are correct. It would be too complicated to put into practice, but it explains the theory correctly. In practice we found that in the region on the map where enemy guns were located, these imaginary hyperbolic curves (the ones the fancy calculations gave them) were fairly straight lines each of which if extended passed through a point midway between the microphones giving rise to the curve in question. So we bored a little hole in the table half way between each two adjacent microphone locations and ran a thread up through it with a lead weight on the table and another below the table to keep it taut. Around the edge of the table were scales of time intervals. All the computer did was to put the string coming from between A and B onto the AB scale on the table edge at a reading (AB), then do the same for the string coming from between B and C, C and D, etc. until all five strings crossed (supposedly) at a single point on the map and there the gun must be. In practice they did not often cross at the same point so we took the center of the bunch of crossings as the best we could do.

A prerequisite of the method Roberts sets out is the availability of accurate maps. By 1918 the level of sophistication of map making had made pre-war efforts look childish, but more important was the development of aerial photography and the distribution of the results of it to front line officers. The ease with which the data could be gathered was diminished by German advances in aircraft design which gave them, for a time, the upper hand. By early 1918 the tide was flowing the other way and the airforces were fairly evenly balanced.

THE INFANTRY

The manual of February 1917, *Instructions for the Training of Platoons for Offensive Action*, was revolutionary. The lines of infantrymen considered standard eight months earlier were to be replaced by a platoon consisting of a command group and four specialised sections. One section consisted of nine riflemen, of whom one was a sniper and another a scout. A second section was made up of bomb (grenade) throwers and their assistants, and a third had four rifle-grenades served by nine men. The fourth was the Lewis-gun section nine men strong, equipped with one of the American-designed automatic rifles and thirty drums of ammunition. The gun weighed twenty-five pounds (11.3kg), about one-third of that of a Vickers machine-gun with its tripod, and so could be carried. The platoon was thus an attacking unit with a number of capabilities ranging from precision marksmanship through a 500-round per minute covering fire facility to grenade-assault ability. It was well-conceived for attacking, as was demonstrated at Messines in June and at Ypres in August and September 1917.

Private Donald Drake Kyler, 16th US Infantry, 1st Division, rose to the rank of sergeant after the war and wrote a substantial memoir of his army experience. His views on the weapons of the infantry are informative:

There were divided opinions and a lot of controversy in the army at that time over the value of bayonet training. It was noted that in the French and German armies, fighting with bayonets had largely ceased. But in certain colonial units of the French Army and the British Empire troops the reverse was true. Our leaders wisely decided to allot time for close hand-to-hand combat training, including bayonet training, in our schedule. Firepower of all kinds, and by all arms is extremely valuable; but in the end it is the infantry, who by various means closes with the enemy, assaults him, and by whatever means destroys him. That is what war is all about. To overcome the enemy and his power of resistance was what we were there for.

In connection with the bayonet training at that time, a new course was introduced. At least it was new to all the soldiers that I was associated with. A few specialists in close contact fighting were brought to our area as instructors. A selected few of us were given the course and we were supposed to teach it to our companions. The course taught us what parts of the body were most vulnerable to pressure, blows, or stabbing. The use of leverage and torque: how to dislocate joints and break bones with the least risk to ourselves. Emphasis was put on killing or disabling an antagonist, and not on controlling him.

Soon we were introduced to several kinds of weapons that were new to us: machine-rifles, hand grenades, rifle grenades, and mortars. We were issued one French chauchat machine rifle to each squad. By machine rifle, I mean those weapons which shoot continuously as long as the trigger is pulled or the ammunition supply lasts. The term, automatic rifle, means those weapons which when fired, automatically load another cartridge into the chamber ready to be fired again when the trigger is pulled. [Note: this is Kyler's definition, not in general use.]

The chauchat rifle weighed over twenty pounds and was recoil-operated. Ammunition was supplied to it in spring-loaded magazines. The magazine could be quickly attached to the gun by spring latches, and held twenty round of French rifle cartridges. One gun could shoot more shots than all the rest of the squad combined for short periods. So it added a lot to our firepower. But it was not accurate at over a few yards, was too heavy, too clumsy to aim, and in general not effective except against very close concentrated targets. About a year later those rifles were replaced by American made Browning machine rifles, which were an improvement.

The Browning weapon was lighter than the chauchat, with an adjustable rate of fire, could be shot singly or in short bursts, and used our own rifle cartridges. The regular magazine held twenty rounds, but magazines were available that held forty rounds. It was a good weapon, but with the same limitations as the chauchat, and had a few faults of its own. One was that it fired too fast on automatic, resulting in the loss of very effective aim. Another was that of frequent jams in the mechanism, and the loss of its use until the jam could be corrected. A little sand or mud getting into the chamber or magazine could cause a malfunction. Also, the gas port sometimes became clogged, causing failure of the extraction and ejection mechanism, which was gas operated. However, in spite of their faults, those weapons were very effective at close range concentrated targets.

But in retrospect of experience in war and in training for a few years thereafter, I was not in favor of having machine rifles in infantry platoons. Self loading rifles yes, but machine rifles, no. I believe that controlled and aimed shooting is more effective than trying to spray the landscape with shots, most of which have no effect whatever, except to deplete the ammunition supply.

We were given instruction in the use of grenades. At first it was by French noncommissioned officers, using their grenades, which were of several types. The first was a training grenade, made of sheet metal, and could be thrown about ten yards away and left to explode with little danger of fragments harming the thrower. But they were not to be closer than that. We had a few cases of men being injured by not throwing quickly enough or far enough. The second type was a fragmentation grenade, made of iron, and with much more explosive power. It was for longer range use, or to be thrown around or behind something, or in a hole or dug-out. It would be dangerous to be thrower if it exploded anywhere near him. Another type, heavier and with more explosive power, was for throwing into the openings of caves or fortifications, etc. Immediate cover had to be taken by the thrower to escape the resulting blast.

Those devices were all pear-shaped, with a pin sticking out of the small end about half an inch. That end had a metal cap covering the pin, secured with sealing wax. When ready to use the grenade, the cap was twisted off and the pin pushed in, which ignited a time fuse. Five to seven seconds after the pin was pushed in the blast would occur. So there was no time to be lost in throwing the grenade. The short time fuse was necessary so that the enemy would not have time to throw the grenade away from him. However, they have been known to do so. Ideally, the timing should be such that the grenade would explode just as it reached the target.

Another type of grenade was the rifle grenade, which was fired from a grenade launcher. The grenade launcher was shaped like a beer bottle with the bottom removed. The neck of the launcher was placed over the muzzle of the rifle and locked in position by a twisting motion. They were issued one to each squad. The grenade had a hole through its center the same size as the rifle barrel, and was placed in the open end of the launcher and let slide down until it came to rest on the decreasing inside diameter of the neck part of the launcher. The butt of the rifle was placed on the ground and was ready for firing. When fired, after the bullet had passed through the grenade, there was an area of high pressure still in the rifle as the bullet left it, which gave the grenade a considerable boost into an arched trajectory. The maximum range could be achieved by holding the axis of the launcher at slightly more than 45 degrees from the horizontal. At more angle than that the range would decrease, until by holding it straight up, theoretically the grenade would come down on the launcher. From the maximum range of perhaps two hundred yards the range could also be decreased by holding the launcher at an angle less than 45 degrees from the horizontal, until at the horizontal the range would be only a few yards, which was impractical for a number of reasons.

The grenade had a time fuse which was ignited when the bullet struck a projection as it passed through the hole in the grenade. To depress the muzzle toward the target would flatten the trajectory and decrease the range and lessen the time of the grenade in flight. The grenade, when striking the ground, would not explode promptly and would thus give the enemy time to take evasive action. It was necessary to have the butt of the rifle against the ground or some solid object, because of the recoil. In no case should it be rested against any part of the body. Some of our rifles' stocks were broken by the force of the recoil when using the launchers.

The rifle grenade, like the fragmentation hand grenade, had a powerful explosive charge. It filled the need for a plunging type projectile beyond the range of the hand grenade and less than the range of the light mortar. It could be fired over the tops of embankments, walls, buildings, or trees. Like the light and heavy mortars, howitzers, and certain high angle guns of the artillery, its fire was of the plunging kind. It was designed to fire at a high angle into the air, and the angle of arrival of the projectile at the target was at a steeper angle than that at which it was fired. Therefore, that type of fire power was very useful in getting into ravines, behind buildings, and in thick woods.

The disadvantages of rifle grenades were that they lacked accuracy, and the difficulty of supply of grenades at the right place at the right time. Their weight made it impractical for a soldier to carry them on his person, so special means of supply had to be adopted when they were to be used.

I had great respect for the value of hand and rifle grenades, but regarded them as secondary in importance to the rifle and bayonet. If the infantry is to be very mobile, and not loaded down with excessive weight, then their use was of necessity limited to defensive positions or to selected and well supplied periods of attack. Like the ammunition for machine rifles, a carried supply was soon exhausted when going forward in an attack. And going forward to attack was necessary if we were to be successful in war.

Grenades of other types were also supplied. For example: smoke grenades for laying a smoke screen, toxic gas grenades, and incendiary grenades.

We used the French grenades until the summer of 1918, when grenades of our own were supplied to us. They did not have a pin to be pushed in, but instead had a small handle to be held down while a cotter pin with a ring on the end was pulled out and discarded, which allowed the spring loaded handle to rise when released. When throwing the grenade, the handle was released when leaving the

*hand which ignited the fuse, which was timed for five seconds. Those
grenades were much safer in use and in handling, than the others
had been.* [The description is of the derivative of the British Mills
hand grenade.]

Heavier machine-guns than the Lewis were operated in a number of
special units. Within the infantry division there was one battalion of
the Machine-gun Corps with sixty-four guns; between four and five
machine-guns to an infantry battalion. The guns were heavy and ill-
suited to mobile operations. The Germans had a sled mount and also a
limber and gun-carriage arrangement like a light field gun. In defence
their great advantage was that, being tripod-mounted, they could be
ranged on fixed bearings to cover likely routes of attack such as gaps
left in barbed wire. Their rate of fire was some 500 rounds per minute,
but as their ammunition belts held 250 rounds and as they had a ten-
dency to over-heat and jam if fired continuously, the rate of fire does
not describe how many rounds actually got fired in a given time.
Attempts to render the weapons mobile included mounting them on
motor-cycle side-cars and in tanks.

It has been said that the British Army was slow to adopt the machine-
gun but it is hard to see how they could have been much faster. The 0.45
calibre Maxim was supplied to the army in March 1887 and when the
.303 bullet with smokeless powder was adopted for the rifle, the Maxim
was modified and went into production at the new calibre in July 1893.
It was used in the South African War of 1899–1902 and before the war
was over a detailed evaluation had been undertaken. Major-General F.
W. Kitchener was particularly enthusiastic, saying that machine-guns
should accompany every company of infantry and that to send them to
fight 'unsupported by machine-guns is nothing short of a crime.' He recommended eight as the minimum and ten the best number for every
battalion. Edmund Allenby, at that time a major of the 6th (Inniskilling)
Dragoons, found the Maxim very effective, up to even 3,000 yards
(2.75km) and said he would like one per squadron. Lieutenant-Colonel
J. H. G. Byng, South African Light Horse, had a battery of six Colt auto-

matic machine-guns attached to his formation and said its behaviour in action and the effects produced by its fire had been excellent. The War Office ordered 1,792 Vickers machine-guns in September 1914 for delivery by the following July, but only 1,022 could be manufactured in the time. By 1918 shortages in machine-guns had been made up to the army's requirements. By this time also Allenby was in command in Palestine and Byng had also become a general, commanding the British Third Army on the front east of Arras and Bapaume.

THE TANKS

Early in the war it had become apparent that the trench systems, protected with barbed wire, supported by pre-ranged artillery and armed with machine-guns, were close to impregnable to infantry and to cavalry. Colonel Ernest Swinton summed up the requirements for a device to overcome trenches, rather than a machine to re-introduce mobile warfare. The bullet-proof vehicle had to be 'capable of destroying machine-guns, of crossing country and trenches, of breaking through entanglements and of climbing earthworks.' The inspiration was found in the machines that had been developed for agricultural use, where the track-laying vehicle had proved its ability to deal with broken ground. The first example, *Little Willie*, was built in 1915. It was high in the body, and mounted on conventional caterpillar tracks low in profile. An improved version, *Mother*, soon followed. A rhomboid profile lowered the overall height, and the tracks ran right round the rhombus, giving improved performance in trench-crossing and dealing with embankments and shell-holes.

The vehicles of 1916 were very primitive, even by the standards achieved later in the war. Weighing twenty-eight tons, they were powered by unreliable engines of only 105 horsepower and could manage a snail-like half-a-mile an hour off the road, consuming a gallon of petrol in the process. Their armour was light, sufficient to withstand small-arms fire but easily penetrated by shell-fire. The impact of machine-gun bullets on the armour caused flakes to peel off, sending metal fragments, 'splash', flying around inside. Crews were issued with bizarre leather helmets with goggles and chain-mail visors for protection. Few bothered to wear these uncomfortable and restricting head-pieces, and veterans could be recognised by the black powdering of tiny scars on their faces. The noise and fumes inside were indescribable.

Two models of the Mark I tank were made. The 'male' was armed with two six-pounder naval guns in sponsons, pods, fitted on each side. The 'female' had twin Vickers machine-guns. To protect it from grenades, the tank had a chicken-wire shield mounted on top; a device soon abandoned as causing more problems than it solved.

Navigation and steering were difficult. Two brakemen controlled a track apiece, and the officer in command used compass bearings and time elapsed to attempt to work out his position. Vision was poor, and on more than one occasion the tanks opened fire on their own troops. Radio communication was not developed until late in the war, and the first tanks could only send messages by using the infantry's systems, where telephone lines were intact and not cut by the tank tracks, or by carrier pigeon. When radio was first introduced it could be used only when the tank was stationary. In spite of all these shortcomings, the new weapons had a significant impact when first deployed on 15 September 1916 in at attack from Delville Wood to Flers in the Somme campaign.

The British had developed two tanks by 1918. The Mark V Heavy Tank was an up-grading of the original Mark I used on the Somme, somewhat more reliable, a little faster and with better armour protection. Rails mounted on the top of the vehicle provided for a wooden beam to pass clean around the tank, chained to the tracks, to enable the machine to unditch itself. The medium tank, the fourteen-ton Whippet, was capable of over eight miles an hour (nearly 13 kph) and was armed with machine-guns. The French had two designs of medium-heavies based on the Holt tractor system, the Schneider and the St Chalmond. Both were designed round the 75mm field gun and were, in effect, self-propelled artillery. Neither was particularly useful cross-country. The chief AFV of the French army from May 1918 was the light, six-and-a-half ton Renault. This was a two-man tank armed with a 37mm gun and was effective if used in quantity, but it was vulnerable to German anti-tank rifles because of its light, 6mm armour. It was also difficult to fight, being under-manned. The driver had a full-time job simply controlling it while the commander had to keep a look-out, issue orders to the driver and serve the gun, leaving too many opportunities for mistakes to be made.

In 1917 the British made use of their tanks at Arras in the spring, with some success, but they were limited by the damage done to the terrain by shellfire. In the Ypres Salient the same problem beset them, compounded by heavy rain. What went unremarked, both then and since, was the success of two actions in which they were precisely targeted on German strongpoints. During the Third Battle of Ypres, which ended with the taking of Passchendaele in November, when the advance was sticking in the mud having come only half-way since 31 July, the Battle of Langemarck opened on 16 August. It left the German blockhouses on the St Julien-Poelcapelle road in enemy hands. The action against the strongpoints called Maison du Hibou and The Cockcroft involved three tank companies with a platoon of infantry following each tank some 250 yards to the rear. The tanks moved up along the roads which, broken up though they were, still afforded a solid footing in the morass. A creeping barrage was used instead of a preliminary bombardment and smoke shells screened the action from the German support lines. The tanks moved off at 0100 hours on 19 August, crossed the Steenbeek with difficulty on a temporary bridge and ground on up the stone block pavé in the middle of the road which had survived the shelling quite well. They were able to approach their targets by road until the last tens of yards, when some bogged down, but still close enough to bring the blockhouses under fire, force their occupants to surrender and cover the capture of the strongpoints by their infantry. On 27 August four more tanks attacked Springfield and while only one came to close quarters with the blockhouse and was hit by a German shell soon after, it had done its work, firing through the rear door of the pillbox and forcing the surrender of its garrison. In his book on armoured warfare of 1937, *Achtung – Panzer!*, the German tank genius Heinz Guderian was to write, 'The tank forces should be committed only where there are no obstacles that exceed the capacity of their machines; otherwise the armoured attack will break on the terrain'.

The terrain off-road was much better suited when the British launched their attack on Cambrai on 20 November 1917. The artillery achieved surprise and the tanks a breakthrough, except at Flesquières where the commander of the 51st (Highland) Division, General G. M. Harper, feared that the tanks would attract shellfire and kept his troops back. As a result the German artillery had a free hand until the infantry came up and eleven tanks were lost. This left a German-held salient which hampered the intended cavalry break-out on the first day and gave the Germans time to mount counter-attacks. The potential of the tank had, all the same, been shown.

THE DISPOSITION OF THE BRITISH FORCES

The Allied plans for 1918 were less than coherent. General Pétain was in favour of a defensive posture while General Foch was all for mounting attacks as being the best method of defence. The proposal to create a general reserve of thirty divisions to be employed in countering any German offensives was sensible, but the ability to contribute to it was lacking. Neither Pétain nor Sir Douglas Haig were willing to lose formations to it and instead they made an agreement of mutual assistance should a crisis strike. Haig, in particular, was dealing with a different problem – the lack of manpower. In consequence the strength of his divisions was in the process of being reduced from twelve battalions to nine, redistributing the men from nearly 150 axed battalions to other formations. This was not merely difficult to organise and implement, but disruptive of personal loyalties and morale. New relationships had to be forged, communication and confidence between infantry, artillery and other branches built afresh and command structures re-established. The greatest impact was on the newest army, Gough's Fifth Army.

The British defence system had been overhauled in theory, drawing extensively on German ideas, and now, with a front stretching as far south as the River Oise, work was in hand to construct it for real. It was intended to consist of an area up to twelve miles (19km) deep with a lightly-held Forward Zone of barbed wire and reinforced machine-gun pits covering the front trench. Behind that was the Battle Zone between one and two miles (1.5 to 3km) wide in which the enemy, slowed and disorganised by the Forward Zone, was to be destroyed by fire from massive redoubts and by artillery. The Rear Zone, a further four to eight miles (6.5 to 13km) back was a second battle zone killing ground. These arrangements were decreed in a GHQ memorandum of 14 December 1917, but then they had to be built. The front of the Fifth Army, with twelve divisions under the command of General Sir Hubert Gough, ran from Gouzeaucourt, between Cambrai and St Quentin, to Barisis, south of the Oise. The northern part had been held by the British for over a year, but from St Quentin southwards it was the former French front, poorly entrenched; moreover, the dry winter had rendered the former marshes passable on the Oise. To the north the Third Army, with fourteen divisions under General the Hon. Julian Byng, was more fortunate, but there was still much to do. The manpower problem was helped to some extent by using Chinese labourers, but by late March Byng's defences were incomplete and Gough's, in the south of his sector, consisted of his front line, some redoubts and very little else. His relatively few troops were, as a natural consequence, similarly deployed, mostly in the front line.

On 20 March, therefore, the British had twenty-six divisions in unfinished defences between Gavrelle, just north of the River Scarpe and the Arras to Cambrai road, and Barisis, south of the River Oise and of La Fère. While an attack somewhere on the British front between the North Sea and the French front was expected, they were not aware of the power they faced here at the southern end of the line. The Germans had arrayed against them the eighteen divisions of Von Below's Seventeenth Army between Arras and Cambrai, the twenty divisions of Von der Marwitz's Second Army between Cambrai and St Quentin and the twenty-seven divisions of Von Hutier's Eighteenth Army between St Quentin and Barisis. New ideas of warfare were about to be tested in the most dramatic fashion.

PART TWO
THE GERMAN OFFENSIVES

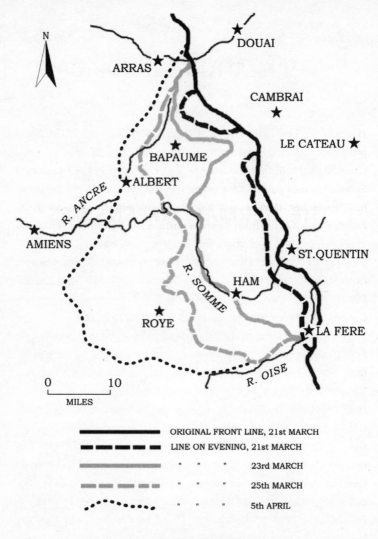

	ORIGINAL FRONT LINE, 21st MARCH
	LINE ON EVENING, 21st MARCH
	" " " 23rd MARCH
	" " " 25th MARCH
	" " " 5th APRIL

Operation Michael
March–April 1918

3

OPERATION MICHAEL

THE DIVIDING LINE between Byng's Third Army and Gough's Fifth Army positions was at Gouzeaucourt on the road between Péronne and Cambrai. North of that, the front bulged north-east in the Flesquières Salient, the area pushed forward in the Battle of Cambrai of the previous November. Here it was held by Lieutenant-General Sir E. A. Fanshawe's V Corps (from south to north, 47th, 63rd Royal Naval and 17th Divisions). To their north was IV Corps under Lieutenant-General Sir George Harper with the 51st Highland and 6th Divisions. Then VI Corps, Lieutenant-General Sir Aylmer Haldane with 59th, 34th and 3rd Divisions and finally, in front of Arras, XVII Corps of Lieutenant-General Sir Charles Fergusson with 15th and 4th Divisions.

The southern flank of the salient, a section of the line centered on Epéhy east and northeast of Péronne, was held by the northernmost formation of the Fifth Army, Lieutenant-General Sir Walter Congreve, V.C, with his VII Corps (north to south, 9th Scottish, 21st and 16th Irish Divisions). To Péronne, the River Somme and its associated canal come from St Quentin in a great loop curving as far south as Ham and the junction with the Crozat Canal heading up from the south-east. The two canals make a triangular area, with the front line between St Quentin and La Fère, while the river runs north through marshy flats cut into the broad, high, rolling countryside which lay behind the British lines. The area east and south of Péronne was held by Lieutenant-General Sir Herbert Watts with XIX Corps, 66th and 24th Divisions about as far as the Roman road that runs due west to Amiens. From there to a point south of the Somme Canal and south of St Quentin was Lieutenant-General Sir Ivor Maxse's XVIII Corps, 61st, 30th and 36th Ulster Divisions, and facing the line down to the Oise River was Sir Richard Butler's III Corps with 14th, 18th and 58th

Divisions. The Cavalry Corps, three divisions including the Canadian Cavalry Brigade, did not operate as a single unit but was divided up for use where necessary and in the event provided an invaluable emergency mounted infantry support. Four divisions would be added from the reserves to the Third Army and three to the Fifth in the first few days of the coming battle.

There were intimations of the start of the *Kaiserschlacht*, the Kaiser's Battle. In spite of the secrecy with which the Germans amassed their forces, aerial observation told the British something was going on. The major concern was to protect what was vital, that is, the Channel ports and their protecting positions at Arras and Vimy and their more southerly flank towards Péronne. Sir Julian Byng was keen to preserve what he had won near Cambrai. But further south, along the River Somme and its left bank, there was little of value before the railway junction of Amiens; just open agricultural country that would prove attractive to tank warfare enthusiasts and airport builders in the next hundred years. On 20 March, near Fayet, just north of St Quentin, a raiding party consisting of A and C companies, 2/6th Royal Warwicks, XVIII Corps, took prisoners from the German 28th Division who revealed that the attack was scheduled for the next day and that the bombardment would begin at 0440 hours – and could they be taken to the rear of the British lines with all speed, please? No general alarm was given.

THE BATTLE COMMENCES

The bombardment was carried out in five phases. The first, from 0440 to 0640, was mostly gas with some high explosive and was widely targeted. From 0530 the fire concentrated on infantry positions with the smaller calibre weapons. At 0600 those alive to see it could watch the sun rise. From 0640 to 0710 a wave of fire every ten minutes, frustrated to some extent by the fog which prevented precise ranging for the next phase, from 0710, seventy minutes fire by all batteries on British strongpoints and redoubts. From 0820 to 0935 they reverted to ten-minute bursts before the final phase, five minutes of heavy explosives

44

on the front line trenches and more general shelling of the zone behind them. To all this the Royal Artillery replied as best they could, but their gunners had to wear gas masks and their observation was compromised by the natural fog and the German smoke shells. Attempts by their own front-line troops to send flares up to call for counter-fire were futile as visibility was close to zero in thick fog.

The overall effect was fairly close to Bruchmüller's objective, although the Germans, too, were frustrated by the lack of visibility which prevented more delicate targeting. British communications were disrupted when telephone lines buried as much as six feet (1.8m) deep were cut and railways and airfields damaged. By 0940 hours, nearly 8,000 casualties had been inflicted on the British. Confusion was achieved by similar bombardments on the British First Army in Artois and Flanders and on the French in Champagne; all or any could be the prelude to attack.

The Flesquières Salient was a major objective for Ludendorff. The Seventeenth Army pressed forward in the valley of the Hirondelle River, west of Cambrai, at the junction of IV and VI Corps. They threatened the village of Bullecourt where the ANZACs had suffered so grievously in the spring of 1917. By the end of the day, the 59th and 6th Divisions had been pushed back to the rear of the Battle Zone as had the right of the 51st (Highland) Division. The main bulge of the salient was put under pressure, but, as the idea was to nip it off with a north and south pincer movement, the defenders suffered only from gas attack. It was to the south that the next fierce effort was made against the northern troops of Gough's Fifth Army. The South African Infantry Brigade of 9th (Scottish) Division were holding the right of the line and the 130 men of 2nd South Africans were defending Gauche Wood. They held it until noon with such tenacity that the Germans retired and left it alone for the rest of the day. Forty defenders emerged fit to fight at the end of the action.

VII Corps' 21st Division held the next section of the line with two good positions at Chapel Hill to the northern end and the village of Epéhy on the southern end of their front. Chapel Hill was held by 1st

Lincolns who endured a heavy assault and were fortunate to have help from the 4th South Africans who moved from their left to reinforce them. Between the two stronger positions, down in the valley, was Vaucelette Farm, held by 12/13th Northumberland Fusiliers. They were ejected from their position by noon having been encircled by their enemy, but then the fog dispersed, exposing the Germans to view from north and south, Chapel Hill and Epéhy. The British fire was withering and the German advance tottered to a halt. The theory of the Battle Zone's redoubts was demonstrated to be sound, provided you could see your targets. Epéhy itself was held by 110th Brigade, three battalions of the Leicestershire Regiment. They had been pulled back from the front line before the barrage by their divisional commander, Major-General D. G. M. Campbell. Lance Corporal S. T. North of 7th Leicesters described the experience once they had resumed their positions. At first the fog obscured everything, but slowly the sun got the upper hand and the mist dispersed. In front of them were their attackers, evidently disorientated and confused by the fog themselves, and trying to get in good order. The infantry were moving forward four abreast, with horse-drawn artillery and supply wagons to their rear. This was certainly not a storm-troop operation as yet, although the infantry might well have been capable of adopting the approved tactics. As it was, unprepared and groping their way forward, they were easy prey for the Leicesters. The Lewis guns opened fire and the riflemen joined in. Soon only riderless horses moved amongst the fallen. Lance Corporal North then looked to the right, the area held by the 16th Irish Division. There the Germans were making a steady advance.

The position on the right of Congreve's VII Corps' front looked down the broad slope towards the village of Bony, to be enshrined in American memory the following September, and Le Catelet at the northern end of the St Quentin Canal tunnel. The tunnel was obviously being used to conceal German stores, equipment, and troops, and Congreve presumably suspected that a major attack could be mounted with extreme speed and total surprise from that quarter. Over-riding the protests of Major-General Sir C. P. A. Hull, the divisional commander, he insisted on having only one of the three brigades held in reserve and five of the six battalions of the remaining two brigades in the front line itself. Three days before the attack, Gough had visited the 16th Division and Major K. S. Mason, the Divisional Machine-gun Officer, had been present when Hull repeated his misgivings. Hull wanted only one brigade on the front line but, Mason reported, 'General Gough would not agree to this and said, "I wouldn't dream of such a thing. The Germans are not going to break my line". I saw quite a lot of General Gough during his visit and came to the conclusion that he was a very arrogant, conceited and pompous man.' To the disadvantage imposed from above were added the handicaps of the division itself. Nearly twenty-five per cent of the men were English replacements sent to make up the numbers of Irish units badly reduced in previous fighting, and an even greater number were inexperienced.

When the bombardment entered Phase Five at 0710 hours what had been relatively occasional shelling became a concentrated deluge of fire on infantry positions. The Irish were concentrated in their forward line and suffered abominably, unlike the Leicesters on their left. At about 0930, when the first parties of German troops came questing forward, they were in no condition to offer serious resistance. One redoubt, Malaisse Farm, garrisoned by men of the 2nd Royal Munster Fusiliers under Lieutenant W. S. Kidd, held out until 1100 hours before being over-run. The 39th Division, in reserve, was ordered up by Gough to plug the gap.

In the centre Watts's XIX Corps was hard pressed, but held on the rear line of the Battle Zone. The 50th Division was ordered to move forward from reserve to support Watts. South of him Maxse's XVIII Corps also held through the day. Of the fourteen redoubts on this front, six of them held for up to five hours, but out of the eight forward battalions, only fifty men made it back to the rear.

In the darkness other units, by-passed but untouched, were able to draw back, amazed they had survived the day. Gunner Maurice Burton of 342nd Battery, Royal Garrison Artillery, had been serving their 6-inch howitzers. He later wrote:

March 21, the opening day of the massive German offensive. As the day wore on first one battery then another on either side of us fell silent and we were aware they were pulling out and falling back. Finally, ours were the only guns firing and even they fell silent about mid-afternoon... There were no infantry in sight, friendly or hostile, no planes flew overhead. There was no sound of rifle, machine-gun or mortar fire, no bursting shells. So it remained until night fell when all hands were mustered to load the convoy of lorries drawn up on the road running beyond our left flank.

Everything was carried on our backs or shoulders including the several hundred rounds of hundred-pound shells. All was done in strict silence and smoking was forbidden.

Then came the turn of the guns. Each had to be manhandled up a slope, all hands to each of the guns in turn. Each gun was fastened to its four-wheel drive lorry to be towed away. Presumably, by the time we came to pull the fourth gun up the slope we were beginning to tire for the procession moved slowly.

One of our sergeants, a schoolmaster by profession, took charge. Now boys,' he bellowed, `Left-r-r-right, left-r-r-right, left-r-r-right,' he called, rolling his r's. It was as if he were marching a class of boys back into school after morning break. I know I inwardly cursed him and I expect everyone else did for giving our position away; but we got the gun up onto the road and hooked to its lorry with no more than a few rounds of machine-gun fire aimed at us, fortunately at random, the bullets buzzing harmlessly over our heads.

Piecing the story together afterwards it became clear we were surrounded on three sides by the enemy.

The convoy of lorries got on the move just before dawn when the enemy laid down a barrage on the road we had just left. It passed through a village a little further on, just as this was being heavily bombarded, or so I was told. I heard nothing of it for I was fast asleep on my feet, standing in one of the lorries.

THE SOUTHERN SECTOR

It was at St Quentin, and southwards towards the Oise, that the Fifth Army was hit hardest on 21 March. The four divisions of Butler's III Corps found themselves up against Hutier's ten from the Eighteenth Army. Here the fog persisted longer than in the north and the silent, gas-masked advance of the German infantry, close behind a creeping barrage, killed and captured the front-line defenders, dazed as they were from five hours bombardment and blinded by the fog. The poor visibility led to the redoubts being by-passed, unable to harrass the attackers and the following German forces with their field guns and mortars moved up, ready to reduce these strongholds as soon as they could see what they were about. The increasing clarity also released the grounded Royal Flying Corps to attack German lines of communication and to spot for their artillery, but already a great deal of ground had been lost.

The German 28th Division moved forward from Fayet towards Holnon, just west of St Quentin on the Amiens road. Their experience was recorded in the memorandum entitled *The Battle in the Intermediate Zone* which was found and republished by the French and Americans. Under the heading of 'Outflanking Points of Support' it speaks of getting past Holnon Wood, one of the British strongpoints. The conditions needed were, it said, either that the infantry could keep far enough away to avoid machine-gun fire of significance or that it could advance in dead ground. Failing these, only covering fire would work, and this was the case with Holnon Wood. The artillery had the range of the wood and could shell it from the positions already held at the start of the action. They therefore laid down a barrage along the southern edge of the wood, and the guns accompanying the attack took that opportunity to move to a position about a mile and a quarter (2km) south-west of the wood, and open fire from there. That allowed the 118th Regiment to establish themselves on the edge of the wood and fire along the southern side, enfilading British positions. It was, the report says, 'obstinately defended by fire and by hostile counter-attacks.' In addition, the 28th's Mountain Machine-gun Section 233 gave covering fire to the 3rd Division on their flank, watching their progress by marking the detonations of their grenades as they advanced through the wood. It was very skilfully done.

The Canal de St Quentin runs from the Somme near St Simon north-east to St Quentin itself. This sector was held by the 36th (Ulster) Division of Maxse's XVIII Corps and was attacked by the German XVII Corps with three divisions. The anti-tank 18-pounders were over-run almost immediately, but three of the Ulster's front line posts held out until 1300 hours. East of Castres, on either side of the railway, were Boadicea and Racecourse Redoubts. By 1230 hours the Germans had passed them, penetrating as far as Contescourt and approaching the railway at Essigny on the Ulsters' right. By nightfall the German 238th Division had got as far as Seraucourt-le-Grand, an advance of four and a half miles (7.25km). The 2nd Royal Inniskilling Fusiliers held Boadicea Redoubt, and it soon became isolated. The 2nd Battalion, 463rd Regiment was left to guard it, but thought it too daunting an objective to attack. Their mobile artillery came up, but before they opened fire a group of four men who could speak English asked permission to parley with the defenders under a flag of truce. White flag aloft, they approached the redoubt with caution and, no doubt, considerable apprehension. They explained that the strongpoint was isolated and by-passed and that, if necessary, they would shell it into dust. After a few minutes the defenders filed out, some 250 officers and men, to go into captivity. The Germans released two carrier pigeons they found with messages reporting the fall of the redoubt. Racecourse Redoubt lasted until 1800 hours and surrendered after its commander, Second Lieutenant Edmund de Wind, was killed. These strongholds had been cut off so quickly, sightless in the fog, that they played little effective part in the day's events. By 2230 the Ulsters had pulled back over the canal to the north-west.

Butler's III Corps had three divisions with which to match Hutier's ten in the area to the right of the Ulsters. The British 14th Division was pushed out of its Battle Zone between 1400 and 1700 hours. Only the reinforcement provided by 5th Dismounted Brigade prevented a collapse of III Corps's entire front.

General Gough was not idle. At 1400 hours he contacted his corps commanders by telephone and then made flying visits to their head-quarters by automobile. The situation was evidently serious, but not yet disastrous. The damage south of the Flesquières Salient had been dealt with, his centre was bent but holding, and only in the south had a sizeable seizure of territory been achieved by his enemies. He gave Butler permission to put into effect the provisional plan to withdraw behind the Crozat Canal which runs down to the Oise, today under the name of the St Quentin Canal, abandoning the wedge bounded by the canal south-west of St Quentin to Hutier's men.

RENEWED PLANNING

Ludendorff had reason to be pleased, but not delighted, with the day's achievements. In the south the advance was excellent, but in the centre and north things had not gone so well, and in particular the effort to pinch out the salient had failed in front of Cambrai, although two big bites to the north and south had been inflicted upon it. Between that salient and St Quentin a massive effort had been made, but no break-through came of it. In fact, none of his armies had managed to reach their planned first-day objectives. Encouraged by Hutier's progress, however, four divisions were taken from the German First, Third and Fifth armies to take position on the Eighteenth Army's left. The cost of the day had been high. The Germans had suffered nearly 40,000 casu-alties, 10,851 fatal. They had inflicted nearly as many on the British, 38,500, of which 21,000 were prisoners. The combined total was larger than that of 1 July 1916, the first day of the Battle of the Somme; this time, however, much more costly to the Germans.

Sir Julian Byng had been able to reinforce his front-line troops, but it was clear that he had to pull back in the Flesquières Salient, and at 1800 hours the order was given for a limited, 4,000-yard (3,650m), with-drawal. The man without reinforcements to feed into his calculations was Gough. He had met the French Third Army commander, General Georges Humbert, in the morning and was dismayed to discover that the troops intended to be available for the assistance of the British should it prove necessary, the agreement made to free both Pétain and Haig from contributing to a general reserve, were not there. They had been parcelled out amongst the French. As Humbert put it, 'je n'ai que mon fanion' – 'I have nothing but my pennant', meaning his flag of office on his car. Not that the French were careless of the problem; the first of their divisions arrived the next day. Gough's orders had been given for withdrawal to the canal lines but he could not have been happy to hear that, although Haig approved his actions, his chief of staff, Lieutenant-General Sir Herbert Lawrence, voiced the languid opinion that the Germans would not 'come on' the next day. Lawrence had already refused Gough's request for two divisions to be moved closer to his front a couple of days before and appeared to be unable to appreciate that the Fifth Army commander was not making demands just for fun.

THE SECOND DAY

That night the fog returned, and early on 22 March, the Germans came on once more. Five of Gough's redoubts still held out and did not fall until 1700 hours. Butler's III Corps stood on its new line along the Crozat Canal and was reinforced by 2nd Cavalry Division. The 1st Bavarian Division mounted three successive attacks in an attempt to cross at Jussy, where the bridge had been blown the previous night. They failed. At noon the Germans managed to get over at Tergnier, close to the canal's junction with the Oise and the French line, and by 1930 they had established a secure bridgehead on the western side. It was to the north of this sector that a severe problem developed. For some reason Sir Ivor Maxse concluded that his southern flank was compromised and pulled the 36th (Ulster) Division back to the Somme River and the rest of his Corps naturally had to march back in concert with the move. By doing so, he in fact gave Butler the real version of the same problem on his left flank and began to lose touch with Watts to the north, having failed to keep him informed. It was a serious error.

Watts's XIX Corps had been bolstered by 1st Cavalry Division to face renewed attack by Second Army's left wing. By 1245 he had to order a retreat to the Green Line behind the 50th Division. On his left, the attacks near Epéhy were renewed and the village fell by 1400 hours. The mass assaults by the German XXIII Reserve Corps were more like the attacks of 1916 than the sophisticated tactics now advocated and losses rose in consequence.

The British Third Army was also under severe pressure. A gap opened north of the Flesquières Salient, through which the Germans however could not make progress, and in the evening a counter-attack with twenty-five Mark IV tanks drove the German 24th Reserve Division back to close it. One of the field artillery brigades, a unit of twenty-six guns, fired 20,600 rounds over open sights that day. At 1630 hours Byng and Gough met at Albert to co-ordinate their movements and Byng ordered V Corps, in the salient, to fall back to keep contact with VII Corps on its right. Later that night, Field Marshal Haig added his weight to keeping the line coherent, authorising Byng to fall back to a line running north of Péronne if need be. Things were looking distinctly shaky.

THE DAY OF ERROR

Ludendorff issued orders on 23 March that changed the campaign entirely. The progress in the north being slow and expensive, he decided to exploit the south. The Seventeenth Army was to head for St Pol, due west of Arras, while the Second was to advance straddling the River Somme towards Amiens. The Seventeenth was to head southwest to prevent repair of the junction between the French and the British. The concept of Hutier's southern force blocking French reinforcements arriving to prevent an envelopment of the British line was abandoned, and each army was off on a jaunt of its own, maintaining only a tenuous contact with its fellows. Ludendorff was scattering his effort, assuming that the British were beaten and that the French would try to secure their own lines. In the latter he was very nearly correct.

The immediate results suggested he might well be right in his new scheme. Hutier's Eighteenth Army was over the Crozat Canal and pushing the French and British back. Maxse's Corps could not hold the Somme, and the Germans crossed at Ham and another bridge further to his right so that by nightfall, the gap between him and Butler was wide open. Further north, Watts's XIX Corps was too thinly spread to prevent the Germans getting over the Somme at Pargny and St Christ, south of the St Quentin-Amiens road, but they had received another division, the 8th, from Flanders which regained the Pargny position. The St Christ bridgehead was also destroyed. Around Péronne VII Corps was retreating and losing contact with Third Army at the same time. Byng's troops had vacated the long-disputed salient, but their movement was pulling them north, with a line on the Ancre running north from Albert as an ultimate defence position in mind.

The Allies rushed into meetings. Haig went to see Gough at Villers-Bretonneux and remarked, somewhat belatedly, that more men were required. At 1600 hours Pétain met Haig at Dury, south of Amiens, and was shocked to be asked for yet more divisions, as General Marie Fayolle was already hurrying thirteen divisions to Gough's right in order to assume command of all Allied forces south of the Somme thirty hours later. The only brightness on the horizon was the news that General Sir Herbert Plumer was sending three Australian divisions.

SAD SUNDAY

Sunday 24 March, Palm Sunday, dawned foggy once more, and in the south Hutier's thrust went on. The French were moving men into the area as fast as they could, but they arrived with only what they could carry, and it was no surprise that, having expended their ammunition, the French 1st Dismounted Cavalry were being forced back by noon. Maxse's XVIII Corps retained a tenuous hold on the Somme north of Ham, but from the Ham bridgehead two German divisions pushed forward, falling on the unfortunate and already much-depleted 36th (Ulster) Division and destroying two more of their battalions. They were supported at Villeselve, due south of Ham, by 150 troopers of 6th Cavalry Brigade who, at 1400 hours, charged the German 5th Guard Division, sabred eighty-eight of them and took 107 prisoners at a cost of seventy-three casualties of their own. The Ulsters maintained their resistance at the village for another two hours. On the northern side of the Ham salient, the British 20th Division were forced to fall back to the line of the Canal du Nord in front of Nesle.

At Béthancourt-sur-Somme, downstream and north-west of Ham, the river crossing was made before dawn by the German 28th and 1st Guards Divisions, using footbridges and by the afternoon the bridgehead had been developed north to Pargny again, against the resistance of the British 8th Division. Along the river towards Péronne other attempts to cross were held off, but a gap had now been forced between XVIII and XIX Corps, the inevitable consequence of Maxse's withdrawal the previous day. Gough hoped to mend the defect with the help of the newly arriving French 22nd Division the next day.

North of Péronne, Congreve's VII Corps was striving to maintain contact with Byng's Third Army while preserving the line with XIX Corps on its right. West of the Péronne to Bapaume road, north of Cléry-sur-Somme, the South African Brigade's 9th Division caused the German 357th and 237th Reserve Regiments of the 199th and 9th Reserve Divisions considerable delay by holding out at Marrières Wood until 1700 hours. The eventual capture of the hundred or so survivors was as a result of running out of ammunition. They were now returning to the battlefield of the Somme of summer 1916, still a wasteland of broken blockhouses, shellholes and rusting wire. The arrival of the British 35th Division from Flanders and a thousand mounted troops from 1st Cavalry Division allowed Congreve to create something of a line in this wilderness.

The most serious problem was the thrust of General von Stäbs's XXXIX Reserve Corps through the space that had opened between Congreve and the Third Army south of Bapaume. Third Army's IV Corps began to pull back astride the town at 1900 hours, and the southwestern movement allowed contact with their comrades to be re-established before the next morning. After Haig met Byng to encourage him to maintain a line up to Arras, he went into conference with Pétain at Dury. The French commander was supplying the troops promised, but Haig hoped for more. They were neither granted nor withheld at this point. It was not an argument over additional men that upset Haig, but Pétain's longer-term intentions, for he had ordered Fayolle that, if necessary, he should fall back on Beauvais, thirty miles (50km) south of Amiens. Such a movement was bound to sever the connection between the British and the French, Haig exclaimed. Pétain agreed, but he evidently regarded the preservation of the integrity of his army and the protection of Paris as his prime duty, and if the eminently desirable objective of keeping in touch with the BEF had to be abandoned, so be it; it was inevitable if events continued in the way they had developed so far. This was, in any case, Haig's impression of his ally's attitude.

In the early hours of the next day Haig got in touch with London asking for the Chief of the Imperial General Staff, General Sir Henry Wilson, and Lord Milner, Minister of War, to come to France to help resolve the crisis this sad day had brought. Meanwhile, in England, the 88,000 men on home leave were being recalled with all speed.

Notwithstanding the divergence of opinion in the high command, the re-organisation of the allied armies took place overnight. All troops south of the Somme, with about two-fifths of the line being held by the French, came under French command, and all troops north of the river became part of the Third Army. The troops now under Fayolle were Gough's Fifth Army, with Watts's XIX Corps on the left and Maxse's XVIII Corps on the right in the north of the sector, and Humbert's Third Army, with General Robillot's II Cavalry Corps on the left and Pellé's V Corps on the right. This description, though, lends a false air of organisation and coherence to what was a turmoil of semi-fragmented units held together by the sheer guts of officers and men determined to halt their enemies.

On Monday 25 March the scheme for regaining ground at Pagny failed even to start when the Germans launched a six-division attack. The French were ejected from Nesle and the whole line was pushed back to Roye by evening. The Germans thrust west of Noyon to force the French back over the Oise in the south of the battlefield. On the left flank of the French sector XIX Corps disputed the Somme crossing at

Brie, near the Roman road, for much of the day but the river was not held at Biaches, close to Péronne and another withdrawal became inevitable. Gough gave orders for work on the Amiens Defence Line, west of Lamotte-Warfusée, to be redoubled and for the line to be garrisoned. He lacked formations to serve here, so Major-General George Carey was charged with the creation of what became known as Carey's Force. It was composed of the staff of the various schools of instruction in the rear areas, the 500 American soldiers of B and D Companies, 6th US Engineers, men from British tunnelling, electrical and workshop units and anyone else he could lay his hands on. In the coming days he would acquire 300 semi-invalids rousted out of hospitals, and 400 Canadian railwaymen.

Third Army, north of the Somme, fought innumerable actions all along its front that day, but by evening it was back on a line including Beaumont Hamel and Albert, the positions from which the British had started on 1 July 1916. The Royal Flying Corps had thrown everything available into the fight. Major-General John Salmond ordered his airmen to 'bomb and shoot everything they can see' east of a line from Grevillers, west of Bapaume, and Maricourt, between Albert and Péronne, and German battle reports bear witness to the enthusiasm with which they obeyed.

ENTER FOCH

The meeting to settle the top-level command problems took place at Doullens on 26 March. The French President, Raymond Poincaré, took the chair. On the French side were the Prime Minister, Georges Clemenceau, and generals Pétain and Foch. The British included Haig, Lord Milner and Sir Henry Wilson. Wilson and Pétain fell out when the latter compared the British retreat in the current battle to the flight of the Italians at Caporetto. Foch advocated fighting where they stood at that moment, not retiring a single inch. From all the emotional rhetoric a practical solution emerged, possibly at Haig's prompting. While the appointment of a commander-in-chief of all Allied armies was going too far, someone with an overall function of co-ordination of Allied efforts was not. Foch was appointed. The Americans, who had not been present at this meeting, were relieved, for they had been unable to understand how the Allies thought they could fight the war in the absence of such an officer. Even now Foch's authority was weak and at Beauvais on 3 April a further meeting gave him all powers necessary to enforce co-ordination as well as the strategic direction of military operations. That the Americans General John J. Pershing and General Tasker Bliss were present on the second occasion may have helped promote sound sense.

While the Doullens Conference was taking place, the Germans were driving relentlessly onwards. The 28th Division had crossed the Roye to Amiens road the previous day, threatening the right of Maxse's XVIII Corps. The 28th penetrated as far as Saulchoy, but to their north XVIII Corps was holding the Germans back, leaving a dangerously long exposed flank of about five miles (8km) in all. On 26 March the British, according to the 28th Division's report, counter-attacked the villages of Bouchoir and Le Quesnoy not only from the west but also from the north, supported by a French force a little east of the British. The attacks from the west were beaten off, but the British from Arvillers and Bouchoir beat the Germans back as far as Erches itself and, indeed, were cutting into the German 28th Division east of that village. The 28th's report continues, 'Hostile units were already appearing in the rear of the division. Persistent bombardments by hostile aviators were causing appreciable losses to our troops, a part of which were in close formation. Some supply wagons near the east edge of Erches withdrew in haste towards the east.' Three batteries of field artillery were brought hastily into action to fire on their forward guns which the British had already engulfed and the attack was driven off. From noon onwards, the Germans were taking the initiative, and the 7th Duke of Cornwall's Light Infantry struggled to hold on at Le Quesnoy until 1840 hours, when eleven remaining men managed to get away. From the British point of view, XVIII Corps had succeeded in making a withdrawal towards Amiens. From the German side it appeared to them that they had survived a dangerous attempt to cut them off from their rear. The

28th were withdrawn from the line three days later with some of their companies reduced to a quarter of their strength, and the division as a whole requiring 2,500 replacements, many of whom were of the class of 1919. Germany's finest troops were being lost at a frightening rate.

Watts's XIX Corps had a difficult day with messages failing to arrive, probably because of the death of the messengers, and consequential failures of understanding. They withdrew to a line running south from Bray-sur-Somme but to their north there was vacant space. Byng had given his commanders permission to fall back further and Congreve issued an order which led to his Corps starting to withdraw from the Albert-Bray sector at 1430 hours. Then, as a result of the Doullens conference, the orders came to stand firm, so Congreve attempted to countermand his own instructions. It soon became clear that even greater disorder would follow such an action with units all tangled up in a massive traffic jam, so he elected to withdraw as first planned. It was fortunate that the German 13th Division was exhausted and forced to halt at Morlancourt, south of Albert and west of Bray, instead of exploiting the open space before them. The 3rd Australian Division slogged south to fill the hole.

Albert was vacated and the 3rd Marine and 54th Reserve Divisions entered, but failed to climb out beyond in the face of resistance from the British 12th Division. Further north, the 24th (Saxon) Division looked as if it was on the point of a breakthrough, but the New Zealand Division fought all night to rebuild the link with the Australians at Hébuterne, north of Beaumont Hamel, by 0630 the next day. By now the Germans were finding the extent to which their lines had been stretched was causing problems. Front line units had been without new rations for two days. The old battlefield of the Somme and the southern area over which the Fifth Army had been driven back were without rail communication, either because there never had been any, or because it had been smashed in the latest fighting. The heavy artillery was lagging far in the rear, and ammunition for the field artillery could not be brought up in quantity.

THE RETREAT CONTINUES

For all this, and in spite of new reinforcements arriving almost by the hour, the Allies were still being forced back. Fayolle was fearful for Noyon on the River Oise, with Compiègne next downstream and Paris beyond, but Foch demanded, and got, priority for the defence of Amiens. The thin line manned by Gough's and Humbert's tired troops cracked, was repaired, and cracked once more. Mondidier was lost and fierce fighting took place to hold a line on the River Avre where the German 28th were putting in their last effort. The last of Maxse's Corps were clinging on south of Watts's whose men were involved in a fierce fight at Rozières-en-Santerre, but the greatest danger came from the area Congreve had vacated the day before. His VII Corps and the RFC aircraft held the German Second Army's advance from Morlancourt at Sailly. The German commander, Von Brauchitsch, turned his 3rd Grenadier and 43rd Regiments sharp left, southwards, by planking over the blown bridge between Chipilly and Cérisy and crossing the river at about 1400 hours. This brought them onto the south side of the Somme in the rear of Watts's men and in front of the line manned by the ad-hoc force under Major-General George Carey. The 3rd Guards attacked Carey's men, the 6th US Engineers, at the Bois des Tailloux on the Hamel-Warfusée road and went on to take the villages of Warfusée and Lamotte on the Roman road by 1900. Gough lost no time in moving his 61st Division by bus to positions to the rear of Carey. The Germans failed to reinforce their advantage and the next day XIX Corps was able to retire, sliding away to the south.

Gough's day was crowned with the news that he was to be replaced by General Sir Henry Rawlinson. He was being made the scapegoat for the failure of the BEF to prevent this depressing retreat and while he was not without fault it is fairly clear that he was given a task that was near to impossible in the face of government policy.

THE LINE STABILISES

It was Gough's great misfortune to be relieved of his command just as the situation was turning in favour of the Allies. Rawlinson assumed command at 1630 on 28 March. Carey's Force was in action again that day, but held off the attacks, and XIX Corps extended the line south of the Roman road to link with the French.

North of the Somme the Australians seem to have become tired of retreat. When attacked by the Germans they were not content merely to hold them, but counter-attacked and forced them back. The long-planned Operation Mars was put into action with nine German divisions striking at the four British divisions at Arras. The Front Line/Battle Zone/Rear Line defence system worked precisely as intended. By 1700 hours the German effort had ground to a halt with heavy casualties. The clear weather coupled with the excellent vantage-point of Vimy Ridge allowed the British artillery to play a full part. Ludendorff cancelled the operation that evening.

Over the next few days a series of relatively minor attacks and counter-attacks took place, but the new line settled until two last battles finally stabilised it.

THE BATTLES OF VILLERS-BRETONNEUX

The pause had been used by Ludendorff to bring up his heavy guns, resupply his troops and put six fresh divisions into his line. At 0515 on 4 April a fresh, gas-laced bombardment began. On the Avre line, south of the Roman road, the French were pressed back at first, but then bloodily, regained their ground. Across the Roman road, east of Villers-Bretonneux, Watts had established his front line of, from north to south, 14th Division, the Australian Brigade and 18th Division with 6th Cavalry Brigade in reserve and there were yet more reserves further to his rear. The German 228th Division broke the 14th's line between the Roman road and Hamel and the fleeing British had to be rallied by Australians and encouraged to regroup. Hamel village was captured by noon. The main Australian force and the 18th Division both threw back three successive German attacks, but with a gap to their left, fell back to trenches close to Villers-Bretonneux in the afternoon. North of the town, the 14th's line was being regained by 6th Cavalry, but at 1600 hours the German XI Corps made a violent attack on the 18th Divison and sent them staggering back into the town through mud and rain. The Australians reeled under the assault. As the battle stood in the balance Lieutenant-Colonel J. Milne gathered not only his battalion, the 36th, but another thousand Australian and British men scattered through Villers-Bretonneux and sheltering in cellars and, with the help of 7th Queens, thrust XI Corps back. North of the Roman road 17th Lancers bolstered the wavering 33rd Australian Battalion and linked 6th Cavalry with the counter-attackers, so that, by 1900, the position was restored. On 5 April further attacks here and to the north on the Ancre failed. Operation Michael was at an end, but fighting stuttered on for another couple of weeks around the village of Hangard on the Roye-Amiens road.

On 24 April the Germans attacked Villers-Bretonneux once more. The bombardment began at 0300 and at 0600 two German divisions moved up from the south-east followed by two more in reserve and preceded by A7V tanks. The Middlesex and West Yorkshires were forced back and the East Lancashires were pushed out of the town.

The Germans advanced tentatively beyond with four of the 13 A7V tanks with which they started that day. The clumsy German vehicles rolled down the slope to the south-west of the village at about 0930 to be met by three British Mark IV tanks. Lieutenant Frank Mitchell was commanding one of the British landships and wrote afterwards, 'There, some three hundred yards away, a round squat-looking monster was advancing, behind it came waves of infantry, and farther away to the left crawled two more of these armed tortoises... So we had met our rivals at last.'

The tanks exchanged fire, and eventually Mitchell's gunner scored a perfect hit with the six-pounder. The A7V heeled over, and the crew piled out. Seven of the new British Medium Mark A Whippets joined the fray and the Germans were forced back to the village. The world's first tank against tank action had been fought.

That night the Australian 15th and 13th Brigades and a brigade of 18th Division counter-attacked. The night was misty. There was no artillery preparation and the troops went forward in the dark with bayonet and machine-gun, fighting one small, bloody action after another.

The 13th Australian Brigade were later commended by Field Marshal Haig for they way they managed to overcome successive belts of barbed wire running diagonally across their line of advance. By daylight the two arms of the attack had the town in their embrace and mid-morning the Germans had been captured or thrown back.

THE COST

Ludendorff had called off Operation Michael on 5 April and turned his attention to his next big push on the River Lys to the north. Here, on the Somme, he had secured nothing of value. Amiens, the key rail link between Paris and Calais, was still in Allied hands. He now had the desert of the 1916 battlefield under his control and the virtually empty lands south of the Roman road from Amiens to St Quentin; country without benefit and hard to defend. He had inflicted substantial damage on his enemy. The British had lost 177,739 men killed, wounded and missing, of whom about 72,000 were prisoners who would have to be fed by a near-starving Germany. The Americans had lost seventy-seven men. The French casualties were about 77,000 of whom some 17,000 were prisoners. The Allies had lost 1,300 guns, 2,000 machine-guns and 200 tanks.

The impact of these losses was not fatal to the Allied cause. Their manpower needs were now being supplied in increasing numbers by American troops flocking into Europe. Winston Churchill had told Haig on 26 March that, by 6 April, 1,915 new guns would be delivered. Machine-guns were being manufactured at the rate of 10,000 a month and tanks at 100 per month. What was to be, perhaps, the greatest Allied gain was a coherent high command in the person of General Foch.

The Germans had lost, to all causes, 239,000 men, of whom a high proportion were the German's specialist *Stosstruppen*. It was a doubtful bargain.

LESSONS LEARNED

The memorandum from the 28th Division, written after their withdrawal from the action on 29 March, provides some interesting insights

into the German experience in this campaign. The fighting was designated 'the battle in the intermediate zone' – the area beyond the rigid
lines of trenches but not yet out in open country beyond. The author of
the memo, one Captain Schmidt, says of the organisation of the troops:

*Instead of masses of infantry and artillery starting out together from
one point as during the trench fighting, there are now nine small
units of all arms (mixed battalions) which fight independently in the
zone of attack. The infantry regiment is not composed of three battalions of infantry but of three battalions consisting of detachments
of all arms of the service and of a regiment of artillery placed at the
disposal of the regimental commander. Three mixed regiments of
infantry of this kind form the divisional infantry of a division.*

*The divisional artillery during the battle in the intermediate zone
is divided up into detachments of artillery placed at the disposal of
the battalions and regiments of infantry and artillery remaining at
the disposal of the divisional commander. Until the infantry battalions are supplied with special infantry guns, it is recommended that
a regimental field artillery group belonging to the infantry division
be distributed among the three infantry regiments of this group.
Each regiment is assigned a battery; each battalion, one section. It
is to be hoped that the accompanying batteries of the infantry will
be increased to six guns so that one section and always the same
section may be constantly incorporated in each battalion.*

*Of the two remaining groups, one may, for example, be under the
orders of the regiment on the right, the other under the orders of the
regiment on the left. This is not laid down as a rule. If in exception-
al cases the division has three regiments of infantry engaged one
beside the other, the second regiment of artillery will assign one
group to the third regiment. The rest of the artillery (the second field
artillery regiment of the division as well as several heavy-artillery
battalions and whenever possible two mixed battalions of heavy
field howitzers and one mixed battalion of mortars) is under the
orders of the divisional artillery commander.'*

Schmidt goes on to consider what happens if the fight tends to revert to fixed position warfare, and how his own 'position', as opposed to mobile, artillery can help:

> *If it is foreseen that, after the first shock, the crossing of the crater area as well as the advance of the battalion and regimental artillery will meet with great difficulties, it is recommended that batteries of position artillery be designated within our own positions, and that the mission of the battalion and regimental artillery be entrusted to them until the latter has regained contact with the infantry after having crossed the crater area. To play this role of the supporting battery it is necessary to designate either the batteries in position well forward, which are able by direct observation to support the infantry attack from the departure position, or it is necessary during the artillery preparation to place batteries for this purpose in position close to our own advanced trenches. If it is not possible to observe the enemy's positions from our positions, these batteries must during the attack push forward their observation posts far enough into the enemy's lines so that it may be possible to observe the terrain of the attack.*

Tactical approaches during the advance are then commented upon:

> *Whenever a point of support and a machine-gun nest is approached, it must always be observed whether it is possible to pass beyond them without attacking them. In this connection, there is no fear of abandoning the zone of combat.*
>
> *When the reduction is absolutely indispensable, each battalion will first of all try to reduce the machine-gun nest and point of support by its own weapons.*
>
> *The following method has given good results: On approaching a point of support or a machine-gun nest the infantry deploys in a thin line of skirmishers, and, accompanied by light machine-guns, seeks to gain contact with the enemy and to establish itself firmly. It must*

approach the enemy as near as possible; an effort is then made to immobilise him with the light machine-guns and heavy machine-guns which have been brought into position. Under the protection of this fire larger forces are engaged... upon the flank and as far as possible in the rear of the enemy. While the infantry is advancing... the light trench mortars are brought into position.

The light trench mortars execute direct fire upon the objective when it is to be taken under fire from the front and plunging fire when it has to be fired on from the flank or rear only.

The accompanying artillery will always try to take up a position at close range (350 to 1,500 meters at most) so as to put the enemy out of action by direct fire. In case it is impossible to bring the batteries into an open position the accompanying guns will be brought up into protected positions; in all cases it must be possible to obtain observation in the immediate vicinity of the guns.

On account of the great precision of fire of the trench mortars or accompanying artillery, firing at short ranges a few rounds is very frequently sufficient to put the enemy out of action or force him to retreat. If this is not sufficient the enemy may, by the fire mortars, be shattered or at least immobilised until the infantry comes into action. The infantry undertakes the assault when it recognises that the enemy is shaken. It makes known its intention to attack by sending up the light signal, `We are attacking'. The machine-guns then cease firing, the trench mortars and accompanying guns likewise stop or lengthen their range.

The possibility of being without the supporting fire of artillery or trench mortars is discussed and flanking movements are suggested, but the most important factor is the initiative of the field commander of the unit immediately engaged. He must act at once, using whatever forces are to hand. Support units, machine-gunners or trench mortar batteries, must be ready to open fire on targets of opportunity and also give support without waiting for specific orders. The necessity of reinforcing success rather than persisting in failure is emphasised:

*According to Paragraph 24 of Section 14 of the 'Collected
Instructions on Position Warfare', it is of advantage to engage
reserves at the place where the attack is progressing most favorably
and never, therefore, where it has been checked. The rules in this
paragraph, which are often lost sight of, can never be too much insisted upon. When they are observed, the reserves appear after a short
time upon the flanks or in the rear of the enemy's forces which are
still resisting and thus also assist in carrying forward the attack at
these points.*

*In open warfare, we seek to gain a decision by outflanking the
exposed wing. In the battle to break through, we strive for the same
result by bringing up the reserves at the points where the advance
has been most rapid, and thus reaching the rear of the enemy, succeed in outflanking him.*

*One of the principal tasks of the commanders of all ranks down to
company commanders is to recognise the point where the enemy is
offering the least resistance. It is there that the effort must be made
to break through, that is, the outflanking of the enemy by the method
described above.*

The problem of the exposed flank is studied and Schmidt says that,
while risks must be accepted, action should be taken to cover the flanks
as soon as possible. He proposes the use of machine-guns until one's
own units on the flank are able to come up into support, and gives the
28th Division's experience at Erches on 26 March as an example of
holding off an attacker on the flank even when that flank was five
miles (8km) long.

What the memorandum does not discuss is how far and for how
long the battle in the intermediate zone can be sustained. The 28th
Division fought for eight days before being withdrawn. At the end of
that time, 2,500 replacements were needed to bring it back to strength,
and many of those were 'Class of 1919', boys who were not even meant
to be liable for military service until the following year. Nor does the
document consider the problems of lengthening lines of supply of

arms, ammunition, rations and medical services. Many German units were disrupted by the unexpected riches they uncovered, storehouses filled with good clothing, sound boots, ample food and, most subversive of all, alcoholic drinks. Thus, while the memorandum is a fascinating exposé of German tactics in practice, it is not, and does not pretend to be, a complete blueprint for success.

The manpower problem was not limited to Germany alone. The fright engendered in England by Operation Michael forced the Government to take action at last. There were about 170,000 men in a reasonable state of readiness to be sent to France and another 50,000 or so were ready in April. Many of them were under nineteen years of age and theoretically not to be sent overseas, but the emergency decreed otherwise. The age of conscription was also changed, dropping from eighteen to seventeen and a half years of age at the lower end and rising to fifty at the other. Even these extraordinary provisions were to be scarcely enough to contain Ludendorff's assaults.

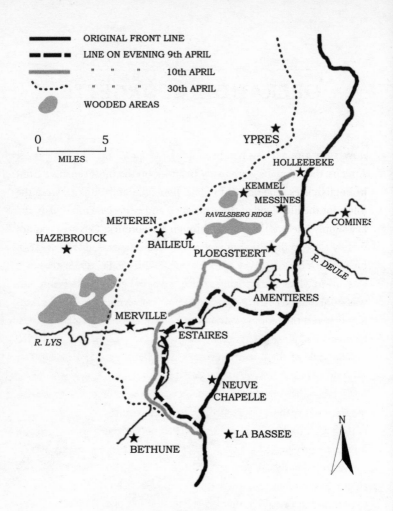

Operation Georgette: The Battle of the Lys
April 1918

4

OPERATION GEORGETTE

NOW THAT THE BRITISH had been drawn away to the south to protect Amiens, the Germans were ready to attack on the most sensitive front in English eyes. The ports of Calais, Boulogne and Dunkirk were the inlets for the life-blood of the army, men and *matériel*. From Calais, the key supply line was the railway through Hazebrouck. This area was not merely close to the junction with the Belgian Army, and thus vulnerable in much the same way as the junction with the French Army, but it was one in which the British feared they might be choked to death. Nor was it the mud-trap of the previous year. The winter had been unusually dry and the land was more open to movement here, just as the Germans had already seen on the Somme.

The scale of the operation to be undertaken was considered. The original plan for Operation *George* was too demanding and a lesser undertaking, *Georgette*, was substituted. It would be concentrated on the flat country in front of the modest north to south ridge west of Lille, bounded on the south by the La Basée Canal and on the north by the higher country north-east of the Armentières to Béthune road, the route followed today by the A25/E42 autoroute from Dunkirk to Lille. The ridge was the same, the Aubers Ridge, below which lay Neuve Chapelle, Givenchy and Festubert, that held harsh memories from earlier in the war. To the north of this area, the so-called mountains of Flanders rose, little hummocks in general terms, but in this low country positions of eminence from which vast tracts of land could be overseen. From the Mont des Cats, north-west of Bailleul, by way of Mont Noir, north of the town, and on through Kemmelberg or Mount Kemmel the ridge ran with a dip before Wytschaete, and then curved away to the north through Hill 60 and Broodseinde to Passchendaele.

Cutting across his intended line of advance, Ludendorff had the canalised river Lys, running a little north of east to Armentières from Aire-sur-la-Lys, halfway between St Omer and Béthune, through Merville, Estaires and Sailly-sur-la-Lys. From Béthune the little stream of the Lawe goes north to join the Lys at Estaires. The Canal d'Aire, known to the British as the La Bassée Canal, makes a diagonal from the north-west, where it extends to the Channel at Gravelines as the River Aa, through St Omer, Aire and Béthune to La Bassée. To the rear of the Lys, behind Merville from the British point of view, is the Forest of Nieppe. None of the waterways is particularly deep or formidable and, in this much-cultivated and industrialised region, bridges are many, so while mobility is affected, it is not rendered impossible by the rivers and canals.

THE PRELIMINARIES

Facing the British in northern France and Belgium, the Germans had General Sixt von Armin's Fourth Army in the north, and General Ferdinand von Quast's Sixth Army in front of the sector to be attacked in Operation Georgette. Altogether, seventeen divisions, Ludendorff planned, would be involved in the assault with fourteen of the Sixth Army, nine in line and five in reserve, pressing the main assault and the balance, the Fourth Army's two corps, enveloping Armentières and giving support in the Ypres Salient. The preliminary bombardment would be a classic firewaltz with a great concentration of gas – 2,000 tons in all, with a mixture of lachrimatory, blistering and lethal substances. The exact purpose of the operation appears to have been ill-defined. Some considered it to be the next in the series of hammer-blows Colonel Wetzell had advocated, while others saw it as a decisive operation in itself.

The victim of the assault was to be the Portuguese 2nd Division. This sorry formation, understrength, and with men denied home leave and consequently suffering from low morale, was holding a line some seven miles (11km) long at Neuve Chapelle and Laventie. The troops were inexperienced and only partly trained and, indeed, the British had small confidence in them. The 1st Division had already withdrawn to Boulogne and the 2nd were preparing to be relieved on the night of 9-10 April, but the blow fell first. To their right, in the south, was the 55th (West Lancashire) Division. The troops now in the line to their left and moving up from the south to reinforce them had still not recovered from the previous great attack. The 9th Division was between Hollebeke, on the Ypres-Comines Canal south-east of Ypres, and Messines, with the 25th Division on their right at Ploegsteert. Armentières was held by the 34th Division, and the 51st (Highland) Division was to the Portuguese rear on the River Lawe. Also in the second line were the 50th, 31st and 40th Divisions, the Guards and the 19th and 21st Divisions, all of whom were reduced in numbers by recent fighting and in need of rest. These dozen divisions were required to face the German seventeen. They were, however, occupying defence-in-depth positions.

THE FIRST DAY — 9 APRIL

The German guns opened up at 0415 hours and the infantry began to move four and a half hours later. The gas shelling caused 8,424 casualties that day, of which thirty were fatal. The high number of non-fatal victims was at least as satisfactory for the attackers as the fatalities, because yet more men were taken out of the line to look after them. The dawn was obscured by fog once again and the ability of the British artillery to respond was, for a second time, severely limited. The front line was penetrated immediately, and those Portuguese who resisted were by-passed in what had become classic German style. A British liaison officer, Captain R. G. C. Dartford, wrote that the front line was taken at about 0830 and the B line at 0845. Half an hour later, the battalion headquarters was under threat. The demoralised Portuguese, for the large part, fled. The Germans pursued and by 1000 hours had taken the third line at Laventie. One battalion held on at La Couture until their ammunition was gone and then resorted to the bayonet, but they were the exception in this sad story. By 1600 hours the Germans were on the River Lys and had crossed it near Sailly. Some 6,000 prisoners were taken in this swift action.

To the south of the Portuguese, the 55th Division stood on ground it knew well. The 1st West Lancashire Territorials, to give them their full name, were familiar with their complex of trenches, and were commanded by a man of skill who had mastered the new arts of defence. Major-General Hugh Jeudwine had brought this formation through two major episodes of the Third Battle of Ypres, the opening day and the Battle of the Menin Road, and the German counter-attack at Cambrai. In the seven weeks since taking position on this front, they had studied and extended their defences, establishing strongpoints and working out fields of fire for their guns. The terrain was cut through with a maze of trenches almost four years old, adding to the defensive opportunities and the confusion of the attackers. In these positions the West Lancashires held on well. Even when men of the King's Liverpool Regiment were forced out of Route A Keep and the Germans occupied it, a counter-attack regained the strongpoint. The refusal of the 55th Division to give way prevented development of the German attack on this flank and left it exposed to enfilading fire from the artillery throughout the battle. It also prevented an attack on Béthune and the precious coal-fields nearby.

On the Portuguese left, the 40th Division had moved into position on the night of 7–8 April. Brigadier-General F. P. Crozier, commanding 119th Brigade, was not impressed by his allies. He visited their trenches, and found rifles and ammunition simply lying around. Men presumably meant to be on duty were sleeping. The next day they ran away. Crozier was obliged to lead his men back to positions near Bac St Maur, east of Sailly. At the same time Major-General Sir John Ponsonby, commanding the 40th, ordered the 120th (Highland) Brigade forward to Laventie rail station, south of Sailly. At Fleurbaix, south-east of Sailly, the men of the Suffolk Regiment stood, fell back, counter-attacked and stood again.

The Germans had made a good start to Georgette. The bite into British positions was ten miles (16km) wide and five miles (9km) deep. Not so satisfactory was the fact that on their left, from Givenchy to Festubert and north along the River Lawe to Estaires, they had been held. The 51st (Highland) Division moved up to the Lawe and the 50th took position to their left and 40th's right on the Lys. On the opposite flank the Germans had not made much impression either. The British were proving rather more stubborn than expected, but at Sailly and Bac St Maur the bridgehead was developed.

THE FIGHT CONTINUES

On 10 April the German Fourth Army turned its attention to Plumer's Second. They shelled the Messines Ridge at 0245 hours and had the village surrounded as the day dawned, but the resistance by the British on the ridge was determined. Messines was lost for a while, but recaptured in a heroic action by South African troops. The advances in the north of the campaign area made the 34th Division's position at Armentières impossible and they had to pull back.

On the Lys the fighting continued, but recent rain had made the ground difficult for the Germans' heavier guns to move and, lacking their support, small progress was made. Estaires was taken by evening and to the east the British pulled back from the Lys to Steenwerck. This left an untenable salient between Steenwerck and Ploegsteert, bulging out towards Armentières.

The need to retreat again was depressing for the British, but worst of all was to see the inhabitants of what had been a stable and relatively safe part of the country being forced to abandon their homes, farms and businesses. Major John Lyne of the Royal Field Artillery wrote home about the farmers near his lines. They had been over-run early in the war by 'the Hun' and the farm plundered. Now they had rebuilt their lives and work to the point of having a dozen cattle, a herd of pigs and a flock of poultry. The fields were newly and expensively fertilised. Now, they faced losing it all again. Captain Harry Graham, staff officer, 40th Division, also commented on the unfortunate French. The mass of civilians not only got in the way of troop movements and made demands on valuable and scarce transport to escape, but they also fell victim to enemy shellfire. 'Even the Hun,' he wrote, 'must have felt stirred to loathing when he reached Bac St Maur and Estaires... and found the bodies of women and children and poor old people lying about the streets – but I do think it is the fault of the French or even our own authorities for not clearing the inhabitants away just as they did in the south.'

BACKS TO THE WALL

Sir Douglas Haig was energetic in his calls for reinforcements from the French, but Foch was not convinced that the British were truly in danger of being broken and Pétain, as usual, was apprehensive about attacks elsewhere, for which he insisted his divisions must be kept ready far from the Lys. Nonetheless, General Paul Maistre's Tenth Army was ordered to take over positions from the British north of the Somme, releasing them for service further north, and soon after General Joseph Micheler's Fifth Army followed suit. Haig, for his part, was looking at an enemy that had just advanced at a rate that, if maintained, would take them to the Channel, just fifteen miles (25km) away, in the next week. It was a very serious situation.

On 11 April Haig issued a remarkable Order of the Day which is frequently quoted in selected parts according to the thesis being promoted by the author concerned. It is better read in full:

To all ranks of the British army in France and Flanders:

Three weeks ago to-day the enemy began his terrific attacks against us on a 50-mile [80km] front. His objects are to separate us from the French, to take the Channel ports, and to destroy the British army.

In spite of throwing already 106 divisions into the battle and enduring the most reckless sacrifice of human life, he has as yet made little progress towards his goals. We owe this to the determined fighting and self-sacrifice of our troops.

Words fail me to express the admiration which I feel for the splendid resistance offered by all ranks of our army under the most trying circumstances. Many among us now are tired. To those I would say that victory will belong to the side which holds out the longest.

The French army is moving rapidly and in great force to our sup-

port. There is no other course open to us but to fight it out. Every
position must be held to the last man; there must be no retirement.
With our backs to the wall, and believing in the justice of our cause,
each one of us must fight on to the end. The safety of our homes and
the freedom of mankind depend alike upon the conduct of each one
of us at this critical moment.

There can be no doubt that Haig chose his words with care. The emotional appeal of this Order is so unusual for the Field Marshal that every word must have been examined, considered and placed precisely where he wanted it. The most usual cuts made by those who quote from it are to remove references to the Germans' objectives, and so make the message less respectful to its recipients, and to omit the remarks about the French support, making it more divisive of the alliance. Readers will form their own views, but the reception the Order received on 11 April 1918 was mixed.

Some of those to whom it was addressed were moved and enthusiastic while others asked 'Where's the ******* wall?' and grumbled that they were well aware that things were serious. In later years Gunner Burton, by then the celebrated natural history writer and zoologist, Dr Maurice Burton, wrote:

Recalling those days, my feeling is that it had no purpose except to let
everyone know that times were grim. Never, as I think back, can I
remember hearing anyone even so much as suggesting that we might
be defeated. At various times, during the retreat, we met men of many
regiments and units, from all parts of England, Wales, Scotland,
Ireland and from overseas. They were infantrymen, engineers,
artillerymen and other branches of the army. I cannot recall anyone
uttering words of despair. They complained of fatigue, of hunger, of
inconvenience: they would utter "Roll on, Blighty", which being trans-
lated meant "I shall be glad when all this is over and we can go home".
But despair or defeat seemed not to have been contemplated.

THE CRITICAL DAYS

On the same day as Haig's message was sent to his troops, Armentières was occupied by the Germans. A brigade of the 29th Division was withdrawn from Passchendaele for rest but instead found itself bussed from Poperinghe and pushed into the line at Merville on the Lys. The 25th Division was retiring from Ploegsteert towards Neuve Eglise. The 34th, having quit Armentières, were on the marginally higher land north of Bailleul which gave their gunners a good view over the salient now occupied by the Germans when the weather was clear enough, and in the late afternoon of 11 April it did, at last start to clear. Now both the artillery and the Royal Air Force, as the flying service had now become, could play a full part.

On 12 April the progress the Germans made in the centre was fairly satisfactory. They got over the Lys at Merville and reached the outskirts of the Forest of Nieppe in front of Hazebrouck, but the salient was growing longer and more vulnerable, and the resistance they faced at the western end of their incursion was being stiffened with new forces. The 31st Division arrived from the Arras sector to defend the forest and at Rocbecq, on the little Clarence River where the Béthune to Hazebrouck road crosses it close to the Aire Canal, the 4th Division came from Vimy to hold the line for the rest of the battle. The German action was being squeezed northwards, and the approaches to Hazebrouck were hardening.

Plumer had already reconciled himself to swallowing a bitter pill. The increasing pressure to the south of Ypres was creating a longer and more vulnerable southern flank to the Ypres Salient. It became clear that the most easterly positions in the salient had to be abandoned; Passchendaele, for which so many under his command had given their lives, would have to be evacuated. As the withdrawal began on 12 April the Germans started a new thrust towards Mount Kemmel and the village of Neuve Eglise or Nieuwkerke to the south-east of it. (The English tended to use the French, rather than the Flemish, place-names; a practical thing to do, given that it was with the French that they had chiefly to co-operate). The assault was along a curving line

from Bailleul to Wytschaete, embracing the high ground and was fiercely resisted. The greatest weight was thrown against the 25th Division
at Neuve Eglise, the junction of the roads enfolding the hills and the
routes northwards to Kemmel and to Ypres.

The attack was made in force and the village was taken but the
Worcesters, Sherwood Foresters and Yorkshire Light Infantry counter-
attacked on the morning of 13 April, a Saturday, and retook it.
Meanwhile, Plumer's withdrawal from the forward positions in the
Ypres Salient was quietly progressing. The Germans renewed their
efforts with yet greater force that same day. At one point the British
were almost surrounded, with only the slender link of the road to the
north-west and the village of Dranoutre between them and the BEF.
Eventually they had no choice but to pull out, the King's Royal Rifles
acting as rearguard. This rendered Wulverghem, between Neuve Eglise
and Messines, untenable, and Bailleul vulnerable.

Six divisions of the Bavarian II Corps made the attempt on Bailleul.
The British artillery on the hills to the north did great damage to the
German artillery and troops and the massing of machine-guns in depth
slowed their advance, but they still came forward. In the end they were
halted by the Royal Newfoundland Regiment, within a grenade's throw
of the Royal Newfoundland's front line.

In the centre, the Germans tried to by-pass the Forest of Nieppe on
its northern side, but were held by the determined stand of a curiously
mixed array of units – Scottish Rifles, Highland Light Infantry, West
Surreys, Worcesters, Middlesex and New Zealanders. Tank Corps men
fought as infantry, and men from various support units joined in. The
Germans were becoming disheartened, and Crown Prince Rupprecht
was to compare the fight with the First Battle of Ypres, in which
Germany's finest troops were stopped by a rag-bag of cooks, grooms
and personal servants who joined the remnants of the regular soldiers.

On 15 April the evacuation of the Passchendaele Ridge was complet-
ed as Bailleul and Wulverghem fell to the Germans, but on that day the
French arrived. Pétain had organised the Détachment d'Armée du Nord,
DAN, to support Haig's hard-pressed men. It consisted of the 2nd

Cavalry Corps under General Robillot, and five infantry divisions under General Henri de Mitry. Two of those divisions were in action alongside Plumer's men the following day. The actions of 16 April increased the German hold on the higher ground by advancing against Wytschaete in the east and Méteren, near Bailleul, in the west. A final attempt to unseat the 55th Division from its positions near Givenchy on 17 and 18 April made some progress at first, but was then thrown back. The axis of effort was twisting northwards, away from the key communication lines and towards the hills south of Ypres.

THE FIGHT FOR MOUNT KEMMEL

The German ambitions in the Battle of the Lys had, like those in Operation Michael, become less substantial with time. Their troops, after ten days' hard fighting, were tired and had lost momentum. Nothing much of value had been gained in Operation Georgette, but one attractive prize stood before them – Mount Kemmel, a height from which the whole area south of Ypres and west of Lille might be overseen.

The Mount itself was held by the French 28th Division and on 24 April, under the cover of fog, the Germans massed seven divisions to take the hill. At 0330 hours, the artillery bombardment, the now usual mixture of gasses and explosives, fell on British artillery positions,. At 0600 the Mount itself was shelled, and the French suffered heavy casualties. The infantry assault by XVIII, X Reserve Corps and the Alpine Corps began at 0700. The assault was made on three sides and the defenders were soon surrounded. The French held out on the summit for eight hours, their final struggle witnessed by a reconnaissance aircraft. The German report of victory at 0840 hours was exaggerated, but eventually came true.

To the west, beyond Locre, the chain of hills ran on through Mont Noir and the Mont des Cats while to the north, on the way to Ypres, the village of Vormezeele lay below the ridge that curled round the much-disputed salient. The last effort of the operation was the attempt to take these crucial positions. On Friday 26 April the Germans took Locre. French cavalry rode sixty miles (100km) to come up in support and, on foot, took the position back. An attempt to take Vormezeele petered out. On 29 April thirteen German divisions attacked the whole line from Méteren to Zillebeke at 0540 hours and also struck at the Belgians north of Ypres. The gains made were trivial. On 30 April Ludendorff ended Georgette.

THE RESULTS

Apart from inflicting damage and a very nasty fright on the Allies, mainly the British, Ludendorff had gained little. Although the Germans stood on Mount Kemmel, they did not control the rest of the line of hills to the west and thus had failed to achieve a domination of the southern side of the Ypres Salient. The rail centre of Hazebrouck remained in British hands. The Canal de l'Aire or La Bassée Canal along the southern side of the battle area, a threatening artillery position, remained British. Casualties of 109,300 men and a loss of 38 aircraft had been sustained. The best of the offensive forces had been sharply reduced in the first two campaigns of the spring.

The Allies had suffered greatly as well, with 6,000 Portuguese among the 29,000 prisoners the Germans had taken. British losses, killed, wounded and missing (possibly as prisoners) came to 76,300 men and more than a hundred guns and sixty aircraft. The French figures were 35,000 men and twelve guns. In manpower the damage was roughly equal, but here the Allies had a massive advantage – America.

CANTIGNY

The Americans had been building their numbers and training energetically through the year. They had gained some front line experience in the relatively quiet areas of the Lorraine front and on the the southern side of the St Mihiel Salient. They had to fight off a few German raids and, notably at Siecheprey on 20 April, did not impress either the Germans or their Allies with their effectiveness. When the *Kaiserschlacht* crisis was at its height, on 28 March, Pershing offered Foch all the assistance in his power to command, but little of a practical nature emerged from that gesture.

The United States had now been at war for a year. In that time, the AEF's fatal casualties in action had been a mere 163 men. It was essential that Pershing take a greater share of the load, and yet more important to gain the confidence of his allies and raise the morale of his troops by making, and succeeding in, an attack. The fighting spirit of the men was not in doubt, but the competence of the regimental officers and staff was. The place chosen for this first American offensive was the village of Cantigny, west of Montdidier, where the German advance had been halted in March. The 1st Division had entered the line here on 23 April, overlooked by the Germans from the village on the ridge, and made their plans to take the position.

The French provided the greater part of the artillery support for the coming attack. The preparations were made with immense care – the American staff, including Captain George C. Marshall, Jr, were determined that everything should go perfectly. A model of the objective was made for the officers and NCOs to study and, well to the rear, the target zone was replicated by tracing it out on the ground so that troops could practise their tasks. The mission was described and repeatedly emphasised – Cantigny was to be taken and held against all counterattacks. The assault on 28 May fell to the 28th Infantry Regiment.

Raymond Austin, an officer of the 6th Field Artillery, wrote home on 1 June:

We adjusted our rolling barrage, etc., as discreetly as possible the day before, and everything was ready that evening... H hour would be at 6.45am – the time when the infantry would go over the top... At 4.45 all batteries... began their final adjustments all along the line and at the first shots the Boche's sausages [observation balloons] went up in a hurry to see what was going on... Then at 5.45 all batteries began a heavy raking fire throughout the zone to be covered by our advance... Then at 6.45... the barrage moved forward at a rate just fast enough for the infantry to keep up with it at a walk. At the same time... the infantry suddenly appeared on the slope of the ridge close behind our barrage – a long brown line with bayonets glisten-

ing in the sun... They walked steadily along... accompanied by the
tanks which buzzed along with smoke coming out from their exhausts
and their guns. As the line reached the crest and was silhouetted in
the morning sun... it looked like a long picket fence. Occasionally a
shell would strike among them and a gap would appear among the
pickets, then quickly close.

The Americans were soon in the enemy's third line trenches, having
carried the first and second lines. As the shellfire passed beyond
Cantigny, Germans emerged from the cellars where they had sheltered,
either of their own volition or flushed out by flame-thrower or grenade,
and a flurry of fights saw them either killed or captured. Now the 28th
had to hold the ground. Counter-attacks were not long in coming, with
immediate German shelling. Counter-battery fire was not undertaken,
for the French artillery had been called away. Only a few hours before,
the Germans had launched their next great assault Operation Blücher-
Yorck, this time on the Chemin des Dames above the valley of the
Aisne, and every French gun was needed to oppose them.

There were two counter-attacks that day, and the 28th fought both
of them off. Two companies of the 18th Infantry reinforced the position that night. In all there were seven attempts by the Germans to
regain the ground. All failed. Some fifty casualties had been the price
of taking Cantigny, but holding it cost the Americans 199 killed, 652
wounded, 200 gassed and 16 missing. Raymond Austin wrote:

Casualty lists of an attack like this don't look very large beside those
of a German fifty-mile front drive, but when you see fine, young
American boys lying dead in heaps of six or eight or twelve here and
there it's more than enough, but it must be if we're going to whip
Germany and the sooner people realise it in America the better – and
we may be able to finish the job sooner.

It was, indeed, a minor action, but it made its point. The Americans
had proved not only that they could organise and carry out an attack,

but also that they could hold their ground. Holding ground was soon to be an American task of immense importance.

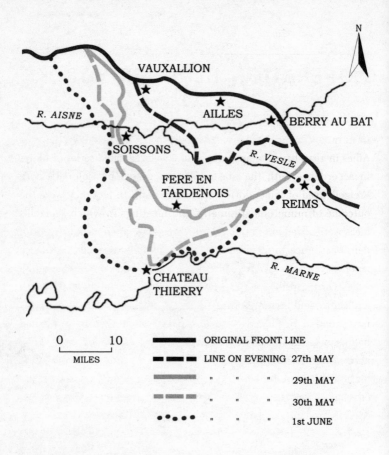

N

VAUXALLION

AILLES

BERRY AU BAT

R. AISNE

SOISSONS

R. VESLE

FERE EN
TARDENOIS

REIMS

R. MARNE

CHATEAU
THIERRY

0	10	ORIGINAL FRONT LINE
	MILES	LINE ON EVENING 27th MAY
		" " " 29th MAY
		" " " 30th MAY
		" " " 1st JUNE

Operation Blücker-Yorck: The German Aisne Offensive
May 1918

5

OPERATION BLÜCHER-YORCK

IN RETROSPECT the successive attacks launched by Ludendorff on the Allies in 1918 have the appearance of a well-regulated series of blows in accordance with the master-plan suggested by Colonel Georg Wetzell, head of Ludendorff's operations staff. In fact they were the outcome of numerous arguments and meetings in which Wetzell's ideas were added to, subtracted from and, quite often, simply over-ridden. Deep uncertainties and severe misgivings were commonplace amongst the German commanders just as they were on the side of the Allies. On 20 April, as the Georgette operation was stalling in the south and centre and turning towards Mount Kemmel, Wetzell drafted his next proposal. He judged that another attack on the British front would be unsuccessful and that the Chemin des Dames, the high ridge road above the Aisne between Soissons and Reims, was the appropriate place. This Operation *Blücher* would be supported by Operation *Goerz* enveloping Reims and followed by a strike on the west, *Yorck*, between Soissons and the Compiègne Forest. After that a third attack, Operation *Gneisenau*, would be carried out on the other side of the forest, between Noyon and Montdidier. By this means French, and possibly some British forces, would be drawn away from Flanders and Artois. That achieved, the original operations could be undertaken once again; a New George and a New Michael. These were given the names *Hagen* and *Wilhelm* respectively. They would result in the splitting apart of the British and the French, their total demoralisation and the negotiation of peace terms before the Americans could tip the balance against Germany. A nice, tidy scheme on paper that was to become unravelled within the next few weeks.

THE SECOND BATTLE OF THE AISNE

The Chemin des Dames sector had been the scene of the terrible slaughter of General Robert Nivelle's supposed master-stroke for the defeat of Germany in the spring of 1917. In a poorly-conceived and badly-managed attack, the French had suffered fearful losses and their army had been brought to the brink of collapse. Mutiny had taken hold of an alarmingly large number of regiments, and it was only the steady and tough but sympathetic approach of General Pétain that had prevented total disintegration. This area was now considered quiet. The same terrain that had broken the French assault was, it appeared, equally unsuited to the kind of lightening assault Ludendorff favoured.

The defence of this line was in the hands of General Denis Duchêne, commander of the French Sixth Army. He was not the most sensitive of men and rejoiced in the nickname of Le Tigre. In 1917 he had been in command of the Tenth Army which had sustained large casualties in Nivelle's attack and had also been harshly handled in the subsequent unrest. He had been specifically ordered to organise his defence in depth. Pétain's Directive Number 4 of December 1917 was clear, but Duchêne would have none of it. Pétain's chief of staff, who was also Duchêne's brother-in-law, General François Anthoine, argued the case with his relative, but he would not give way, leaving Pétain the choice of conceding or removing him from command. Once again the man on the spot had his way.

The forces at Duchêne's disposal included four French divisions and one British Corps in his front line. The British IX Corps under Major-General Henry Jackson had not liked the defensive arrangements any more than the French High Command, but when Jackson protested packing in all the infantry and artillery on a narrow band of land which fell away to a river and a canal in his rear, his French superior brushed him off with the abrupt remark 'j'ai dit!' In spite of that, the environment in which the British found themselves was very pleasant, if unmartial. An officer of the Devonshire Regiment observed that in some places there were rose-covered arbours, and another officer of the Middlesex Regiment compared their trenches to an underground Savoy

Hotel. After the blasted wilderness of the Somme, Artois or Flanders, this must have seemed a paradise, and no more than they deserved.

The 50th Division, in which were found the 2nd Devons, 2nd Middlesex and 2nd East Lancashires, had provided the vital bulwark on the southern flank of the German advance in Georgette, and now held the line climbing to Craonne on the eastern end of the Chemin des Dames. On their right was the 8th Division, also down from the north and now defending Berry-au-Bac and then came the 21st Division, which had fought at Epéhy and in the retreat to Bray-sur-Somme, now in the area of Berméricourt, north of Reims. To their right the French defended the northern and eastern sides of the city. In reserve the British had the 25th Division, badly mauled in its defence of Kemmel and the 19th, also bruised in the Battle of the Lys. Their chance to enjoy this paradise was to be short.

Early in May, Ludendorff withdrew thirty-two divisions to be trained and rested for the new assault. In the days leading up to the operation they moved forward under cover of darkness, bringing their artillery forward and assembling the few tanks they possessed. Operation Blücher was the business of General Hans von Böhn's Seventh Army, using five corps and leaving one to work with First Army. On the west were General Hermann von François's VII Corps and General Larich's LIV Corps, charged with advancing towards the Aisne west of Soissons. In the centre were General Wichura's VII Reserve Corps and General Winkler's XXV Reserve Corps, with General Conta's IV Reserve Corps to their left. LXV Corps, under General Schmettow, was on the extreme left. On the east of the Seventh Army's front, was the right wing of General Fritz von Below's First Army, ready to play its part in attacking Reims in Operation Goerz. Operation Blücher's attack would be made by fifteen divisions, rested and fresh, with another seven in support. Three further divisions would take part in Operation Goerz.

The British captured a prisoner on the evening of 26 May and were aware of the coming battle. Their report reinforced others received at Duchêne's headquarters over the previous few days, and was accorded the same neglect. The operation opened with one of Bruchmüller's trademark firewaltz bombardments. At 0100 hours, for ten minutes, according to a German report, all possible targets were shelled with gas. This was followed with sixty-five minutes of both gas and explosive on the Allied artillery positions while the trench mortars set about the front line defences and barbed wire. The infantry was scheduled to advance at 0340 hours on 27 May. It was extremely successful. The Allied front collapsed almost in its entirety.

There were some, small but notable, points of resistance. At Pinon, north-east of Soissons on the Canal de l'Oise à l'Aisne, the forest was fortified with pillboxes held by three French battalions. They held out for two full days, grimly fighting on when all hope of relief must have gone. On the British end of the line the shelling had been very effective, but the German advance was not without problems. On the Craonne plateau the Durham Light Infantry and the Northumberland Fusiliers put up a stout resistance and at Ville-aux-Bois-les-Pontaverts, in the wood called the Bois des Buttes, elements of the 2nd Devonshire Regiment made a stand. Under Lieutenant-Colonel R. H. Anderson-Morshead, and supported by 5th (Gibraltar) Battery, 45 Brigade, Royal Field Artillery, as one witness said, they were '... an island in the midst of an innumerable and determined foe, fighting with perfect discipline, and by the steadiness of their fire, mowing down the enemy in large numbers.' The resistance was heroic but ineffective. The centre of the line had already broken and the British were outflanked on their left as the Germans poured across the Chemin des Dames and down to the Aisne. Those who could withdrew towards the River Vesle.

Major-General von Unruh, Chief of Staff of Conta's IV Reserve Corps, wrote:

Against the onslaught of three German divisions, which were quickly followed by two others, it was humanly impossible for the extended and surprised English troops to stand up... Our losses were remarkably small. The enemy had no time to resist. The English, who could usually be relied upon to hold out in shell-holes, firing to their last

*cartridge, were given no opportunity by the violence and activity of
our combined artillery and trench-mortar fire to display their cus-
tomary coolness. They were up against `force majeure', and, first
blown out of their trenches and then surrounded, sentry-posts, Lewis-
gun teams, and whole platoons saw that resistance was hopeless and
were reluctantly obliged to surrender. Everywhere one could see
groups stumbling down from the high ground to be taken prisoner by
our waiting troops.*

By evening most of the Germans were over the Aisne, on which the
bridges had been left intact, and had advanced as far as the Vesle in the
centre of the front. The River Vesle runs from Reims to join the Aisne
above Soissons, and thus men on the eastern flank had further to go.
The two Corps in the centre, Winkler's and Conta's reached Braine and
Fismes respectively, while Schmettow's men were held up by the
British, the Devons amongst them, to some extent and found that the
bridges on their line of advance had been destroyed. Having eventually crossed the Aisne they ran into more British resistance in the woods
south of Gernicourt. Operation Goerz had few problems in crossing the
road running north-west from Reims, but then ran into the British on
the eastern flank of those same woods, here overlooking Cormicy. To
the west, the Germans had encountered rather greater difficulties. First,
they had been forced to bypass the strongpoints at Pinon, and then
Wichura's men had run into heavy fire from Condé on the Aisne.
Larisch's Corps lagged behind because of efficient French shelling, but
reached Soissons by the end of the day, and François's men established
a bridgehead on the Ailette at Leuilly, north of Soissons. It was a satisfactory first day for the Germans.

On 28 May General Pétain appealed to Foch for reinforcements and,
while the commander-in-chief was wary of weakening the line in
Flanders, he did remove the French Fifth Army from Haig's sector.
Pétain then toured the headquarters of his troops in the area under
attack and concluded that the line of the Vesle could not be held. His
instructions were then to hold the flanks, just as the British had done

against Georgette, and permit the Germans to extend themselves into a potentially vulnerable salient. The French and British proved difficult to push back on the eastern flank that Tuesday and the following day the British 19th Division came into the line. The battle here developed into a struggle for the heights south of Reims, the Montagne de Reims, a forested area that had to be held if the city was not to be abandoned. By the end of the week, 31 May, the hill at Bligny, south-west of the city and overlooking the valley of the River Ardre, had become the key point of contention. The Cheshires and Shropshires, with the support of the Staffordshires of 19th Division, eventually secured the village. A series of actions on the opposite side of the growing salient, around Villers-Cotterets in the Forest of Retz, defined the western flank. On 31 May the French attacked with three divisions and thirty of the new Renault light tanks. Three of the machines were lost, but the relative speed and mobility of the vehicles caused the Germans problems. Ludendorff again changed his plans. The intoxicating success of the assault had taken his troops across the Aisne and the Vesle to the Marne in five days. He turned his eyes to Paris, already under shellfire from the massive 21-centimetre gun nicknamed Wilhelm. Who would stop them now?

CHÂTEAU THIERRY

On 31 May General Conta held a position facing west with his left near Château Thierry on the River Marne and his right north of there, at Brécy. To his east, Schmettow's Corps was also on the river. Paris was fewer than sixty miles (100km) away. The French and British had no fresh troops to bar the way, and it was to fall to the Americans to make the difference.

The Headquarters unit of the American 3rd Division, under Major-General Joseph T. Dickman, had landed in France on 4 April 1918 and the formation was thus without front line experience, a cause for hesitation on the part of Pétain in asking General Pershing to put them in the field. The crisis was so severe that there was no choice. The 7th Machine-Gun Battalion of the Division was commanded by Captain J.

R. Mendenhall, and while still in France after the end of the war he
toured the area of his first battle with Captain Joseph A. Minturn, who
wrote a detailed account of what Mendenhall told him. The account
given here follows Minturn's report closely.

'We arrived in France,' Mendenhall said, 'about April 15, 1918. I was
captain of Company B, 7th Machine-gun Battalion, 3rd Division.'

The two officers went to the area in which the 3rd Division had
been training and retraced the route taken in those first days of June:

> Our organisation was the machine-gun battalion of the division, and
> had two companies with twenty-four active and eight reserve guns;
> twenty-four officers and 353 men. Our motor equipment was not
> received until May 20, when we got twenty-four half-ton Ford trucks
> and two Ford touring cars for each company and six trucks and one
> touring car for battalion headquarters. We began at once to teach
> the men how to drive the cars. Our other training schedule called for
> two months of preliminary, followed by a short period of trench duty
> in some quiet sector of the front. This should have put us on trench
> duty about July 1, 1918.
>
> Around 10 a.m. of May 30, Decoration Day at home, an order came
> to our major, Edward G. Taylor, to go at once on our own transporta-
> tion to Condé-en-Brie, and report to the French officer commanding
> that sector. Speed was urged because the German drive was forcing
> back the French and the British troops, and all reserves must be
> thrown in at once to stop the enemy and save Paris.
>
> When loaded we found that our cars had on three times their capac-
> ity, but the battalion left La Ferté [St Aubin, south of Orléans,
> perhaps?] at 2:55 p.m. in good order. Major Taylor went ahead, fol-
> lowed by Company A, and then by Company B, after which came several
> three-ton trucks with extra ammunition, gasoline and equipment.
>
> We had difficulty in making the steep grades on account of
> unavoidable overloading. In many cases the rear springs touched the
> axles, and blow-outs were frequent because the tires could not stand
> the extra pressure and we were soon badly strung out along the road.

We made no stop for supper and reached Arcis-Sur-Aube by 8:30 p.m. We were out of gasoline and hoped to get some there, but could not, and had to wait for our three-ton trucks, which came in near midnight. Our route was by Mery-Sur-Seine, Anglure, Sézanne, Montmort and Orbais. We came out of Sézanne... about 5 a.m. of May 31. It was blocked with refugees with their household goods, babies, old women and little children, crowded and piled on carts, to which cows and donkeys were hitched. Many pulled the carts themselves; and loaded wheelbarrows and dog carts were in the jam. Men and women carried their heavy loads with frightened children clinging to what they could to keep themselves from being trodden down or lost. The expressions on the faces of the refugees were most pitiful, and we began for the first time to realise something of the real meaning of war. Farther on, spaces between cars were forced and filled by small detachments of French and British troops, all looking thoroughly demoralised and discouraged. Following these came artillery, blocking the road entirely at times, the faces of the men showing signs of great fatigue and many sleepless nights. Some of the light batteries were going into position there on the slopes of these hills and were firing vigorously, which added to the confusion and frightfulness.

This appalling jam of terrified traffic made it impossible for us to keep our train intact, and as a result our arrival at Condé-en-Brie was very fragmentary... By 2 p.m. the entire battalion except the three-ton trucks had arrived here at Condé. We were again almost out of gasoline and our major reported to General Marchand, of the French army, at Janvier Ferme. We were told the enemy was expected to begin shelling Condé at any time, and were ordered to evacuate Janvier Ferme. Our gas tanks were so nearly empty that our Fords would not pull the hill southwest of the town. So, filling a few tanks by emptying gasoline from the others, we moved as many of our companies as we could and the remainder marched on foot, carrying their guns, equipment and packs. They were later picked up by the cars who had filled their tanks upon arrival of the three-ton trucks.

Major Taylor, with his two company commanders, went ahead to Nesles-la-Montaingne, a village overlooking the flood plain of the Marne south of Château-Thierry, where he met a French general commanding a colonial division. He briefed the Americans on the defences of the town and told them that detailed orders would be given by the lieutenant-colonel they would find when they got there:

> We left instructions for our battalion to rendezvous in Nesles, and, proceeding to Château Thierry by automobile, found the lieutenant-colonel had crossed to the north side of the River Marne, where he had been captured by a German patrol. The officer, a French captain, who gave us this information, urged us to bring our troops into the town with all speed to prevent the enemy crossing the bridge to the south side of the river.
>
> When we got back to Nesles about half of each company had arrived from Condé-en-Brie, and, assembling gun squads as quickly as possible, we transported them hurriedly in what cars were still in running condition to Château Thierry, where we reported to Major Taylor in the Place Carnot [south of the river and of the island north of which is the main part of the town]. By 6 p.m. about six gun squads from each company were available, and were assigned positions which roughly divided the town into two sectors – Company A on the west toward the cathedral and Hill 204; Company B on the east toward the sugar factory and Brasles – each being responsible for the defense of a bridge, the local river margin and one flank.
>
> Second Lieutenant Cobbey of Company B had a machine-gun in a two-story brick house on the bank of the river, ready to fire from a lower window and cover the river bank from the bridge east, and one in a shed on the east of this building with range to the northwest. Second Lieutenant Paul T. Funkhouser had three guns in a wooded peninsula about 600 yards to the east of the bridge we were defending; two guns ranging west along the river, and one east. Two guns, under First Lieutenant Charles Montgomery, were in a sunken garden 200 yards south of the bridge, which also enfiladed it. The other

guns of Company B were held at battalion headquarters as a reserve. My post of command was established under the railroad bank, giving me a covered line of communication to all my guns and to the battalion post of command, located in a house facing Place Carnot. This arrangement was completed by 3 p.m. June 1.

About 4 a.m., just as daylight was getting strong, a column of German infantry was observed marching west of the town of Brasles [just to the east] along the road paralleling the river toward Château Thierry. They apparently did not know they were in danger... The guns under Lieutenants Cobbey and Funkhouser opened fire when the enemy arrived at a slight bend in the road. The German discipline was such that the soldiers continued to advance until our positions were apparently located, when they deployed into the wheat fields between the road and the river. The grain stood waist high and the men were lost to view. However, our men whipped the field continuously with machine-gun fire, causing heavy casualties to the enemy. At 5 a.m., or within an hour, our guns on the peninsula were located and fired upon by enemy machine-guns, wounding a man and forcing the rest to withdraw. Our other guns continued their effective fire. Making a rapid reconnaissance with First Lieutenant J. W. Ransdall, I placed him with two guns near some small buildings where the railroad crosses the Crezancy highway. By this time the enemy machine-gun fire was much heavier, coming apparently from the high ridge in the north distance across the Marne from us. A call by phone to the French artillery brought a response within just two minutes, in the form of a `75' barrage on the north, or opposite side of the Marne, and extending from the railroad bridge we were defending, 500 yards east toward Brasles, and creeping north for 500 yards toward the long ridge there. It was the prettiest job you ever saw from our point of view and practically cleared the wheat fields of all Germans. A general artillery duel now commenced, which lasted through the next three days. This shelling made it advisable to move Lieutenants Montgomery and Cobbey's guns.

At nightfall of June 1 the enemy machine-gun and artillery fire increased tremendously, and we increased ours in the same proportion, keeping at least one gun firing on the bridge at all times. About 11 o'clock that night I heard a terrific explosion, shortly after which all of my guns ceased firing, and in a little while Lieutenant Bissel of Company A came to my post with several wounded men belonging to his company. He said he had taken part in a counter-attack by the French and got left on the north bank of the river; that the French had blown up the west bridge to keep the Germans from following them and this had prevented his retreat, forcing him to make a run for the railroad bridge we were defending. Lieutenant Cobbey controlled the fire of our guns on the railroad bridge but knew the Germans had enfilading fire from their side of the river. He heard Lieutenant Bissel's call for Company B to hold its fire; that some of Company A were about to cross. But not being satisfied with holding his fire, Lieutenant Cobbey unhesitatingly crossed the bridge in the face of the enemy fire, found Lieutenant Bissel with his men preparing to swim the river, and dissuading them led them back over the bridge to safety. This act of heroism was characteristic of all our men.

Mendenhall and his men remained there for another two days, firing as necessary on the few Germans who exposed themselves on the hillsides above the town:

We were supported by French colonial troops, among them the Senagalese sharpshooters – wild, fierce, dark-skinned, silent fellows, who gave you constant thrills at night by unexpectedly challenging at the point of a wicked-looking bayonet. By day also their conduct excited my curiosity. A group would be sitting silently under cover, when, without any command, one of them would get up at intervals, face the enemy ridge across the Marne, gaze intently for a minute or two, raise his rifle and fire, then go back and sit down. After some observation with the glasses I learned what they were doing. They could see incredibly far, and when they located a gap in a far-away hedge back of which the Germans were moving, up came a rifle and down dropped a German!

We were relieved at 3 a.m. on June 4 by Lieutenant Hose and Company A, 9th Machine-gun Battalion, 3rd Division. My company left town for the woods south of Fontenelle in three large trucks, over a road being constantly shelled. The firing was so heavy during the early part of the night that it was necessary to change the guns under Lieutenant Cobbey for cool ones and these fresh guns became so hot after a couple of hours of firing that they could not be dismounted and were left with the relieving company.

The Machine-gun Battalion had performed a vital part in halting the German attempt to cross the Marne, and had suffered remarkably few casualties in the process. One officer and four enlisted men, or 'other ranks' as the British call them, had been killed and thirty-two were wounded.

BELLEAU WOOD

The advance on the northern bank of the river had also to be checked. The American 2nd Division had been formed in France the previous year and comprised one infantry brigade and one brigade of US Marines, this strength only recently attained. The 5th Marines had disembarked at Brest on 6 May 1918. On Friday 31 May they were taken by train to Meaux, twenty-three miles (38km) west of Château-Thierry and went on by truck and then on foot to the village of Lucy-le-Bocage, only five miles (8km) west of the town. Marine William A. Francis wrote of his experience:

It is now dark; a company of Marines has just passed, everyone silent, for we realise that most of us will never return. We followed behind this company, no one being allowed to speak above a whisper. We are marching single file, it is very dark and we have to march with one hand on the shoulder of the man in front of us to keep from getting lost. After marching this way for several kilometers we were given two bandoliers of ammunition, although we already had one hundred rounds in our belts. It started to rain a slow drizzling rain, the Germans were shelling us very hard. I could hear men cursing from falling into shell holes. The line has been broken several times; runners have gone out to find the other part of the line; word has been passed for us to keep closed up and for no one to speak above a whisper, for we are very close to the German lines and they may have men on scouting duty. It has settled down to a slow, steady rain, and we are soaking wet. We finally reached a little town named Lucy (a town every soldier will remember if he was at Château-Thierry); the Germans are shelling us pretty hard and the town is practically destroyed.

The road from Château Thierry to Paris climbs the steep hill westwards, leaving Hill 204 to the left, passes through the village of Vaux and away between Coupru to the south and Lucy-le-Bocage to the north. Parallel to it some three miles (5km) north, the little River Clignon runs through a narrow valley, passing through Torcy-en-Valois and Bussiares, affording a sheltered route west for forces driving from the east. On 1 June General Jean Degoutte, commanding the French XXI Corps, charged his 43rd Division with the defence of the line from the north-west to the south-east astride the valley through the villages of St Gendeloulph, Bussiares, Torcy, Belleau and Bourresches. They could not hold it. He had been given the 2nd American Division to solve the problem and ordered them to hold south of the Bois de Belleau – Belleau Wood – and to block the main road. This had brought the Marines to Lucy-le-Bocage on the Belleau side, and the US 3rd Infantry Brigade took on the southern sector, with the French 167th Division on the 2nd Division's left.

On the evening of 2 June, the Marines had come up to Lucy-le-Bocage as night was falling and hastened to get organised. Seeking advice from a French officer, a Marine was startled to receive counsel to retreat. 'Retreat, hell! We just got here!' was the response. Just who gave that answer is not clear; Colonel Wendell C. Neville, Captain Lloyd

S. Williams and Lieutenant-Colonel Frederick Wise have all been credited with the remark, but whoever said it expressed the American attitude exactly.

For the next three days and nights the Marines consolidated their positions and beat off repeated German attacks. William Francis tells of three nights of raids:

> *The Germans came down the hill firing everything at us, machine-guns, rifle and hand grenades. We opened up immediately with our rifles and threw hand grenades as if they had been baseballs. We could not see them, but we knew they were only a few yards away and they were set upon taking our trench... This lasted all thru the night... We were nearly exhausted for sleep, none of us having slept for days...*

On 5 June Brigadier-General James G. Harbord was ordered to take Belleau Wood. French sources declared it to be lightly held and to have little artillery support, and thus vulnerable to a surprise attack. In actual fact it was occupied by the whole German 461st Regiment, more than 1,000 men. On the morning of 6 June the Marines moved forward and established a position facing the wood across a wheatfield. They attacked across the field in daylight, bravely and with heavy casualties.

Marine Malcolm D. Aitken wrote of that attack:

> *...one morning, we found out later it was on the third day, we sauntered down the hill and across the wheat field to the other side, went through the forest of trees and rocks to beyond the crest. The enemy could not be seen except occasionally but their presence was sorely felt. Several faces were here but Duke and Jim as well as my bunckie [buddy] had mysteriously disappeared. I saw my first death, and it was a shock. There were so many more that suddenly dropped and were gone within the minute, however, that I did not notice it anymore. They were dropping all around me, and I noted the peculiar whispering sound [passing bullets] again and again throughout the*

advance. The trees and rocks of the hill were infested with buzzing bees and crackling twigs and branches. How the handful ever reached the hill top I never knew, but there we were. Night came, and no chow yet. So we drank some water and waited for something to happen. It happened immediately and this time I saw the enemy for the first time, and they came very close before they broke and ran. We paced it off the next morning and the closest dead one was within 50 feet (15m). On roll call the middle of the morning, there were twenty of the 250 that sacked here. It was a silent and solemn lot that again stood-to that night. Twenty had to replace 250 on the line. We all realised the possibility of another attack which started at daylight, and if it had not been for some engineers who handled our extra rifles, we had no machine-gunners left, I might easily be writing a very different story.

They took the edge of the wood and the village of Bourreches at the south-eastern corner, at a cost of 1,087 men killed, wounded or captured. Just to the south the 23rd Infantry, misunderstanding their orders to maintain contact with the Marines' flank, had pushed too far forward in their enthusiasm and had been badly mauled, losing 27 killed and 225 wounded or missing. On 8 June the Marines tried again, but gained no ground.

The attacks of the following days were preceded by artillery bombardments that shattered the trees and struck sparks off the rocks, but did little to shake the Germans. Units repeatedly lost orientation in the confusion of smashed woodland and rocky outcrops. They crawled across open areas but were caught in sudden gunfire, huddling behind rocks for survival. The wounded could not be brought in, and the Marines had to listen to cries for help fading into silence in the night as death overcame the isolated men.

William Francis left an evocative account of the fighting:

On Sunday morning [9 June] our lieutenant called us together and explained an attack we were to make that afternoon at 5.05 p.m. to feel the enemy out, and try and find out how many machine-guns and men were on the hill. We spent the rest of the day camouflaging our helmets; we cut our blankets into squares and tied them around our helmets to keep them from making a noise when we hit a dead limb or brush. We were talking and planning the attack, when one of the boys said he felt that he would never come back, and sure enough he was killed. We realised that most of us would not go through the attack and live, and in one way we dreaded to go over (for life is sweet when you think you are going to die) but we were losing men every day and night, and never had a chance to sleep, so I am sure we would not have had the orders changed for anything. So Sunday at 6.05 p.m. (Zero hour) we were standing by to go over. I was given a bag of bombs, and also had three hundred rounds of ammunition. We went over in a column of squads, each squad about fifty yards [46m] apart. We crawled on all fours, Indian fashion, and kept going without seeing the enemy. Everything was as still as death. We had crawled a good piece in this way when all of a sudden it sounded as though all hell had broken loose – all the machine-guns the enemy had opened up on us. (If you can imagine fifty riveting machines going at once, you can imagine what we were into). They knew as soon as we had left our trench and had waited until we had gotten far enough out so we couldn't get help from our lines. I was the third man in our squad. As soon as the Germans opened fire, I knew we were outnumbered by a large majority, and never expected to get through alive, but I kept crawling forward as best I could, hugging the ground as close as possible. I don't know what became of the man leading us. A machine-gun was at my right, and also a sniper; I saw a little rock in front of me that would afford a little protection so I made for this. It was only high enough to protect my head. I was trying to work close enough to use my bombs, for a rifle was useless on account of the brush being too thick. The machine-gun was playing a funeral march on the rock; my light pack I had on my back was riddled with bullets, and then the sniper opened fire on me. A little tree was only about six inches from my head and the sniper was clip-

ping the bark off the tree. My face was peppered with bits of rock; a piece hit me under the eye, causing it to turn blue, and for two days after I could hardly see through it. The boy in front of me had been hit, and crawled over to me trying to make it back to our lines; he was hit in the side and bleeding badly. Every time I would make a move the Germans would try for me again, so I decided to keep perfectly still, as if I had been killed. They stopped firing for a few minutes. I looked around to see if I could locate some of our men, and about this time a boy crawled up to me – we were the only two left of our squad. I asked him if he had seen any of our men and he said that he had seen two or three to our left, so we decided to make a run for a big tree that had fallen to our left. I saw a red and green flare go up and I knew it was a signal for a barrage. A big shell hit a few feet from me, covering me with dirt and knocking my helmet off. It shook me up pretty badly but I was unhurt. Another signal went up and I knew it was a signal to stop the barrage for the German shells were killing their own men, who were only a few yards from us. When the smoke had cleared away we crawled to our left to find some of our own men. I tried to crawl under the tree and my pack caught, so I left it there. If I had gone over the tree I would have been hit sure. About five hundred feet from here was a big rock, we slipped around this to see if our men were there – or Germans and to our great relief we found eight of our men. It was now dark and we had no idea where we were so we decided the only thing to do was to stay and defend ourselves as best we could in case of an attack. I crawled on my stomach for two hundred yards and found a small rock; I got behind this, and in case we were attacked we were to crawl back to the rock (if we could) and make a stand there. I was so close to the Germans that I could hear them talk and work their bolts in their guns. I had my trench knife in one hand and my rifle in the other, waiting to be either killed or captured, for I was sure that they would find me in the course of time. I often wonder who was the more afraid – the Germans or I. They kept the sky lighted with flares all night through. These flares went up not more than fifteen feet away and *many a time I thought that they would fall on me, but I dared not move for I knew it would give my position away. They kept firing all night with their rifles, one-pounders, trench mortars and heavy artillery. I will never forget this Sunday night as long as I live – in `no-man's-land' – not knowing where the Germans were, expecting to be captured or killed any minute. I was soaking wet from perspiration and the night was very cold.*

The Germans were as determined as the Americans to win at Belleau Wood. They regarded it as vital to show both their enemies and their own comrades that the much-feared Americans could be beaten. But after two weeks of gruelling combat both sides were exhausted. As the Germans relieved their severely battered troops the Marines were also granted a brief respite, being relieved by the 7th Infantry from 3rd Division. It gave them a chance to bury the dead. Even that activity was disturbed by shellfire.

When the Marines moved back into the line on 22, 23 and 24 June no great change in position had been achieved. Renewed attacks simply confirmed the strength of the German positions. At long last the desire to take the wood was to be supported with the means to do so. The 2nd Division now had three French batteries – two of the 37th Light Artillery and one of the 333rd Heavy Artillery – and for fourteen hours from 0300 hours on 25 June they pounded the German lines in the northern half of Belleau Wood. At 1700 the attack went in behind a rolling barrage. William Francis recalled:

About 700 of us went over this time – all that was left of our battalion... We had orders to take no prisoners... We had a wonderful barrage from our artillery which was falling only a few yards in front of us... We finally made it to the top of the hill; the Germans were entrenched at the bottom of the hill and just beyond the hill was a large wheatfield, the wheat being about waist high. After we had reached the top of the hill the Germans opened up with their machine-guns, hand and rifle grenades and trench mortars. Just then we all seemed to go crazy for we gave a yell like a bunch of wild indians and started down the hill running and cursing in the face of the machine-gun fire. Men were falling on every side, but we kept going, yelling and firing as we went. How any of us got through... I will never be able to figure out... I found a bunch of Germans in their dugout and ran them out... How we did cut the Germans down when they tried to cross the wheatfield. The wheat was just high enough to make good shooting, and when we hit one he would jump in the air like a rabbit and fall. We had orders to take no prisoners, to kill all of them, but it was impossible for we had no idea there were so many Germans there.

The great German effort towards the Marne had, in fact been halted at the end of the first week of June with the help of Captain Mendenhall's machine-guns at Château-Thierry and the arrival of the Marines at Lucy-le-Bocage. The campaign in this region, between 27 May and 6 June, had cost the Allies 98,160 French, 28,703 British and 474 American soldiers killed, wounded and missing. The American figure grew to 9,777 by the time Belleau Wood fell to them. About 800 guns had been lost, together with more than 2,500 machine-guns and 130 aircraft. The German casualties were very similar, 130,370 to 6 June, of whom a significant proportion were from the recently trained attack divisions. The erosion of strength was easier for the Allies to bear than their enemies, but Ludendorff's attacks were not yet finished.

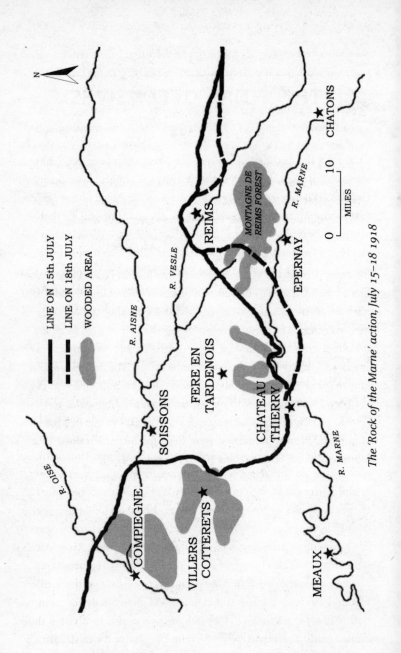

LINE ON 15th JULY

LINE ON 18th JULY

WOODED AREA

CHATONS

R. MARNE

REIMS

MONTAGNE DE REIMS FOREST

EPERNAY

R. VESLE

R. AISNE

FERE EN TARDENOIS

CHATEAU THIERRY

R. OISE

SOISSONS

COMPIEGNE

VILLERS COTTERETS

R. MARNE

MEAUX

10

MILES

0

The 'Rock of the Marne' action, July 15–18 1918

N

6

THE FINAL OFFENSIVES

ON 6 JUNE the German advance on the Marne had been brought to a standstill, its last energies drained away by American opposition. Ludendorff had now made two large dents in the Allied line at Amiens and on the Marne, and a small one on the Lys, but still he had not achieved the grave wound he had to inflict before the Americans made victory for Germany unattainable. His next effort was the extension of the Blücher-Yorck operation westwards with Operation Gneisenau. The main attack was to be made by General von Hutier's Eighteenth Army on a line south of Mondidier to Noyon, west of the River Oise. A secondary attack on the eastern flank of the area, south-west of Soissons, was to be made by the Seventh Army. The intention was in part to join the Marne and Amiens salients, and in part to tempt more reserves away from Flanders to render that region vulnerable to a decisive blow.

The River Oise runs towards Paris from the north-east and to its west the River Matz runs parallel to it until it turns eastwards to join the larger stream. Further south another little river, the Aronde, cuts into the plateau to the west and flows eastwards towards the Oise. Thus, between Montdidier and Roye-sur-Matz the front to the south-west offers a prospect over the plateau towards Méry-la-Bataille, while the other half of the Mondidier to Noyon front faces the wood and hill-filled pocket defined by the Matz. East of the Oise and south of Noyon are the forests of Ourscamps Carlepont, de Laigue and, south of the River Aisne, Compiègne. The confluence of the two large rivers is at Compiègne.

The preparations for this operation were evident as the artillery required was moved into position and it was increasingly common, on both sides, for prisoners, sickened and worn out, to divulge their armies' plans. The French were, therefore, ready for the onslaught.

ATTACK ON THE MATZ

The defenders of this sector were the men of General Humbert's Third
Army. Humbert had been encouraged to adopt the modern practice of
defence in depth and had, rather reluctantly, conformed to a substantial degree. The impact of Bruchmüller's latest firewaltz was, therefore,
muted. It began at 0050 hours on 9 June and, all the same, the 750,000
rounds of gas and explosives accounted for 3,918 casualties, of which
thirty-two were fatal. At 0420 the German infantry started their
advance in approved style, by-passing hard positions. The valley of the
Matz was the principal axis of advance, the shattering bombardment
and light forward defences coupled with the terrain drawing the
Germans into an arrow-shaped probe. They took the important position of Gury hill, south-west of Lassigny, and thrust on down the valley
for some four miles (6.5km). The left wing of the German advance
swarmed around a dismounted French cavalry regiment at Plémont,
where they were to hold out for some days while on the other wing, at
Courcelles on the edge of the plateau, another strongpoint remained
defiant. On the far west, at Cantigny, the American 1st Division held its
ground. The French artillery had been placed to command the intermediate zone and did considerable damage to the German infantry.

Hutier pressed on the next day, crossing the Matz at Marquéglise
and forcing the French to fall back on the Aronde. With Soissons, east
along the Aisne, in German hands, the troops on the east bank of the
Oise were now in danger of being surrounded and Foch withdrew them
from the Carlepont forest into the Laigue woodland. To the west of the
Oise, the hills at Dreslincourt and Thiescourt were abandoned, and the
French fell back in line with their comrades to their right. The German
progress had been impressive, but as yet did not endanger any vital
French position and, once again, lines of supply, particularly in restricted terrain, were becoming stretched. They were also losing men as a
result of the French policy of working their field guns until the last possible minute, then putting them out of action and withdrawing their
gunners. Guns could be replaced.

General Foch conferred with General Fayolle, commander of the

Army Group of Reserve, and agreed with him that a Tenth Army should be formed from reserve units under the command of General Charles Mangin. He had commanded the 5th Infantry Division in the First Battle of the Marne in 1914 and had risen to the rank of General by October 1916 during his service at Verdun under General Nivelle, where he was responsible for the recapture of forts Douaumont and Vaux. He was under Nivelle again in the Spring Offensives of 1917 and, after their disastrous failure, was subjected to an enquiry which exonerated him, but he had been without significant field command since. His aggressive attitude had not endeared him to the soldiery who had nicknamed him 'Butcher'. In the present circumstances, Foch clearly felt he was the man needed. When he arrived at the meeting with Foch and Fayolle, the Commander-in-Chief immediately asked him if he planned to attack. Mangin not only affirmed that as his intention, but declared he would do so the next day. He was surprised when the others laughed, unaware that Foch had predicted his reaction.

There was no preliminary bombardment before the attack on 11 June. On a front of some seven and a half miles (12km) from Rubescourt, south of Montdidier, to St Maur, to the south-east in the direction of Compiègne, Mangin fell on the unsuspecting Germans. General von Eben was himself formed up to attack the French and found himself facing four divisions and more than 150 tanks. The villages of le Frestoy, Courcelles and St Maur were retaken and a thousand prisoners and ten guns fell into French hands. The fiery French general was keen to continue the action, but he had cleared the Germans from the best of the tank country, the open plateau, and Pétain had no interest in getting into a battle of attrition. The counter-attack was halted on the evening of 12 June. Gneisenau was halted as well.

In the scale of casualties to which combatants had become adjusted, the losses were not great. In terms of individuals killed, maimed, missing or taken off into captivity they were still substantial. The French lost about 35,000 men, of whom around 15,000 were taken prisoner. In *matériel* they lost seventy tanks, sixty-two aircraft, including some British, and more than two hundred guns. German losses came to

30,000, a score of guns and a dozen aircraft.

For the Germans the results of their great offensives on the Aisne, the Marne and the Matz had been unsatisfactory. They had, indeed, inflicted heavy losses on the Allies, but they had not succeeded in forcing them to concentrate their troops on the southern front in sufficient quantity to endanger their hold on the northern front, Flanders. In addition, they had themselves lost many of their finest troops. The French intelligence service, the Deuxième Bureau, calculated that on 27 March their adversaries had eighty-five divisions available, of which sixty-two were fresh. By 27 June the total had dwindled to sixty-six and the number of undamaged units had fallen to thirty-nine. These fresh troops were not of the first quality, being made up of young and inexperienced men. It was the French forecast that the Germans could not mount a new offensive until 15 July; a remarkably accurate prediction.

The Germans themselves were becoming increasingly anxious. The plan had been to follow up these operations north-east of Paris with a new strike, Hagen, in the north. Here the Allies were, frustratingly, still strong, and to create a new firewaltz in support of a new attack a great deal of *matériel*, guns, ammunition and so forth, would have to be moved northwards. The suggested date for Hagen, 20 July, was clearly impossible to achieve in these circumstances, and German eyes turned back to the Marne and to Champagne. On 14 June planning was ordered for operations Marne and Reims with the intention of keeping the Allies involved around the city of Reims, while at the same time making ready for the Flanders operation which was rescheduled to follow the renewed onslaught further south. Over the next few weeks the plans were constantly modified and the schedules changed. Uncertainty prevailed. In July Ludendorff observed, '...not only had our March superiority in the number of divisions been cancelled, but even the difference in gross numbers was now to our disadvantage, for an American division consists of twelve strong battalions...' It was not only war that was sapping German strength; illness was also taking its toll. Europe, indeed the whole world, was falling victim to an influenza pandemic that would kill more people than the entire war before it had run its course. By June the Germans had between one and two thousand cases per division, and the eventual total of deaths was to be 400,000 German civilians and 186,000 servicemen, more than twice the number of British that died and the mark of a people worn down by lack of food and the shortages of other comforts resulting from the war.

FRICTION AMONGST THE ALLIES

Uncertainty also gripped the Allies. Foch agreed with Haig that Flanders was the likely objective of the next offensive and that reserves should be transferred to that sector. Pétain, on the other hand, insisted that Paris was certain to be the the target and the reserves should stay. Both of the national army commanders wanted the return of their own men from the other's regions and grumbled that they were carrying an unjust burden in the battle against Germany. Foch was not a man to be envied. In one thing they were united: the contention that America should now shoulder a greater load.

Pershing's orders from Secretary Baker on leaving America for Europe were entirely clear. He was told to keep in mind '...the underlying idea... that the forces of the United States are a separate and distinct component of the combined forces, the identity of which must be preserved.' He therefore worked to create an American army in all its complex detail, from the doughboy in the front line to the most distant supply source and all stages in between. To some extent this was the inevitable outcome of the inability of his allies to give the Americans certain things, railways, for example. To move supplies to the army in the east of France the Americans had to build lateral links in the Paris-centred rail network. To serve troops to whom neither wine nor tea provided cheer, coffee-roasting plants had to be installed. Pressure was brought to bear by the Allies to persuade Pershing to increase the numbers of men being shipped across the Atlantic and to draw on the French and British for guns, ammunition and other needs; in short, to worry less about independence and more about putting troops in the field.

On 17 June Foch suggested that his chief-of-staff, General Maxime Weygand, and Pershing's G-3, Colonel Fox Connor, should work together on plans for the shipment of American troops. Foch had it in mind that American regiments should be added to French division to stiffen them, but Pershing replied that he was already working on schemes to get three million men into France by 1 April 1919 and that 'all soldiers like to be with their own people.' The American general was also sensitive to criticism of his officers and staff and remarked, 'We had now been patronised as long as we would stand for, and I wished to hear no more of that sort of nonsense.' His attitude was not, in fact, a healthy one as events would show; the Americans had a good deal yet to learn about the successful conduct of operations in this war, lessons that the Europeans had spent nearly four years and an immense number of lives in learning.

After a number of meetings, and a certain amount of bad temper, it was agreed that the American First Army should come into being in August and that its principal area of operations should be in the east. Pershing's political duties were to become the responsibility of General Tasker Bliss, thus freeing him to devote his time to the army.

VAUX

The long haul to take Belleau Wood had cost the Americans dear, largely because of the lack of artillery support and of experience in using shellpower co-ordinated with manpower. The capture of Vaux on 1 July was a very different business. There had been a month to become familiar with the territory and to regroup after the scramble to block the German advance. There was time to make precise plans. The displaced citizens of the village were quizzed to reveal the exact layout of every street and house in the place; the village stone-mason had worked on every dwelling and public building. The artillery was in place and communications were well organised.

The Germans they faced were now VIII Corps, under General Schoeler, which had relieved IV Reserve Corps on 21 June. They had diligently prepared the village of Vaux as a defensive position.

The American 23rd Infantry was on the left, from Bourreches to the Triangle brickyard north of what is now the N3 road, the 9th on the right with the 2nd Engineers in support, and the French beyond them with Hill 204 as their objective. A thirteen-hour artillery barrage started at 0500 hours on 1 July. This converted to a rolling barrage when the attack went in and a standing barrage beyond the village to prevent counter-attacks once it had been taken. Vaux was in American hands in an hour.

Private Ralph L. Williams was with the 2nd Engineers. After the war he wrote his memoirs in which he records that, just before they moved forward:

> ...A newsreel photographer worked his way along the ravine bottom, stopped in front of us and said that this looked like a good place. He asked if he could get past us and I asked him where he was going. He said, "Over the rim. I'm going to take movies of the attack." We gave him a hand and right in the thick of the firing, the chap crawled over and we handed the rest of his gear to him. What guts that fellow had!

The attack went in at 0600 hours. The first thing Williams saw was the scattered equipment and dismembered body of the photographer where a shell had made a direct hit.

'My squad had demolition equipment: dynamite, triton, caps, drills and a magneto with which to blow up buildings,' Williams writes.

> We found out later Joe was carrying the dynamite, which weighed about 25 pounds, and was right beside me. I was carrying a sack of percussion caps, more dangerous than the dynamite, and the magneto. None of us knew what we were carrying at the time. Joe was knocked down twice when shells landed in back of him, and he fell again crawling over some German wire. Luck was with us all, and our squad made it...

They had orders to blow up the German headquarters building if the occupants did not surrender, but surrender they did when an irate Irishman who had lost his best buddy started lobbing grenades through the windows. Williams was ordered to take the prisoners to the rear, and when he returned was deeply disappointed to have missed the souvenir hunt. There were Lugers, spiked helmets, and dress uniforms with long flowing capes. 'It seemed every soldier had gotten some souvenir out of it – except me!'

American losses were one officer and forty-five men killed. Their wounded totalled six officers and 264 men wounded, with one officer and eleven men missing. American intelligence reports said that the Germans had lost one officer and 253 men killed, three officers and 159 men wounded and ten officers and 500 men missing, this last figure tallying closely with prisoners the 23rd Infantry had taken. From the American point of view it had been a tidy operation.

The French 153rd Infantry Regiment had a harder time against the heights of Hill 204 and were forced to dig in without clearing the hill. When the US 2nd Division was relieved on 4 July a small gas balloon floated over from the German lines and landed; attached to it was the message, 'Goodbye, Second – Hello, Twenty-sixth.' Their information was correct. The 2nd Division was not, however, sent back to Meaux but kept in close support. A German attack on a large scale east of Château Thierry was anticipated and they had to be available in case of a sudden emergency.

OPERATION FRIEDENSTURM

While the Germans were making their plans for their next assault, *Friedensturm*, the Allies were also making plans to attack. Foch and Mangin made a particularly aggressive team, and the plan was made to reduce the Soissons-Reims salient with a strike on the western flank, to be followed by another on the east before rolling it up from the southwest. Information about this reached the Germans but without details of the date, and they hoped to get their blow in first, Operations *Marne* and *Reims*. On the west, facing the river from Château Thierry to a point upstream of Dormans was the Seventh Army under General Hans von Böhn while General Fritz von Below's First Army had Reims facing its centre and a front to the east as far as Aubérive, beyond which

General Karl von Einem's Third Army's front ran to the hills of the Argonne Forest. It was this section, east of Reims, that was to be hit most heavily and Châlons-sur-Marne captured as a result.

The French defences comprised the French Sixth Army in the west, under General Jean Degoutte, General Henri Berthelot's Fifth Army in the centre and the Fourth Army of General Henri Gouraud on the east. Degoutte's left, at Vaux, was held by the American 26th Division and the line south of the river and east of Château Thierry up to Varrennes, opposite Jaulgonne, by the American 3rd Division. Beyond that, the French line ran to the junction with Berthelot's men in the hilly, wooded terrain of the Mountain of Reims held by the French 14th and 20th Divisions, 1st Colonial Corps and Italian troops of the II Army Corps. The wide, open country east of Reims was defended in depth at Pétain's insistence, with the proven thin front line and deep intermediate zone. Here General Gouraud had the American 42nd 'Rainbow' Division in the line near Suippes.

THE ROCK OF THE MARNE

Major-General Joseph T. Dickman's 3rd Division was in the sector from Château Thierry to Varennes, at the top of the great northerly curve in the river. In fact, the river does a double curve northwards, from west to east, first around the hill south of Mézy, then a dip south to the mouth of the little River Surmelin, then north once more to Varennes to curl round another high hill before heading off north-east to Dormans. On Dickman's right were the French, in whom he reposed small confidence, and next to them he placed his 38th Infantry, under Colonel Ulysses Grant McAlexander, to hold a line from Varennes and the valley of the River Surmelin to the south, and along the Marne to Mézy, where the river turns south-west. To their left were the 30th Infantry, the 7th Infantry, opposite Gland, the end of the bend, and finally the 4th Infantry, all with the bulk of their troops well back from the river. Degoutte, however, did not approve of a deployment that placed so few troops on the river bank; the Americans should, he insisted, receive the Germans with 'one foot in the water'. The American units therefore made an appearance of compliance, and then resumed their former positions when the Frenchman had departed.

Fully informed of the impending attack, the French and American artillery beat the Germans to the punch just before midnight. The gathering Germans were hit before their own barrage started and the first minutes of 15 July were filled with the flash and crash of the guns of both sides. At first light, Colonel William Mitchell took to the air in his Nieuport XXVIII and flew low along the river, where he saw the pontoons and German troops deployed in readiness for the crossing. Orders were given for the bombing and strafing of the crossings. On the right, the French were quick to fall back, and the detachments of the 28th Division with them were, through some failure of communication, left isolated to fight on and die or become prisoners. Colonel McAlexander had foreseen the collapse of his support on the right flank and his F Company was facing east on the ridge overlooking Reuilly. They were supported to the south, in the Bois de Condé, by part of the retreating French divison – to be precise, the Pennsylvanians of 109th Infantry, US 28th Division. Corporal Edward Radcliffe of 109th Infantry later wrote of the action at St Agnon, just north-east of Condé-en-Brie:

...There was a brief lull in the enemy firing and we decided to proceed, soon reaching the edge of the bois which overlooked the village of St. Agnan and the slopes of La Chapelle. To the left face Lt. Hunt, sometime battalion adjutant, was holding a shallow trench grimly enough. He appeared frayed and weary from the desperate clashes with the Germans since they crosst the Marne at dawn on their corduroy bridges which they rolled down the north bank of the river and quickly stept over, sometimes with machine-guns on litters borne by Huns with red crosses on their arms. He shouted a warning not to expose ourselves too much as we would draw fire from the big German guns. They must have had the co-ordinates of the hill crest position for they soon laid down box barrage around us that threatened to cut us off. Sitting with my back to a stout tree I jestingly

*echoed General Grant's words in the wilderness, "We'll fight it out on
this line if it takes all summer".*

The 109th held their positions for another two days.

Captain Jesse W Wooldridge of G Company, 38th Infantry, placed
the platoon commanded by Lieutenant Calkins on the river bank east
of Mézy. The rest of the company was behind the railway line overlooking the wheatfield that lay between them. To their right, up
towards Varennes, H and E Companies adopted similar positions. At
0100 hours the Germans had their pontoon boats afloat and crossing,
only to run into heavy automatic fire from the opposite bank. It was
not until an hour had passed and countless men had been lost to bullet
and grenade, that the Germans finally overcame Calkin's isolated unit,
shipping its wounded commander back for medical help; he survived.
By 0700 three German companies had established a bridgehead on the
railway embankment at Mézy. By 0800 the 38th Infantry had destroyed
them with a wild charge. This unexpected resistance of the Americans
would, their attackers felt, surely crumble against the crack troops of
the German Guards Division. Two regiments were sent across the
Marne against the 38th Infantry as dawn broke, gained the bank and
worked forward through the wheatfield. The fighting broke into a confused pattern of small units of Americans who refused to yield,
shooting, bayoneting and bombing the elite forces attacking them.

West of the 38th were the 7th Infantry and one of their number,
Robert St James, gave an account of the day:

*The German artillery preparation commenced at 12.15 a.m. July 15,
1918. High explosive, gas & shrapnel in terrific intensity, commenced
with a rush at this hour and continued with equal strength until 8
o'clock the next morning... All means of liaison, except runners, were
put out of action immediately, including the wireless telegraph, of
which the antennae was twice shot down during the night...*

*In the hours before dawn, when the Germans began to cross the
river on the right, the 7th, tho badly punished by the bombardment*

was in readiness to receive them. At 7 a.m. July 15, 1918 word was received that the Germans had crossed the Marne & were proceeding west toward Fossoy in large numbers. At this time the German batteries, which had been firing, were plainly visible on the forward slope of the north bank of the Marne, where they had been placed during the night, in order to fire point blank at the target...

Before a new right flank line could be organised, a force of Germans (about one company) came south along the river and railroad. Another larger force came across the fields south of the railroad. To oppose both of these forces were one platoon of Co J and one platoon of Co F in position along the railroad between two advancing forces. These platoons were under 2nd Lt E W Gray of Co J and 2nd Lt A H Baker of Co F. The platoon of Co F had been in process of relieving that of Co J when the bombardment commenced, and in the emergency, both platoons stayed on the front line. The Germans pressed on toward them in skirmish formation. The attack never passed beyond this position. Their heroic stand against superior forces can best be told by the number of dead Germans who lay in front of the R R line, circling the bodies of those two platoons who gave their lives to stem the German advance. It must have been that these men disdained to wait the German's advance but advanced to meet the enemy, for in front of the American line, mingled with German dead, were the bodies of men from these two historic platoons that had died fighting...

Of the heroism of individual men of these two platoons too little is known. They halted the Germans and died. One automatic rifleman, Clarence Hensley of Co J fired his Chauchat until ammunition and crew were gone. A broken Chauchat and the bodies of Germans beside his dead body told the story of his last fight...

As the day drew on McAlexander ordered supporting troops forward. Billy Mitchell's airmen, joined by two French squadrons of Breguet XIVs, machine-gunned troops attempting to cross the river and dropped 10-kg and 20-kg bombs, 45 tons of them in all, on their pontoon bridges. By nightfall the Germans could claim no more than a fin-gerhold on the southern bank in the American sector.

With the help of the British, Mitchell brought new pressure to bear on the Germans the next day. Four RAF squadrons of DH9 day bombers from the British 9 Brigade raided the German supply dumps at Fère-en-Tardenois, escorted by two squadrons of SE5As, two squadrons of Sopwith Camels and by US First Pursuit Group. The German airmen came to the defence, shooting down twelve British bombers, but left their forward troops at the mercy of other Allied aircraft. The 7,500 German troops south of the Marne, mostly in the French sector, were pushed back over the next three days. The US 3rd Division had earned the honorific 'The Rock of the Marne'.

THE CHAMPAGNE FRONT

East of Degoutte's valiant Americans, General Berthelot's men were not putting up so much of a fight. The Germans swarmed over the river and pressed him hard in the hills and woods, but Foch remained cool in the crisis. Pétain was so worried that he ordered the cancellation of Mangin's attack at Soissons, scheduled for only two days later. Foch immediately countermanded the instruction, conceding only a day's delay. He then proceeded to a meeting with Field Marshal Haig and persuaded him to part with four divisions, 15th, 34th, 51st (Highland) and 62nd, forming XXII Corps under Lieutenant-General Sir Alexander Godley for the Champagne front.

While the centre, west of Reims, was sagging back, the French Fourth Army to the east of the city was fighting a classic defence in the modern style. The orders from General Gouraud had been typical:

ARMY H.Q. JULY 7TH 1918

SPECIAL ORDER TO THE FRENCH AND
AMERICAN SOLDIERS OF THE FOURTH ARMY

We may be attacked at any moment. All of you feel that never was a defensive battle started under more favorable conditions. We are forewarned and we are on the lookout. We are strongly reinforced in

Infantry and Artillery.

You will fight on the ground that your steady work has changed into a powerful stronghold, invincible, if all the passages are well defended.

The bombardment will be terrific, you will stand it unshaken.

This assault will be terrific, in a cloud of dust, smoke and gas; but your position and your armaments are formidable.

Within your breasts beat the hearts, brave and strong, of free men. No one will look back, no one will withdraw an inch, all will have but one thought; to kill, to kill so many that they have enough of it and this is the reason that your General says, 'You will break down this assault and it will be a grand day'.

(signed) Gouraud, 4th Army Commander

This was supplemented with a more down-to-earth missive circulated to commanding officers:

ARMY H.Q. JULY 7TH 1918

MEMO NO. 6.653813
SECRET

The Commander-in-Chief's orders are explicit. The enemy must be stopped on the intermediate position. Accordingly, under no circumstances shall any of the troops be authorised to withdraw.

To prevent acts of weakness it is the duty of all the unit commanders to have back of the position they occupy trustworthy officers and non-commissioned officers, capable of preventing, even by force, any withdrawals.

(signed) Gouraud, 4th Army Commander

Although no doubt uplifted and reassured by Gouraud's Gallic eloquence, Norman R. Summers of 167th Infantry, 42nd Division, was evidently much shaken by the actual experience as he recorded in his diary immediately afterwards:

On midnight July 14-15th 1918 the heaviest bombardment since the war began. From information gained from prisoners captured the afternoon of July 14th, this attack was to be the last drive by the Germans. They expected complete victory. They expected to surprise the Allies but we were well fixed for them as we had been preparing for their attack for weeks. Following was the strength of our artillery: 600 3-inch guns every 7 sq.mi. and 1 6-inch or larger gun every 50 yds. This was a great surprise to the Germans and when they opened up their guns we did the same. We knocked out some of their Divisions because they were massed ready to come over. We also knocked out a great deal of their artillery. They shelled one entire area for eleven hours without ceasing. In our position we had two very small dug-outs and one larger one which was Battalion P.C. [post of command] *The men were all in a ditch about 8 feet deep. Many of our men were injured and only one killed...*

One of our gunners in the machine-gun company is credited with killing a whole company of Germans. He was so sick of so much slaughter he had to be carried from his gun.

The French were very proud of the way we stood up under fire and a French General said we were as good as any of his storm troops. They were using the `Blue Devils' as storm troops and when they heard that the 42nd Division were backing them up they cheered. After the battle the French would put their arms around our men and say `Bon camarades'.

On the night of July 19-20 we were relieved. We quietly but very quickly marched to La Cheppi [la Cheppe, south of Suippes]. *We were shelled on coming out but suffered no losses. We spread our blankets out on the side of the road and slept until 12 o'clock. Then we had breakfast and went to the creek to wash our face and hands for the first time in two weeks! Water was very scarce in the ditch and we could hardly get enough to drink and on one occasion we went for two days without water.*

I know God was with us because if he hadn't been we would never suffered as light as we did.

I offer up a fervent prayer of thanks to the All Powerful who saved us from a horrible death. Nothing can bring a man closer to God than an occasion like this and I believe we have more Christian men in our army today than ever before. I more fully realise the Power of God and his mercy and if any man goes wrong after what God has done for him he is very ungrateful. It was through Him that we were victorious and more fully do I realise that nothing worthwhile can be done without his aid.

Although they were out of the line they were not safe from all harm:

At La Cheppi on the night of the 20th we experienced our first bombardment with airplanes. They came about 10 p.m. and stayed until about midnight dropping bombs. The civilians and a few soldiers went to the fields for protection but the planes flew over them dropping flares and by this light fired on them with machine-guns. There were no casualties here but it was rather exciting...

The results of a defence-in-depth deployment were felt by the medical services which, obliged to be as close to the front as they could reasonably be, could find themselves engulfed in the fight. Dr W. W. van Dolsen of 117th Sanitary Train wrote to his mother of just such an occasion, describing it so graphically that his letter deserves to be quoted extensively:

As I wrote you about the 13th we were in a French hospital near the front and were expecting a drive. We had been re-enforced from the base by some operating teams and a mobile unit. Well at ten on the night of the 14th I went to sleep and at about twelve I jumped up wide awake. My gas guard outside was shouting gas and ringing the bell but of all the noise never can I describe what that German barrage sounded like; if you put 100 base drums in a line and had a dozen men hitting each drum at the same time and continuously you might get some idea. Of course these were firing on our lines but worse for us was that about every ten seconds we would hear the singing of a high explosive shell as it sailed over our hospital, they sounded like a high wind through the trees, that means that they are shelling our hospital but have not yet found the range. I knew by the sound that they were not gas shells so I ordered all the masks off. The nurses were rushed into the dug-out and we put the gas curtains up at the doors. As we had a big red cross on the roof of the hospital we thought that they might really not be trying to hit us but to reach the road in hopes of catching reserves coming up. Of course we knew that we would have patients in a short time so we left the nurses in the dug-out and went up to get our wards ready, operating rooms etc.

As the night went on casualties started to arrive and, still under shell-fire, the doctors and nurses went to work. Some of the men brought in smelt of gas, but the wind was from the south so that the gas shells falling on the intermediate zone to the north of the hospital did not cause them inconvenience.

About that time it got daylight and we had about two hundred [patients] in all from the guns, although the ambulances could not get through to the infantry as the pigs were shelling the road too hard. Two drivers were killed trying it. Well, they sent up an observation balloon and saw they were not hitting us so they started giving the range. I saw the shells coming closer and closer. One landed about fifty yards away.

It was necessary to decide what to do next, and orders were given to move everyone to the shelters.

The lights failed. Van Dolsen grabbed candles and ran about distributing them and seeing that the litters loaded with the injured were carried off. He then:

...noted the nurses refusing to leave the wards until their patients were all out. I reported to the director and he ran in and grabbed two

of them by the neck and rushed them into the dug-out. I started for the candles and about that time a shell hit the corner of the hospital killing three patients, I was about sixty feet away and just heard it as it hit. I wish that you could have seen me dive, I rammed my self into that floor so hard I pretty near split the boards. While I was in the kitchen getting the candles another one hit tearing the end off the dining room and that time I dived between two soup boilers. On the way back I saw Capt. Cogland and my gas sergeant knocked flat by the explosion of one. He jumped up picked up a piece of the shell for a keep-sake and dropped it quick, it was so hot he scooped it up in his tin hat and beat it for the dug-out. I was right on his back and when we got there we found that one of the nurses had not come down so I went up to find her. She was under an operating table not having heard the order to got into the dug-out. As we get into the yard half a hall was shot up into the air and she and I took a nice roll in the dust. Well we got down into the dug-out and my dear Mother such a shambles I never hope to see again. A long black tunnel lighted just a little by candles, our poor wounded shocked boys there on litters in the dark, eight of them half under ether just as they had come off the tables, their legs only half amputated, surgeons trying to finish and check blood in the dark, the floor soaked with blood, the hospital above us a wreck, three patients killed and one blown out of bed with his head off.

The Rainbow Division fought fiercely over the four days of the battle. The 165th Infantry were called upon to make a number of counter-attacks and the Germans, taking them for green troops, tried to trick them. Dismounted cavalrymen, Uhlans, attempted to pass themselves off as French troops and were shot for their pains. In the dark the following night they tried the trick again, only to discover that the Americans had been thoroughly trained in the use of the bayonet. It was not without a stern cost to the doughboys, for more than 1,500 casualties were sustained.

It soon became evident that the operation had failed. As early as 16

June a German staff officer, Captain Rudolf Binding, was writing, 'I have lived though the most disheartening day of the whole War, though it was by no means the most dangerous. This wilderness of chalk is not very big, but it seems endless when one gets held up in it, and we are held up. Under a merciless sun, which set the air quivering in a dance of heat, and sent wave after hot wave up from the grilling soil, the tree-less, waterless chalk downs lay devoid of all colour, like stones at white-heat. No shade, no paths, not even roads; just crumbling white streaks on a flat plate. Across this wind rusty snakes of barbed wire. Into this the French deliberately lured us.' He goes on to describe the lack of front-line resistance and the emptiness of the trenches that they had bombarded so diligently. The concealed machine-gun nests were, he remarked, like lice in a garment and the French artillery smothered all efforts to advance. In a whole day they had managed less than two miles (3km) and Binding was evidently shocked and disheartened to a remarkable degree.

On 17 July the decision was taken that the Germans would pull back across the Marne and prepare to go on the defensive. Another, and the last, of Ludendorff's major offensives had failed, this time having made very little progress at all. The initiative was passing from the Germans to the Allies for good.

PART THREE
THE GERMAN ARMY DESTROYED

7

THE SOISSONS SALIENT

The events of the first six months of 1918 were largely initiated by Germany in the succession of attacks that made up the Kaiserschlacht. The Allies, however, had launched offensives of their own, of which the taking of Belleau Wood and Vaux by the Americans and the tank assault on the Matz by the French are examples. One of the most significant attacks of the whole war took place on 4 July and was carried out by Australian, British and American troops. It took place around the little village of Hamel, north-east of Villers-Bretonneux, east of Amiens.

COMBINED OPERATIONS

Since 1914 much had changed in the way war was waged. New weapons, aircraft and tanks among them, and new techniques in the use of artillery had transformed the opportunities available to commanders. The Germans had achieved a notable advance in infantry and artillery tactics while both sides had developed the arts of defensive deployment to a remarkable degree. Before 1918, however, no one had orchestrated all elements of offensive power to create an attacking force capable of smothering the opposition. No doubt there were many aware of how it might be done, but the man who did it in what was quickly to be recognised as a classic action was Lieutenant-General John Monash, commander of the Australian Corps.

Monash was not a soldier by profession, but an Australian territorial militiaman who was commissioned in the Australian Citizen Forces in 1887 and became a colonel in 1913. In civilian life this Jewish businessman was a civil engineer with expert knowledge of concrete construction and business administration. In short, he was from a background Regular soldiers could usually be expected to hold in contempt.

That he was not so regarded by the British military and political leaders, or by the allegedly snobbish Sir Douglas Haig, demonstrates how unreliable are modern stereotypes of First World War commanders. Monash received his commission in the Australian Imperial Force in September 1914 and commanded the 4th Infantry Brigade at Gallipoli. He arrived in France at the end of 1916 and served in the Ypres Salient in 1917. He was appointed General Officer Commanding the Australian Corps on 30 May 1918, following the promotion of General Sir William Birdwood to head the new Fifth Army.

On part of the front that became his responsibility, between the Roman road through Villers-Bretonneux and the River Somme to the north of it, a number of small actions had been undertaken to improve the Allies' front line as Monash himself had done north of the river. One problem in particular gave cause for concern, the German presence in the valley around Hamel, creating an open flank on the Australian left which restricted any attempt to make progress on the higher ground along the road. This area had to be brought under Allied control.

The views of the correct use of infantry held by Monash may have been shared by others, but now the means to realise then was to hand. He wrote:

I had formed the theory that the true rôle of the infantry was not to expend itself upon heroic physical effort, nor to wither away under merciless machine-gun fire, nor to impale itself on hostile bayonets, nor to tear itself to pieces in hostile entanglements – (I am thinking of Pozières and Stormy Trench and Bullemont, and other bloody fields) – but, on the contrary, to advance under the maximum possible protection of the maximum possible array of mechanical resources, in the form of guns, machine-guns, tanks, mortars and aeroplanes; to advance with as little impediment as possible; to be relieved as far as possible of the obligation to fight their way forward; to march, resolutely, regardless of the din and tumult of battle, to the appointed goal; and there to hold and defend the territory gained; and to gather, in the form of prisoners, guns and stores, the fruits of victory.

This is, perhaps, the concept that lay behind the attack of serried ranks on the first day of the Battle of the Somme on 1 July 1916, but then the confidence reposed in the destructive power of the artillery bombardment was fatally misplaced. Monash would now demonstrate to what extent things had changed.

He set out the essentials of his plan for the reduction of the Hamel salient in a proposal addressed to General Sir Henry Rawlinson on 21 June. It was to be primarily a tank operation, for which he would need two battalions of tanks, in which the machines would capture the ground and the infantry would assist in reducing strongpoints, mop up and consolidate the gains. The operation would take place under the command of a single Divisional Commander. The artillery would provide counter-battery fire, a smoke screen to shield operations from view from the north and also a creeping barrage adjusted to the timetable of the tank/infantry advance. Air support would include both fighters and bombers. The detailed plans were to add significant improvements to this concept.

The Australian soldiers were not fond of tanks. At Bullecourt, in 1917, the tanks had failed them, leaving the infantry terribly exposed. However, the latest version of the heavy tank, the Mark V was a greatly improved model. Its propulsion system had been upgraded and the gearing improved, the unditching beam had been introduced and it was altogether a much more effective mobile gun platform than its ancestors. By today's standards, of course, it was unbelievably clumsy, slow and primitive. Most of these beneficial changes were hidden within the structure and Monash took special steps to familiarise his men with the modern weapon. The Tank Corps entertained the Australians, battalion by battalion, at Vaux-en-Amienois, a village to the north-west of Amiens. They all spent a day there to rehearse attacks but also to have fun. Monash recalls:

...red flags marked enemy machine-gun posts; real wire entangle-
ments were laid out to show how easily the Tanks could mow them
down; real trenches were dug for the Tanks to leap and straddle and
search with fire; real rifle grenades were fired by the Infantry to
indicate to the Tanks the enemy strong points which were molesting
and impeding their advance. The Tanks would throw themselves
upon these places, and, pirouetting round and round, would blot
them out, much as a man's heel would crush a scorpion.

By the end of all this a bond was forged. Each infantry company gave
a name to the tank with which it was to work and chalked it on the side
of the machine.

The innovation did not stop there. With the agreement of the commander of 5th Tank Brigade, Brigadier-General Courage, Monash
introduced new tactics:

Firstly, each Tank was, for tactical purposes, to be treated as an
Infantry weapon; from the moment that it entered the battle until
the objectives had been gained it was to be under the exclusive orders
of the Infantry Commander to whom it has been assigned.

Secondly, the deployed line of Tanks was to advance, level with
the Infantry, and pressing close up to the barrage. This, of course,
subjected the Tanks, which towered high above the heads of the
neighbouring infantry, to the danger of being struck by any of our
own shells which happened to fall a little short. Tank experts, con-
sulted beforehand, considered therefore that it was not practicable
for Tanks to follow close behind an artillery barrage. The battle of
Hamel proved that it was.

Complete written orders for the conduct of the attack were prepared to
Monash's exacting standards and all subjected to discussion at confer-
ences convened by and addressed by the GOC himself, who was also
open to questions so that all understood exactly what the final orders
meant. Then they were set in stone – no alterations were permissible.

The final conference was on 30 June and the date was set for 4 July, in part to honour the American 33rd Division which had been training with the Australians and from which eight companies were intended to take part in the battle. On 1 July Rawlinson told Monash that only four companies were to be used, and on the afternoon immediately before the attack another instruction arrived saying no Americans were to be involved. Monash argued that the plans were too far advanced to permit of change and that if no Americans were allowed to fight the entire operation would have to be cancelled. A grudging acceptance of his ultimatum was forthcoming, to the relief not only of the Australian Corps, but of the 33rd Division as well, for they were extremely keen to take part. Monash's submission had to go all the way up to Field Marshal Haig himself, for it was Pershing's wish to pull the Americans out and the matter had to be settled at that level.

Pershing's view of the incident was that it was another regrettable attempt by the British to make unauthorised use of American forces which they had under command for training purposes only. Use in an emergency was fair enough, but this was not an emergency. Pershing recorded in his memoirs that he 'advised' Major-General George W. Read of II Corps, the formation in which the 33rd Division served, to decline the use of the troops when on a visit to him on 2 July. He mentioned the decision to Haig when the two met in Paris the next day. The order to Read was reinforced in a telephone conversation when direct instructions were given for the men of the 33rd to be withdrawn. Pershing writes, 'It was, therefore, somewhat of a surprise to learn on the following day that four companies... had taken part in the attack.'

It appears that Pershing accepted that, rather than upset the Australian plans, Read permitted the 33rd to fight, but he took steps to make sure nothing like this would happen again. That the Americans took part in a notable, even an historic, action he was unaware. His entire interest was in preventing Americans fighting under the command of another. Pershing's failure to understand the military importance of the battle of Hamel is emphasised by his throw-away line, 'It seems needless to add that the behaviour of our troops in this operation was splendid.'

The principal force taking part was the 4th Australian Division, with the addition of the machine-gun battalions of the 2nd, 3rd and 5th Divisions. Sixty Mark V tanks and 600 artillery pieces were used. Each unit was allotted specific tasks. The creeping barrage was precisely defined and there was no preliminary bombardment. The tanks, having assembled under the noise cover of aircraft, advanced through the mist at 0310 hours, with the infantry, close to the creeping barrage. The machine-gunners followed to pre-determined locations to secure the positions taken against counter-attack. The greed of machine-guns for ammunition made supply a problem for men advancing on foot. The problem was solved with the first air-drop of munitions in history; the Royal Air Force delivered 100,000 rounds. Monash wrote, 'Most of the machines of the Corps Squadron were fitted with bomb racks and releasing levers. It required no great ingenuity to adapt this gear for the carrying by each plane of two boxes of ammunition simultaneously, and to arrange for its release, by hand lever, at the appropriate time. It remained to determine, by experiment, the correct size and mode of attachment for a parachute for each box of ammunition, so that the box would descend from the air slowly, and reach the ground without severe impact.' When the machine-gun crews reached their appointed positions they spread a large, canvas 'V', for Vickers, and the airmen were able to drop the supplies within 100 yards (91m).

The fight was still a fight. Two Australians won V.C.s that day. Private Thomas Axford, M.M., of 16th Battalion, and his comrades got through the smashed wire on their line of advance, but the platoon alongside was less fortunate and the German machine-gunners opened fire on the struggling men. Axford ran forward and threw grenades into the enemy trench before jumping into it himself and attacking with the bayonet. He killed ten men and took six prisoners. Private Henry Dalziel of 15th Battalion was Number 2 of a Lewis Gun Section. His company came under heavy fire from a strongpoint, Pear Trench, which had survived the barrage. His Section engaged a German machine-gun, but another opened up from a different direction. Dalziel attacked with only his revolver and captured the gun and its crew. He was wounded then, and once again when loading magazines with air-dropped ammunition.

Will Judy of Chicago was serving as a clerk with the staff of the 33rd Division. He wrote, 'Companies A and G of the 132nd Infantry marched into our headquarters this morning, dirty, tired and wild-eyed... The men were quiet; they seemed in melancholy; the glory of battle was not on their faces. Every one carried a souvenir – a cap, a button, a badge, a gun captured from the enemy... The battle has historical importance for I believe it is the first time American troops fought side by side with their enemy of our own revolutionary days, the British.'

The whole action was over in 93 minutes. Forty-one German officers and 1,431 other ranks were captured, two field guns were taken, 171 machine-guns and 26 trench mortars. Australian casualties numbered 775 and American 134. The British published the complete battle plan as a Staff brochure. Hamel was a model for future set-piece, combined operations.

In the next month the Australians failed entirely to permit the Germans a quiet life. A constant series of minor operations took place. This was not dramatic fighting, indeed, the men themselves termed their activities 'peaceful penetration'. It led to German Second Army Headquarters issuing a number of reports, this of 13 July:

During the last few days the Australians have succeeded in penetrating, or taking prisoner, single posts or piquets. They have gradually – sometimes even in daylight – succeeded in getting possession of the majority of the forward zone of a whole Division. Troops must fight. They must not give way at every opportunity and seek to avoid fighting... The best way to make the enemy more careful in his attempt to drive us bit by bit out of the outpost line and forward zone is to do active reconnaissance... If the enemy can succeed in scoring a success without any special support by artillery or assistance from special troops, we must be in a position to do the same.

It seems to have escaped the attention of the Germans that the Australians were, in fact, special.

SOISSONS – THE GATHERING

Foch had planned to attack the Germans in their salient north of the Marne first on the western flank, south of Soissons, and then in the south, driving up from the river. The Soissons operation was entrusted to the energetic General Mangin, using his French Tenth Army's XX Corps, which consisted of the US 1st Division, the 1st Moroccan Division and the US 2nd Division. Major-General Charles P. Summerall now had command of the 1st and Major-General James G. Harbord had command of the 2nd Division. Neither force was, a week before the attack, anywhere near their start line and they had to make a hasty approach through the Forest of Retz astride the Paris-Soissons road. On the evening of 17 July they were still making their way up for the next day's surprise attack.

Major Raymond Austin, 6th Field Artillery, 1st Division, wrote to his mother on 31 July:

We were relieved [from Cantigny on the Mondidier line] *at midnight about 7 July... We marched all night... We put in three more long night marches... I saw many a driver asleep in the saddle and at every halt men would drop sound asleep on the ground or leaning against trees...* [I] *got dull in thought and action, and the last night I began to `see things'. Distant objects like stars, lights, lone trees, etc. would move back and forth and the road would seem to creep like the track when you look at it from the end of a train... When I reached Crépy* [-en-Valois] *I began to realise the immensity of the operation that was about to commence. Truck trains in endless numbers moved along every road, batteries of light artillery, immense tractor-drawn 6-, 8- and 12-inch guns, staff cars hastening in all directions, blue snake-like columns of French infantry, regiments of Senegalese troops, brown-skinned Moroccans in olive drab uniforms similar to ours, groups of Indo-Chinese laborers, strangely camouflaged tanks,* *military police at all turns and cross roads directing traffic, like policemen in a big city... The entire distance from Mortefontaine to Cœuvres [et-Valsery] was one solid mass of tanks, ammunition trains, trucks, infantry and artillery.*

The infantry had a hard time of it. Private Francis of the 5th Marines, 2nd Division, wrote:

At dusk [on 17 July] we started our hike, which proved to be one of the hardest the 2nd Division ever undertook, if not the hardest ever undertaken by any AEF troops. It was raining and we were tired and hungry. We were forbidden to eat our emergency rations. The road was narrow and literally overrun with equipment going to the lines. I know Broadway never saw such a night for congestion; it was impossible to see two feet in front of us... The last five miles we had to double time all the way to the jumping off place. In the meantime I had such a pain over my heart that I had to drop out for an hour and rest for I was hiking practically doubled over, but I managed to catch my outfit just at the Zero hour, at 4a.m.

Malcolm Aitken, also 5th Marines, was in a group forced off the road and obliged to march along a ditch. It was knee-deep in cold water and muddy. They kept within arms-length of each other, able to maintain contact, and rested from time to time, ten minute breaks, timed with care. On one occasion, when time was up, the man in front did not move, so Aitken gave him a shove. Still he stood. Suspecting something was wrong, Aitken lit a match. He had been nudging the rump of a dead mule.

Second Lieutenant John D Clark, 15th Field Artillery, 2nd Division, saw the infantry coming up:

...There seemed to be a darker shadow approaching and I reined in the horse just in time to avoid running into a column of infantrymen who were dog-trotting in the mud with each man holding onto the

shoulder of the man in front of him. They were to reach the front just
in time to shed their packs and go over the top.

The need for secrecy was the principal cause of the hurry and confusion. Mangin was determined to get his troops into place without the Germans knowing about it and by and large he succeeded. There were, however, other factors. In his paper on Franco-American Relations Colonel Goddard singled out the parsimony of certain French officers as a serious handicap, especially in times of crisis. He cites, in support of his contention, Pershing's observation on the need for men to run to reach their start points at the battle of Soissons. 'One unnecessary cause of delay reported was that the French officer in charge of the truck trains insisted upon counting the men carried and obtaining receipts for their transportation,' Pershing wrote. The receipts were demanded so that the French army could charge a fee for each man carried in their trucks.

MANGIN'S ATTACK

Coming up from the south, the Soissons-Château Thierry road runs past Villemontoire, Buzancy and Berzy-le-Sec, along the edge of the plateau that stretches to the west. The high flatland is cut by numerous steep little valleys, in which the fortified villages of Vierzy, Ploisy and Missy-aux-Bois formed forward defences for the towns that dominated the main road. It was towards that road that the Allies launched themselves behind a creeping barrage at 0435 hours, the dawn of 18 July. Major Austin wrote:

I never realised that there was that much artillery in the world... The
infantry went forward in a long line extending as far as could be
seen to either side, the successive waves following each other at inter-
vals... My PC and that of the 16th Infantry were in a trench on a high
ridge on the forward side of Cœvres, just across the town and valley
from my batteries... I studied out on the map an approximate
advance position to which I could take the battalion as soon as the
infantry had advanced far enough into German territory... When the

16th had reached its third objective of the first day, I started out...
[They] had advanced as far as the range of our guns would permit us
to support them and it had become necessary to move the guns for-
ward... We had changed from the stereotyped trench warfare to a
warfare of manoeuvre...

The 1st Division's Progress was swift at first but the German artillery
soon responded and the wheatfields proved to be peppered with
German machine-gun nests. In the south the 2nd Division pushed forward to the edge of the Vierzy ravine. William Francis said:

Our advance for the first few miles was nothing but a hike... Late in
the evening we had orders to take a town on our right which was very
large and was quite a railroad center. We had to wade through a
swamp over our waists, and immediately beyond was the town of
Vierzy. We had to go up a steep embankment; we crawled to the top
and the Germans opened up, but we couldn't find their machine-guns.
We finally noticed that they were firing from the top of the buildings
and we dislodged them, and also got one out of a tree... On our left
was a big prairie. I watched the rest of the boys go over with tanks
and cavalry. It was a beautiful sight to see the French with their long
lances go after the Germans... The night of the 18th was freezing cold.
I was soaking wet from wading in the swamp. Gas shells were falling
all around so we had to sleep with our gas masks on.

Francis makes it sound easier than it was. The lack of any interval
between arrival and attack left the 2nd Division's communications in
complete confusion, and the taking of Vierzy was much more costly
than it need have been. There was none of the careful combination of
infantry, artillery, aircraft and tank abilities that characterised the
Hamel action. None the less, they had advanced nearly four and a half
miles in the day.

In the centre the progress of the Moroccans was checked by strong
resistance, but they had still managed to push forward more than three

miles, while the 1st Division on their left had been held back by the poor performance of the French 153rd Division to their north. The terrain they faced was particularly difficult and their recent arrival had given them no time for reconnaissance. By the end of the first hour of the attack, the men of the 28th Infantry, mapless and disorientated, were thoroughly lost. Part of 2nd Battalion strayed left into 153rd Division's sector, possibly drawn by the need to supress heavy fire from St Amand Farm, which they succeeded in taking by 0700 hours. This brought the Battalion into line with the Missy ravine across their front which the canny French had been careful to avoid. It took two and a half hours to get through the swamp-filled ravine. To their rear, near Mont d'Arly, Company M, 3rd Battalion was in reserve. Suddenly they saw a crowd of Germans coming out of a cave in which they had been hidden during the American advance. They opened fire and drove the enemy back into the cave from which they eventually emerged to surrender at about 1600 hours, twenty officers and 500 men. By the end of the day the 153rd had relieved the 2nd Battalion and the organization of the front assumed its proper form. As night fell Raymond Austin was at Missy-aux-Bois working out positions for his artillery the following day. He was shocked by the suffering of the wounded:

> *The ambulance service didn't work very well the first day. The road between Croix-le-Fer and Missy-aux-Bois was thickly lined with wounded, tagged (name, injury and first-aid treatment) awaiting transportation. Many died there before they could be got to the dressing stations... That surely was a bad night. The big bombing planes would fly low over us, escorted by small fast fighting planes... they dropped wonderfully brilliant illuminating shells that hung in the air... then... they dropped heavy bombs that burst with terrific concussions... I have never felt so helpless in my life...*

At 0400 on 19 July the Allied attack continued. The objective was to cross the north-south road, the 1st Division north of Buzancy, the 2nd around Hartennes. Neither of them made it. The Germans had taken command of the skies; the crack *Jagdgeschwader I*, Richthofen's 'Flying Circus' (although its leader had become a fatal casualty on the Somme in April and it was now commanded by the young Hermann Göring) was more than a match for the inexperienced pilots of the US First Pursuit Group. Overnight, artillery and machine-gun reinforcements had stiffened the German lines and two fresh divisions had been brought up. The US 1st Division was again hampered by the failure of the French 153rd Division to clear the Missy-aux-Bois ravine, and the supporting tanks were halted by the Ploisy ravine. As the day wore on the situation became increasingly confused and the 1st had to postpone it efforts until some semblance of organization could be recreated.

Sergeant Earl R. Poorbaugh, 26th Infantry, who had until then enjoyed the luxury of liaison duties because of his ability to speak French, and had thus avoided menial tasks, was pinned down by machine-gun fire:

> *As was my usual custom, I had discarded my pack, retaining only my cartridge belt, gas mask and pistol, knowing that I could always find an entrenching tool carried by some unfortunate comrade who would have no further use for it. However, on this day the only thing I could find was a messkit lid and I was really making the dirt fly with this improvised shovel when Major* [Theodore] *Roosevelt* [eldest of the four sons of former President Teddy Roosevelt who came to France] *crept up beside me and inquired, with his usual grin, 'What's the matter, Poorbaugh, did you forget how to speak French?' I didn't even slow down – I just kept digging. Major Roosevelt was later wounded, as I also was, and purely by chance we went to the Evacuation Hospital in the same ambulance. Between us we had one cigarette which we shared.*

Major Austin was on the move, seeking new positions for his guns:

> *I heard a lot of noise which I mistook, at first, for the chirping of sparrows...* [it] *proved to be made by the bullets of a machine-gun*

barrage going over our heads... We went on to the crest and took
cover beside a disabled tank... Through the big shell hole torn in its
side the 75 [-mm] gun, the same size as our field guns, was visible.
Hanging over it and lying beside it were the bodies of the crew. They
must have been instantly killed by the shell... While I was waiting for
[the battery] to come up, Major Roosevelt was brought to the road
slightly wounded in the leg, and, when the battery limbers went back,
I put him on one and sent him to the rear.

The 2nd Division had an equally tough day. The Moroccans between
the 1st and the 2nd kept pace with the former, but their right made
poorer progress, leaving the 2nd exposed. William Francis experienced
the result with the 5th Marines:

About dusk, the Germans began flanking us on our left with artillery.
One shell hit in a dug-out and carried away our lieutenant... They
found one of his limbs about one hundred yards from his dug-out.
Now the Germans were killing lots of the boys. The company on our
left lost practically all their men.

What Francis does not say is that they had fought their way across the
wheatfields to the outskirts of Tigny, just short of their objective.

The 6th Marines had also been in action that day, passing through
the lines of the 23rd Infantry across the broad, open plain, following
the tanks. Their gas officer, Second Lieutenant Daniel Bender, had been
forward earlier to see if there was a danger of gas and, as he crawled
forward on his stomach, he was wounded. He sent a message back to
his command post, 'No gas. Shot in the ass. Bender.' The tanks drew
artillery fire to which the French and Americans seemed unable to
summon a reply. As the tanks were destroyed the Marines pressed on
only to be shot or pinned down by machine-gun and artillery fire. The
advance stalled. The cost had been high, the 2nd Division reporting
casualties of 3,788 men.

They were relieved that night by the French 58th Colonial Division, with which the 15th Field Artillery stayed in support. John Clark was making ready to move the guns forward as the Algerians advanced:

> ...We proceeded according to plan and had just pulled out on the road when Major Bailey galloped back and yelled, `Get back in there and resume firing. Those god-damned sons o'bitches are not advancing. They're retreating'... That day each of our guns fired a thousand rounds. The gun barrels got so hot that we were firing three of them and pouring water over the other one... By the end of the day we had halted the infantry retreat... The Algerians were reputed to be ferocious soldiers on attack but they were not very reliable on defense... But the Algerians, assisted by fresh French troops, held... Finally, on July 25th, we were relieved...

For the 1st Division the battle was not over. They fought on for two more days, finally crossing the Château Thierry road and occupying the heights north of the River Crise, dominating the town of Soissons. It was not a well-managed affair. They were under constant shellfire from the left, the French sector, in which the progress was slower, exposing their flank. Curiously Summerall, an artilleryman, was either unaware of the problem or felt it was one to be solved by the French, so no American counter-battery fire was brought into play. On this, the second day of the battle, tanks were scarce. But what was deeply unsatisfactory was the breakdown of the 1st Division command communications systems. Brigadier-General Beaumont B. Buck, commanding 2nd Brigade, spent much of the day wandering around the battlefield, entirely inaccessible to his subordinates or his commanding officer. Numerous officers became separated from their men, or vice versa, in the confusion of combat.

During the night of 22–23 July they were relieved by the British 15th (Scottish) Division, having lost nearly 1,000 killed out of a total 7,000 casualties. The bravery of the Americans was now impossible to doubt, and their achievements had been worthy of the fulsome praise heaped upon them by General Mangin, but the action was fought in a manner that suggested none of the lessons learned in the past four years had penetrated the minds of American commanders. Pershing had declared that the British and French were too malleable in accepting trench warfare and that American-style open warfare was the answer to ending the war. His experience in Mexico was a poor foundation to rely on and at Soissons failure in command communication, failure in adequate artillery support and failure to work effectively with tanks all contributed to needless loss.

THE AMERICANS ON THE MARNE

The failure of the Germans against the 3rd Division south of the Marne coincided with the opening of the Allied offensive at Soissons. The Germans immediately started to withdraw from the southern side of the Marne Salient, and on 21 July the 3rd crossed the river. The Germans were pulling back along the road from Jaulgonne north towards the valley of the River Ourcq, a fighting retreat designed to permit the recovery of the massive supplies they had gathered to support their recent offensive.

Robert St James wrote by hand an account of the 7th Infantry, 3rd Division experience on the Marne, in which he says:

The morning of July 21st saw a patrol, `C' Co and 2nd Lt. Isham R Williams, cross the Marne to learn the extent of the enemy's retirement on the north bank of the river. From the south bank the boat was seen to be riddled by Machine-gun fire from two guns until it sunk as the patrol reached the north bank. Lt Williams took his men to a sheltered position up the hill and then, having orders to withdraw the patrol in case of meeting fire, Lt Williams calmly swam back across the river, found another boat, rowed over the river, put the patrol in the boat one man at a time and brought the men across the river again, all the while under heavy fire from German Machine-guns...

July 26th saw the unfortunate attack made by the 1st Bn on Le Charmel Chateau, in conjunction with the 4th Infantry on the left and the French on the right. The Battalion suffered heavy losses from

high explosives and gas while forming in the woods for the attack
and when the village south of the town of Le Charmel was reached,
the 1st Bn was reduced to 200 men and 5 officers. 1st Lt David J
Erving who commanded Co D after Lt Brown became Bn Cmdr, was
killed in this attack. 1st Lt Malvern J Nabb, Comdg Co M was killed
in Argentol about the same time. After the dangerous patrolling
which Lt Nabb had so meritoriously conducted, it seemed the irony
of fate that, after returning from the patrol he should be killed by a
stray shell...

The 3rd Division had forced the Germans out of Le Charmel and, on the night of 26–27 July the enemy retired again, this time to a line on the Ourcq, prepared to make a stand.

THE EASTERN FLANK

While attacks were taking place on the west, near Soissons, and in the south of the salient above the Marne, the east, near Reims, was also the scene of bitter fighting. The front in the Mountain of Reims was held by French and Italian troops of Berthelot's Fifth Army. There, the attack of 18 July by Mangin was matched by a bombardment and attack by the 14th Divison in the Bois du Courton on the south-western side of the River Ardre. Progress was slow in the close, wooded country, but the pressure prevented the transfer of German units here as reinforcements in the west. Soon, however, the Italian II Corps was at the end of its strength, and Pétain called for reinforcements from the British. On the evening of 18 July the 49th (West Riding) and 51st (Highland) Divisions of XXII Corps were sent to relieve the Italians, joining the French 62nd Division. The British 15th and 34th Divisions were also available, and they too were sent to Mangin's front.

The 51st Division was ordered to prepare to attack in the valley of the Ardre at 0800 hours on 20 July, but they had scarcely arrived by the previous evening and had to take position to the rear of the Italians, alongside the 62nd. The Highlanders were to operate on the left bank of the river and the Yorkshiremen on the left. The guides, French and

Italian, gave both language and navigational problems – they often could not be understood, and sometimes did not know where they were. The valley was steep-sided and ran between heavily wooded hills which offered cover for defenders and attackers alike, and were as confusing to those who were meant to know them as to newcomers. The 51st met fierce opposition both in the Bois de Coutron and in the valley at Marfaux village which the 62nd was attempting to surround. Neither made much progress; nor did the French 9th Division, on the 51st's left, which was trying for Paradis. To the north, closer to Reims, the French did a little better and the German plans to counter-attack had to be abandoned. In the days that followed, the British renewed their efforts, suffering from the enfilading fire brought down on them by German formations in the woods above and alongside.

On 22 July the West Riding Division winkled out the Prussian Infantry from their fox-holes in the woodland above Marfaux and Cuitron. The 2/5th Duke of Wellington's Regiment captured over 200 men and 40 machine-guns as they cleared the woods. The remains of the 8th West Yorkshires and the New Zealand Cycle Corps chipped away at the defences of the villages themselves. By 23 July the 62nd's front ran from north to south as a result of their progress on the higher ground to their right and on this day Berthilot decided to narrow the thrust on this front by pushing the British forward with French support on the flanks. The attack was only marginally successful. The French artillery cover was on time but much of it fell short, causing British casualties, and the fighting in the woods was as confusing as ever. The frustration of the 62nd's aims prevented the 51st from progressing on their left. Espilly held against the 6th Seaforth Highlanders which was reduced to a single company.

Thursday 25 July saw a pause. It was clear that, without taking the south-western side of the valley, no further advance could be made. The Highlanders spent the day in preparations, and a battalion from the West Ridings was sent to add to their numbers. By this time the Germans had been forced to recognise that their grip on the salient as a whole was slipping and they started to pull back. On 26 July the

Highlanders cleared the Coutron Woods at last, took Espilly and entered Nappes while the 62nd were pushing up to the Reims to Ville-en-Tardenois road at Bligny.

The attack on Bligny and the hill known as the Montagne de Bligny was undertaken by the 8th West Yorkshires at 0400 on 28 July. At first they advanced without opposition. Then they crossed the Bligny to Chambrecy road and continued over the cornfields. Suddenly, they came under fire from machine-guns and rifles from the high ground. Lieutenant Burroughs of B Company recalled:

> *Our advance received a decided check. The delay did not last long for each section changed its steady marching programme to one of quick rushes and short rests... section after section darted up in the corn, rushed a few yards, dropped down and opened fire... Then up on the road, where we joined up with the Devons, a cavalry patrol galloped towards us and, to the cheers of the men, dashed past us... Snipers and machine-guns began to thin our ranks. Some sections lost heavily... One gun section consisted of a gunner, his gun and a pannier of ammunition which he hauled along when not firing at the Bosches to keep them down until his pals made their rush forward... The German fire...finally wavered. Fixing bayonets, the West Yorkshires charged the enemy who eventually broke and fled... helped on by fire from their own captured machine-guns.*

The battalion was awarded the Croix de Guerre by the French for this action. It was the final fight for the British on this front and they were returned to Haig at the end of the month.

THE AMERICANS ON THE OURCQ

On 28 July the US 28th Division were in the line at Courmont, over-looking the broad valley of the Ourcq, on the 3rd's left, while the 42nd (Rainbow) Division stood on the 28th's left on a line looped round the village of Villers-sur-Fère. The same day, on the Soissons-Château Thierry road, the heights to the east fell into the hands of the Allies.

The German choice of line was, as usual, carefully made. The Ourcq runs from Ronchères north-west to Fère-en-Tardenois, east of which, towards Seringes, rises Hill 184. Halfway along that length of the river, and on the far side from the Americans, is the village of Sergy, south-east of which is Hill 212. These hills dominate the valley. The river itself was swollen by rain to a depth of eight feet (2.4m) and a width of forty feet (12m). The bridges had been destroyed. The three American divisions advanced to force a crossing early in the morning of 28 July. The 3rd Division's 4th Infantry had little difficulty in taking Ronchères, but there was some confusion about how quickly the objective was attained. Sergeant-Major Paul Landis was serving with 76th Field Artillery and wrote of his experience:

One day word was received that Ronchères was captured, and the General ordered us to establish our P.C. [Post of Command] there. Next morning early, two Lieutenants and myself with the chauffeur proceeded to go there to pick the house. We went in the General's car, a Cadillac eight. By this time the line had advanced far beyond the P.C. so we had about ten kilometers to go before we caught up with the artillery. Finally we came to Le Charmel where our artillery were in position just beyond the town, but as they were not firing we thought they were out of range and awaiting orders to move up. We waved to them and passed on, when a little farther on, just across the crest of the hill, we passed a line of infantry in a shallow trench with rifles laid on the parapet but we imagined that it was the second or third line, the lines of reserve, and didn't stop to ask. We were ordered to go to Ronchères, and an order is an order. From there on there wasn't a living thing in sight and a kilometer further on was a cross-roads where we must turn to the right. On our left were woods and machine-guns were merrily rattling away, which made us prick up our ears.

A thousand yards further on was a farm house and we decided to turn in there and inquire what was going on. The town of Ronchères was now only about a half kilometer ahead and could be easily been across the fields. At this farm we found about 200 doughboys. We inquired whether any Americans were in Ronchères, and they replied that there were not. They were there last night, but on account of Fritzie's heavy shelling moved out and that at 10 o'clock they would go up there and chase the Germans out again who had moved in during the night after they discovered that the Americans had left. Just then an American soldier came running into the yard, all out of breath and pale to the gills, saying that his motorcycle and a Signal Sergeant with him had been captured by the Boches in Ronchères. The 3rd Division had sent them ahead also, to put in the telephones in preparation to moving up there.

After hearing this, it was evident we couldn't get into the town, and neither did we feel inclined to present the Germans with a Cadillac touring car in addition to the motorcycle. We turned around and leisurely returned the way we had come, but the Germans had seen us come up and were now ready for us. Shells dropped in front and in rear and it wasn't very comfortable, so that one of the Lts. told the chauffeur to `step on her' and the order was most cheerfully obeyed. We fairly flew. The road was perfect, due to the rapid advance, but at one place we hit an awful hole, nearly breaking the springs. A shell had landed right in front of the left wheel, but didn't explode, making a hole about a foot deep and two feet across. Another landed right in back of two Red Cross men making them jump like scared rabbits, but it also was a `dud' and harmed nobody. They merely grinned at us when we passed.

Our headquarters was already on the way, so we went as far as Le Charmel, which was just in rear of our artillery and established the P.C. there. I have never heard of anybody driving through no-man's-land in a Cadillac, actually being between the two front lines, and we feel very proud of our unique experience. Here was open fighting at the time on account of the rapid advance, or this exploit would never have been possible. Also in stable warfare the lines are closer together, and not two kilometers distant as in this case.

The 28th Division was delayed by a faulty relief of the French 39th Division which was late in sending guides, so the sun was up before they could move. They ran into fierce fire from La Motte Farm and did not bridge the river before 1500 hours. Once over, the German fire from Hill 212 and the Bois des Grimpettes, north of Ronchères, pinned them down only a quarter of a mile from the riverbank and they were forced to dig in.

The 42nd went forward to meet heavy fire from Sergy and Meurcy Farm from which they recoiled at first, but they were over the river by 1030 hours. Here German spotter aircraft directed artillery fire on them from batteries on the southern edge of the Forêt de Nesles. Their foothold in the outskirts of Sergy was battered by fire from Hill 212 and the woods of les Jomblets and la Planchette which crowned it. A counter-attack by the German 4th Guards Division threw them out of the village, but a fresh attack got them back into the western edge of Sergy. All day attack and counter-attack saw the village change hands until, at about 2000 hours, the 42nd managed to establish themselves in at least part of it. Corporal Norman L. Summers, 167th Infantry, was not in action until the afternoon:

We dug small holes which very much resembled graves. These afford-ed protection from shells unless one bursted over us. At 5p.m. we received orders to advance. We started thru a heavy counter-barrage by the Germans. Shells, high explosives, were bursting all around us and it was pitiful to see the sights. Some of our men were blown to pieces, some had their legs or arms blown into tatters. Dead horses were lying everywhere and the stench was awful. Dead Americans, French and Germans were lying everywhere... The Germans tried to flank us on our left but were soon discouraged as our machine-guns and rifle fire would leave a line of dead as they advanced.

Raiding parties from both sides harried each other through the night, and as the next morning broke the Germans' heavy bombardment and a determined attack by the 4th Guards drove the Americans out of

Sergy once more. Colonel Isaac G. Walker was commanding the 42nd's 151st Machine-gun Battalion:

Machine-guns were emplaced with about 200 yards between section on the terrace commanding a field of fire to the north of about 500 yards [457m] and the right section (Sgt Williams) a field of fire of about 2000 yards including the village of Sergy. Sgt Merritt commanded the left section. Hours turned into minutes every man dug in. Sometime about noon thin lines of skirmishers drifted back through our front, no officers among them. They stated they could not hold the ground at the crest and many of their company had become casualties. Wounded that could be assisted were among them. [I] observed about this time [my] left section with Sgt Merritt beginning to withdraw with the members of the 167th Infantry. It required only a short time to cause them to assume their former position in time to break up a counter attack in force. We had good shooting at less than 400 yards. It did not last long in our immediate front, the Germans withdrawing running and crawling for cover to the north. Those four Hotchkiss machine-guns certainly were worth their weight in gold.

On our right at Sergy it was a different story. That place changed hands several times during that day and was shelled by artillery fire by both sides during the day. [My] platoon was the means of breaking up a determined counter attack by the Germans from the northwest of Sergy that afternoon. This attack, consisting of about ninety men in two wedge shape formations, moved over the crest to our right front in an orderly manner. The first wave was equipped with French helmets, so we withheld our fire until they were about 800 yards from Sergy when we recognised through glasses German helmets and uniforms. We placed the fire of three Hotchkiss on them and almost to the man the entire force hit the ground; and began crawling for cover to a sunken road to the east. It was the best, and largest target we had that could be observed.

The whole 42nd Division struck back, both at Sergy and also at Meurcy Farm and Seringes-et-Nesles on the left. Sergy was in American hands by noon and the other objectives, including Hill 184, by the end of a day of desperate fighting. On their right the 3rd Division had made no progress north of Ronchères against Meunière Wood, and the exhausted unit was relieved by the 32nd Division that night, while the battered 42nd was reinforced by two battalions of the 47th Infantry, 4th Division. All through the night German shelling pounded the American lines.

The 28th Division succeeded in reaching the outskirts of Cierges and the 32nd in clearing Gimpettes Wood. The 28th was now exhausted by two weeks of fighting and the 32nd took over, extending its line to the left alongside the 42nd. The battle ground on, with the Americans making repeated attacks, winning small gains and stubbornly refusing to yield under constant German shell and machine-gun fire and in the face of persistent counter-attacks. Then, on 1 August, the German fire slackened. They had been pushed out of their principal positions facing the River Ourcq and had no choice but to withdraw. The battle-scarred 42nd Division was relieved by the 4th, which, with the 32nd, moved forward against minor resistance from the retreating enemy.

The cost for both sides in the battles of 15 July to 5 August had been heavy. The Allies suffered 160,852 killed, wounded and missing. Of these the greatest burden was borne by the French, 95,165 casualties. The British total came to some 16,000 and the Italian to 9,334. For the Americans the loss was 40,353 men. German losses totalled some 168,000, of whom 29,367 were prisoners. With the German divisions taken from the former Russian front expended in the great offensives, such a loss could not be made good. And for Ludendorff's armies worse was to come.

8

THE SOMME FRONT

THE FINAL DAYS of the retaking of the Soissons salient were relatively quiet as the Germans pulled back behind the River Vesle as fast as the Allies advanced. The failure of their last initiative at Reims depressed many back in Germany, and a fair proportion of those in France, but Hindenburg remained calm and Ludendorff bustled about to work out where he could attack next. Neither seemed ready to accept that they had already done major damage to their own strength. Since the start of the *Kaiserschlacht* to the end of July Germany had lost 227,000 killed or missing, 765,000 wounded and 1,960,000 ill, many from influenza. Although some two million would, in time, be able to return to duty, the irrecoverable deficit came to 951,000, one fifth of the army. Individual formations were thus well below their textbook strength so that an infantry battalion which should have had 850 men actually had, on average, 600. This could not be made good. Hindenburg proposed taking men for the army from industry and replacing them with women. It was pointed out that it was industry that generated the supplies on which the army relied and that to take the skilled workforce and replace it with inexperienced workers of whatever sex was not going to help. Nor was the idea of raising the age of military service to sixty likely to improve the power of the army. Irrational though the proposals might have been, their rejection led to the myth of civilian sabotage of the fighting men being responsible for Germany's defeat.

In the circumstances a defensive posture appeared the best course for the Germans, but on 2 August Ludendorff, while confirming defence as the prime task, also demanded planning for a number of attacks. The possibility of a major offensive by the Allies did not receive consideration.

AMIENS

At the head of the salient driven into the junction of British and French lines by Operation Michael in March, General von der Marwitz's Second Army stood guard. To his left was Von Hutier's Eighteenth Army. Facing them were the British III Corps north of the Somme, the Australian Corps south of the river and the French First Army along the River Avre down to Montdidier. To the west was the ghost city of Amiens, within range of German guns and largely abandoned by its inhabitants. What was operationally important was that the direct railway route from Paris to Boulogne passed through the city and was denied to the Allies while it remained within range of the Germans.

On 21 July, as the pressure was squeezing the Germans out to the Soissons salient, General Rawlinson called a conference to discuss an attack with the corps commanders of his Fourth Army. On 24 July the Allied commanders-in-chief met at Melun, south-east of Paris, with General Foch. Out of these meetings came the plan to hit the Germans at a number of places in succession and regain lateral mobility in the railway system from the Channel to the Vosges. The Amiens operation was scheduled for 10 August, a date that was brought forward to 8 August soon after, with the objective of pushing forward as fast as possible in the direction of Roye. Lieutenant-General John Monash's Australian Corps was to be in the forefront of the coming battle on the British side and the French First Army alongside, but Monash was not happy about having them on his flank. He preferred a British unit because fewer problems in co-operation would be encountered. His request was granted and the Canadian Corps were to be on his right with a corps of Debenay's First Army next to them. At the time the Canadians were near Arras and, in order to avoid alerting the Germans to the coming assault, they would have to move in the greatest secrecy.

The first step was for the Australians to extend their front southwards from Villers-Bretonneux to Thennes, a task carried out by the 4th Division. The Canadians would take over on the very eve of the attack and the vital familiarization with the terrain would have the cover story of an eventual relief for the entire Australian Corps by the Canadians.

In this way no apparent increase of strength would be taking place.

The measures taken by Lieutenant-General Arthur Currie to ensure secrecy were elaborate and effective. He held a meeting to discuss an attack on Orange Hill, east of Arras and argued stoutly with one of his divisional commanders over the allocation of tanks in an undertaking he knew was not going to take place. When preparations for an offensive action were obviously being made and could not be kept form his troops, each man's pay-book had a notice pasted in with instructions to remain silent if captured under the headline 'Keep Your Mouth Shut'. He even sent the 4th Canadian Mounted Rifles and the 27th Battalion with their signal and medical units to Flanders on 29 July and they threw themselves into a flurry of signalling and preparations that made it appear they were the advance party of the whole Corps. So convincing was their performance that King Albert of the Belgians complained he had not been consulted about the attack planned on Belgian soil.

PREPARATIONS

The Allies had made sure of having superiority in manpower, twenty-one divisions against the fourteen they faced, and their supplies and equipment were similarly substantial. The French artillery comprised 780 field guns and 826 heavy guns while the British had 1,386 field guns and howitzers and 684 heavies. In his book Monash described the organization of his heavy guns into two task groups, one concerned with strategic shelling of enemy strongpoints and communication centres and the other with counter-battery work. The latter were guided by sound-ranging and other observation techniques, but were careful, in the days before the battle, to show no sign of having observed the relocation of enemy artillery, but to go on shooting at the old emplacement. The German gunners were to get an unpleasant surprise once the battle commenced. The field artillery was, in part, to become mobile immediately after the first objective, the green line, had been taken. This meant, in effect, that all the teams, limbers, battery wagons and ammunition wagons of these twelve Brigades, waiting in their wagon lines far in the rear, fully harnessed up and hooked in at the opening of the battle, had to advance during the progress of the first phase, so as to reach their guns just at the right time, but no earlier, to enable these guns to be limbered up, and the batteries to become completely mobile in order to join and advance with the Infantry of the second phase.

The Australians were already familiar with the Mark V tanks with which they had taken Hamel a month before. The Fourth Army had 324 of these for the new attack and 96 medium Whippets which were a little faster, more nimble and armed with machine-guns. In addition there were a number of the new Mark V (Star) vehicles, stretched versions of the Mark V capable of carrying two complete Lewis gun detachments, according to Monash, or an infantry officer, a scout, and three machine-gun detachments (two Lewis of three men each and one Vickers of five men) in the Canadians' case. Their official history states:

> But this scheme to transport foot-soldiers in tanks did not work out well. Jolted about in their cramped quarters, the men suffered severely from the unaccustomed heat and fumes from the engines; many became sick, and a number fainted. More than half the infantry detachments were obliged to seek fresh air and follow on foot.

The British 4th Tank Brigade provided three battalions of forty-two fighting tanks to the Canadians and 5th Tank Brigade the same number to the Australians, which, with other types taken into account, gave Monash 168 armoured vehicles plus sixteen cars of 17th Armoured Car Battalion. Seventy-two Whippets were deployed with the French forces.

The German airforce was massively outnumbered with only 365 machines against 1,349 French and 800 British. The RAF component was made up of 239 heavy bombers, 376 fighters and 185 reconnaissance aircraft. Aircraft were used by Monash to monitor the progress of his troops. 'Contact Patrols' were flown by No. 3 Australian Squadron's two-seater aircraft from which the action below was observed and marked in conventional signs on a map, often with added explanatory notes. The information was then flown to Corps Headquarters and dropped nearby 'wrapped in a weighted streamer of many colours.' The need for dependence on vulnerable telephone lines was done away with. The heavy bombers were also used to distract from the noise of tank movements, the sounds being similar and the aircraft an obvious threat that commanded the full attention of the enemy.

On 2 August the Australian 4th Division took over the front to their right from the French and the British III Corps took over the north bank of the Somme, freeing the Australian 5th Division to move south to join their comrades. Monash was not happy with having the river as a boundary. He wrote:

It is always, in my opinion, undesirable to select any bold, natural or artificial feature – such as a river, ravine, ridge, road or railway – as a boundary. It creates, at once, a divided responsibility, and necessitates, between two independent commanders, and at a critical point, a degree of effective co-operation which can rarely be hoped for. It is much better boldly to place a unit, however large or small, astride of such a feature, so that both sides of it may come under the control of one and the same Commander.

Events in this battle would reinforce this view.

The plan was to fight the battle in three phases. The first was to take the British to the green line, so called because that was the colour of it as drawn on the planning maps. It ran from the Somme at Cerisy along the ridge through Lamotte-en-Santerre and on south-west by way of Marcelcave, Demuin and Mézières-en-Santerre. The second phase was to reach the red line from Méricourt-sur-Somme to Harbonnières, Caix and Hangest-en-Santerre. The third, and most difficult, was the exploitation phase, beyond the red line as far as it was possible to go – open warfare. Monash observed:

The open warfare Infantry Brigades were also to be provided, out of their own divisional resources, each with a Company of Engineers, a Company of Machine-guns, a Field Ambulance, and a detachment of Pioneers, so that, in the most complete sense, they became a Brigade

Group of all arms, capable of dealing, out of their own resources and on their own ground, with any situation that might arise during their advance of nearly three miles [4.8km] from the green to the red line. A detachment of five tanks completed the fighting equipment of each of the four front line Brigades destined to capture the red line... Each of the Exploitation Brigades was equipped similarly... except that they were provided with a special contingent of 18 Mark V (Star) Tanks of the very latest design.

On 4 August the Germans carried out a raid on 13th Australian Brigade of the 4th Division south of the Roman road. The Australians were spread thin here and could not maintain a continuous, fully-manned trench. Instead they were in a series of small, isolated posts. One of these was surrounded that night and a sergeant and four or five men were taken prisoner. The fear was, of course, that, even inadvertently, they might give away the planned arrival of the Canadians. It was subsequently discovered that they had refused to give any information beyond their names, ranks and numbers. A more serious German foray took place on 6 August when a Württemberger division of Second Army struck at III Corps north of the Somme and pushed them back. The Germans then consolidated their positions and were to give the British real problems two days later.

On 7 August the final preparations were made. The Canadians moved into position under cover of darkness, the 1st Division in the centre, the 2nd on its left against the railway and the 3rd astride the Amiens-Roye road. The terrain before them was open and rolling country, with the exception of the valley of the River Luce which cut across their line of advance. The clandestine transfer of the Canadians to this front had not been an easy task. Herbert L. Witherby of 20th Lethbridge Battery, Canadian Field Artillery wrote of his experience. 'The night marches were most fearfully hard on us, especially towards morning, it was so hard to keep awake... I had to keep riding up and down, shaking the drivers and gunners to keep them awake, and this helped me keep awake myself.' They made camp at about 0500 hours each morning, saw to the horses, ate and slept before passing the afternoon in relaxation and small tasks, them a final meal and they were back on the road for the next night's march:

> We had about three days and nights like this, then we arrived at some large woods before it was light early one morning. We pulled all vehicles right up into the underbush, and then as a further precaution cut branches and covered them all over, the horses were tied close into the bush, and we were cautioned to keep cover during daylight.

They went through Amiens and on the night of 6 August moved out towards Villers-Bretonneux on the main road:

> We soon turned off... down a sunken road, with all the evidences of war, trees knocked about, shell holes, broken wagons, etc. Shelling was going on just ahead of us, eventually we got through, and got our guns into the woods, losing one man, Bombardier Pearson, who was killed. We were very close to the line and had to be careful to cover up the guns and equipment against enemy observing planes... all day of the 7th we rested well, had the last orders and laid low. This was all we had to do; keep out of sight.

The Australians took position with the second wave divisions forward of the first wave. A double leap-frog was to be made, the initial attackers passing through the lines of their comrades to advance to the green line, when the next wave would come through in turn to take the red line. In this way the distance to be marched by each wave would be equalised and those destined to move furthest forward started furthest forward. The eighteen Mark V (Star) tanks had moved up the night before to a position about half a mile (800m) north of Villers-Bretonneux. That afternoon they were heavily shelled and fifteen of them destroyed. A chance shot had ignited the cans of fuel one of them carried and the resulting conflagration had drawn further fire.

THE BATTLE OF AMIENS

The operation was to begin at 0420 hours on 8 August. Monash later wrote of the last minutes before the action started. With perhaps excessive modesty, he said:

It needs a pen more facile than I can command to describe, and an imagination more vivid to realise the stupendous import of the last ten minutes. In black darkness, a hundred thousand infantry, deployed over twelve miles [19km] of front, are standing grimly, silently, expectantly, in readiness to advance, or are already crawling stealthily forward to get within eighty yards [73m] of the line on which the barrage will fall; all feel to make sure their bayonets are firmly locked, or to set their steel helmets firmly on their heads; Company and Platoon Commanders, their whistles ready to hand, are nervously glancing at their luminous watches, waiting for minute after minute to go by – and giving a last look over their commands – ensuring that their runners are by their sides, the observers alert, and that the officers detailed to control direction have their compasses set and ready. Carrying parties shoulder their burdens, and adjust the straps; pioneers grasp their picks and shovels; engineers take up their stores of explosives and primers and fuses; machine and Lewis gunners whisper for the last time to the carriers of their magazines and belt boxes to be sure and follow up. The Stokes Mortar carrier slings his heavy load, and his loading numbers fumble to see that their haversacks of cartridges are handy. Overhead drone the aeroplanes, and from the rear, in swelling chorus, the buzzing and clamour of the Tanks grows every moment louder and louder. Scores of telegraph operators sit by their instruments with their message forms and registers to hand, bracing themselves for the rush of signal traffic which will set in a few moments later; dozens of Staff Officers spread their maps in readiness, to record with coloured pencils the stream of expected information. In hundreds of pits, the guns are already run up, loaded and laid on their opening lines of fire; the sergeant is checking the range for the last time; the layer stands silently with the lanyard in his hand. The section officer, watch on wrist, counts the last seconds, "A minute to go" – "Thirty seconds" – "Ten seconds" – "Fire." And, suddenly, with a mighty roar, more than a thousand guns begin the symphony.

THE ADVANCE

The German defences south of the Somme were not the sophisticated alignments of trenches, battle zones and secondary positions their own doctrine demanded. With depleted manpower and lowered morale, the work done had been well below their own standards. Apart from some fortified villages and woods there were three lines of unimpressive trenches. After the front line they relied on the old Amiens Defence Zone trenches dug by Carey's Force during Operation Michael and this was the system the British designated as their green line. The last organised line was designated as the red line and forward of this the Germans had laid out a complex of machine-gun nests.

The British barrage came as a complete surprise to the Germans and the speed with which the troops advanced was startling. The Australians were on the green line by 0700 hours, hidden from the Germans by the morning fog, but to some extent held up by the poor visibility themselves. The Australian 2nd and 3rd Divisions halted and the 4th and 5th took up the challenge. On the Canadian right the 3rd Division had only moved into line at 0200 that morning and, because the River Luce divided their front on the Amiens-Roye road, they had one brigade on each side of it. The infantry were less weighed down with equipment than in previous engagements, but even then carried a haversack, 250 rounds of ammunition, of which 100 were in bandoliers, a gas mask, water bottle, iron rations of corned beef and biscuits, an entrenching tool, two Mills bombs (hand grenades) and two sandbags. By 0730 9th Brigade had reached the green line, though not without some sharp resistance from the woods. On their left the fog delayed the tanks and a number of machine-gun posts had to be overcome, but the green line was attained by 0815.

At 0820 the Canadian 3rd Division resumed its progress along the

Roye road, the 49th Battalion on the left, the 42nd in the centre and the Royal Canadian Regiment on the right. There was little opposition to the 49th on its way to the red line, and the 42nd mopped up two German gun batteries before swarming over Hill 102, an important look-out in this broad terrain, and gaining the red line by 1020. The Royal Canadians made equally impressive progress. The major cost was borne by the Tank Corps, for of forty-two that had started with the 3rd Division only eight remained operational, and those owed thanks to the vigour with which the infantry had dealt with German field guns firing over open sights. To the north the gullies around the Luce delayed the advance but the red line was reached by 1130, and the Canadians pushed on to the old Amiens Outer Defence line, their planned objective for the day, by 1330 hours.

The speed with which they moved forward took them quickly out of range of their supporting artillery. Sergeant Witherby, with 20th Lethbridge Battery, had to hurry to bring his guns up:

We were travelling fast, the sweat was rolling down my face, the shells were bursting everywhere, some of them very low, only just seeming to skim our heads and to burst not far from the road we were travelling on. Machine-gun bullets also whistled over us from the left flank, where the advance had been held up for a while. We had not gone far up this road before out of the smoke came a team of horses alone, trotting down the road with their harness on. I knew them at once, for one of the teams had gone ahead of us; I knew by this that things were happening somewhere ahead, through that awful smoke.

They soon found their comrades lying dead or wounded among their horses. They had been hit by shellfire. Witherby concentrated on his job, drove round the carnage and pressed on:

The mist and smoke were lifting fast now, and we could see further around us – on our right was a shallow trench, used by the Germans that morning, and some dead Germans lying there. Bunches of pris-

oners were coming across country, in some cases absolutely unat-
tended, only too glad to get out of battle. We halted. We soon got our
range and angle, and then started firing, the orders coming through
by phone from our Observing Officer ahead who was in touch with
the Battery.

The day grew hot and the sun was bright. They endured some shelling
and were ordered to take cover for a while. Then the fire died down
and they had a chance to rest. 'We had some bully beef and drank water
from out bottles, and then had a chance to look around, and there was
a great sight of tanks, infantry, cavalry, transport, all going forward, a
wonderful sight.'

On the Australian front the advance was as impressive and Monash
records that their flag was raised in Harbonnières at noon. Captain
Henry Smeddle commanded one of the Mark V (Star) tanks of 15th
Battalion, operating in support of the Australian advance. He started
forward an hour after the battle opened, refuelled in the Warfusée valley and pushed on. A German aircraft machine-gunned them and
Smeddle's runner was fatally wounded. One shell struck their machine,
but bounced off. Later that year Smeddle wrote:

The enemy were evidently quite unaware of the rapidity of our
advance, for just as we were about opposite Harbonnières we saw an
ammunition train steaming into the station as if nothing was the
matter. It was immediately shelled by all the 6-pdr guns of the
approaching tanks. One shell must have struck a powder van for sud-
denly the whole train burst into one great sheet of flame... It was
followed by another one, a passenger train rushing up fresh troops;
this was running on another track and ran right into our lines where
it was captured, complete with personnel.

The Light tank, the Medium Mark A, known as the Whippet, weighed
14 tons against the Mark V's 35 tons, and was said to be capable of 8.3
m.p.h. (13.3km.p.h.) on the road, outpacing the battle tank by nearly

four miles per hour. The crew of three had four Hotchkiss machine-guns at its disposal. Lieutenant C B Arnold, Gunner Ribbans and Driver Carney of B Company, 6th Battalion, were going along in the tank *Musical Box* next to the railway line that divided the Australian from the Canadian sector when they saw two Mark Vs hit by a four-gun field battery between Warfusée and Bayonvillers. Arnold wrote:

> *I saw clouds of smoke coming out of these machines and the crews evacuate them. The infantry following the heavy machines were suffering casualties from the battery. I turned half-left and ran diagonally across the front of the battery, at a distance of about 600 yards [550m]. Both my guns were able to fire on the battery, in spite of which they got off about eight rounds at me without damage, but sufficiently close to be audible inside the cab, and I could see the flash of each gun as it fired. By this time I had passed behind a belt of trees running along a roadside. I ran along this belt until level with the battery, when I turned full-right and engaged the battery in the rear. On observing our appearance... the gunners, some thirty in number, abandoned their guns and tried to get away. Gunner Ribbans and I accounted for the whole lot.*

The Australians took full advantage of demise of the battery. Arnold then dealt with one group of Germans who were troubling his cavalry further down the railway line before seeing a second cavalry patrol pursuing fleeing soldiers:

> *The leading horse was so tired that he was not gaining appreciably on the rearmost Hun. Some of the leading fugitives turned about and fired at the cavalryman when his sword was stretched out and practically touching the back of the last Hun. Horse and rider were brought down on the left of the road. The remainder of the cavalrymen deployed to right, coming in close under the railway embankment, where they dismounted and came under fire from the enemy, who had now taken up a position on the railway bridge, and*

were firing over the parapet, inflicting one or two casualties. I ran
the machine up until we had a clear view of the bridge, and killed
four of the enemy with one long burst...

This took place somewhere just east of Guillaucourt. As he was now
alone Arnold then turned north, cruising off between Bayonvillers and
Harbonnières where he strafed a crowd of Germans packing up to leave.
Ribbans counted more than sixty dead and wounded. They had been
receiving rifle and machine-gun fire from the infantry they had been
attacking, and at this point in his report Arnold breaks off to suggest
that, in future, no fuel is carried on the outside of a tank; the cans he
had were being hit by enemy fire and were filling the tank with fumes.

Further east, at about 1400hrs, he opened fire on retreating trans-
ports, motor and horse-drawn, on the roads crossing the railway before
turning to engage another target. 'On the way across we met the most
intense rifle and machine-gun fire imaginable from all sides. When at
all possible we returned the fire, until the L.H. [left-hand] revolver port
cover was shot away. I withdrew the forward gun, locked the mounting
and held the body of the gun against the hole. Petrol was till running
down the inside of the back door. Fumes and heat combined were very
bad.' Suddenly there was a loud bang and the tank burst into flames.
The crew got out, on fire, but Carney was immediately shot. Arnold
and Ribbans rolled on the ground to put out the flames and were surrounded by Germans. 'They were', observed Arnold, 'furious.'

This was real mobile warfare, but Arnold had made the error of out-
running his infantry support and, though *Musical Box* had done great
damage, the end was inevitable.

The attainment of the red line opened the way for open warfare and
the armoured cars took their opportunity, as Lieutenant-Colonel E. J.
Carter reported. They made their way forward finding the road in good
condition but blocked with felled trees which a tank hauled out of their
way. They caught up with the advance on the red line and then ven-
tured beyond:

When we got past our leading Infantry we came upon quite a number of Huns and dealt with them. Had then to wait a little on account of our barrage, but went through a light barrage. When we got to the Blue Line we detached three sections to run down to Framerville [north-east of Harbonnières]. When they got there they found all the Boche horse transport and many lorries drawn up in the main road ready to move off. Head of column tried to bolt in one direction and other vehicles in another. Complete confusion. Our men killed the lot (using 3,000 rounds) and left them there; four Staff Officers on horseback shot also. The cars then ran down to the east side of Harbonnières, on the south-east road to Vauvillers, and met there a number of steam wagons; fired into their boilers causing an impassable block. Had a lot of good shooting around Vauvillers.

They then returned to the Roman road and shot up troops eating in the houses of Proyart and Chuignolles. The shell-fire had ceased. They rounded up prisoners and got a group of them to start towing a broken-down armoured car back to base. They were now way beyond the day's objectives but it was only 1030 hours. They turned back to the west to re-establish contact with their own forces:

Saw no trace of any organised system of defence of any kind and no troops. My people saw no formed bodies of troops of any kind during the day coming towards us, but very large numbers of fugitives hastening in the opposite direction... I saw, from the hill, open country...

Carter, too, had outrun his support but, more fortunate than Arnold, was able to regain his own lines.

TROUBLE ON THE FLANKS

While the centre of the combined Australian and Canadian effort had made a magnificent advance, the flanks gave cause for concern. On the north of the Somme III Corps was responsible for preventing fire on the Australian flank by taking the Chipilly spur, the ground embraced by a great meander in the river south-east of the village of that name. The Corps was formed of tired divisions, all of which had been severely mauled in the actions of March and April. They had lost significant numbers of their experienced officers and non-commissioned officers, and had a high proportion of young replacements in the ranks. It is, perhaps, understandable that they failed entirely in their task that day. Monash observed:

> There was only one blemish in the whole day's operations. Not serious in relation to the whole, it nevertheless gravely hampered the work of the left Brigade of the Fourth Division. In short, the Third Corps Infantry failed to reach their ultimate objective line, and the enemy remained in possession of the Chipilly spur and of all the advantages which that possession conferred upon him.
>
> The advance of my left flank... remained under the domination of his rifle fire, at quite moderate ranges. But worse than all, a battery of his Field Artillery emplaced just above the village of Chipilly remained in action, and one after another, six of the nine Tanks which had been allotted to the 4th Brigade were put out of action by direct hits from these guns.

To the south of the railway the cavalry had moved forward after the initial attack and crossed the River Luce at Ignaucourt and reached the Roye road at 1030 hours. Lord Strathcona's Horse took over a hundred prisoners at Fresnoy-en-Chausée, but the village was soon reoccupied. Beaucourt-en-Santerre was taken by the Canadian Cavalry Brigade, and to their left, in the centre, the cavalry made fine progress. The Queen's Bays almost secured Harbonnières, but had to leave it to the Australians to finish the job. The 5th Dragoons captured an 11-inch railway gun and 600 prisoners while 15th and 19th Hussars charged 2,000 yards ahead of the cheering Canadians in Guillaucourt to seize the trenches beyond and hold them until the Whippets and infantry came up. It was 'worth all the years of waiting', said an officer of the 15th. The idea of teaming the Canadian cavalry up with thirty-two Whippets tanks was not a success.

When the going was good the horses moved much more quickly, but as soon as machine-gun fire was to be faced only the tanks could advance. Separately they performed much more satisfactorily. The German reoccupation of Fresnoy permitted support fire for another German unit, Regiment Bellman, in the wood to the east of Beaucourt. The infantry slowed and a battery south of Bellcourt picked off ten tanks. The remainder shepherded their infantry back from the heavy fire emanating from around Le Quesnel. It was only with steadfast courage and determination that the Canadian infantry eventually, by about 1630, cleared Beaucourt Wood, but there was no prospect of taking Le Quesnel in the face of copious machine-gun fire and they dug in about a mile (1.6km) to the north-west. This was the only Canadian objective not taken that day. Further south the sluggish performance of the French 42nd Division gave their army commander deep disappointment, but like the men of III Corps, these were tired troops, battle-weary and quite unable to match the verve of their allies on their left.

Later Ludendorff was to refer to 8 August as 'the black day of the German Army'. Five German divisions were broken. The Australians had taken nearly 8,000 prisoners and 173 guns while the Canadians took over 5,000 prisoners and 161 guns. Total Allied losses were about 6,500. The German Official Monograph estimates their losses at about 30,000, and described the battle as the greatest defeat the German Army had suffered since the beginning of the war. The Australians said, 'It was a très bon stunt.'

THE FOLLOW-UP

On 9 August the Australians pushed forward in the centre towards the ridge that runs through Lihons with the support of three battalions of tanks. Progress was slow, for the Germans had been able to reinforce the ridge, but they reached it by dark and contact was made with the Canadians on the railway near Rozières. More important was the problem on the Somme flank. 13th Australian Brigade had done duty screening what became the Canadian start-line on the night of 7/8 August, and were thus reasonably fresh on 9 August. Monash got his wish to command on both sides of the river and ordered them across at Cerisy to deal with the problem. They were too late. The American 33rd Division was serving with III Corps and, in accordance with General Pershing's now well-known wishes, had been held in reserve against emergencies.

The attack on the Gressaire Woods and the Chipilly spur was made by 131st Infantry, 33rd Division at 1730 hours. They had been brought forward after a night march and double-timed their way to their start line. Against machine-gun fire they threw the Germans off the northern end of the ridge and the southern part of the wood. The Australians crossed the river to climb the spur from the south-west and to take the village of Chipilly. The next day the Americans were officially attached to Monash's corps, and with the Australians took the rest of the wood. In these two days the Americans took 700 prisoners, 30 guns, more than 100 machine-guns and one aeroplane. On 13 August both units worked together to take the village of Etinehem.

On the Canadian flank matters were not going well. On 9 August there was confusion over the availability of troops, the British 32nd Division being made available and then withdrawn from the Canadian Corps. As a result the attack on 10 August to clear Le Quesnel involved the Canadian 3rd Division which had already fought long and hard two days before. The 4th Division's attack went in at 4030 hours and a tough hour's fight the village fell. Pockets of continued resistance accounted for more of the tanks and, although they remained in harmony with their Australian comrades on their left, it was becoming clear that, with no chance of surprise and the stiffening German defence as reserves were brought into the line, further progress was going to be costly. The 414 tanks that had started the battle on 8 August had been reduced to 145 on 9 August, one third destroyed by the enemy and the rest broken down, ditched or temporarily incapacitated. On 10 August there were eighty-five machines still operational. By 11 August the reserves were all committed and thirty-eight tanks went into action, working at the limit of endurance of both machines and crew. Six tanks were available on 12 August. The battle was clearly over.

GEORGE KING

The American 33rd Division remained in the area long enough to be recognised, congratulated and have some of their number decorated by King George V on 12 August. Will Judy witnessed the ceremony:

> *At eleven on this sunny morning the heralds came up the hill and soon the royal car shone in the sunlight as it moved between the two rows of poplars that for a quarter mile border the road to the chateau at the top of the hill. An American soldier near me rushed back and called to his comrade, "Hurry, here comes the king." "What king?" "George King." We crowded the sideways, silent in expectancy. The long limousine, black and sleek, drew near and one American called out loudly – "So that's the big stiff!"*
>
> *King George V of England led the procession to the green back of the chateau. General Pershing walked on his left; then came General Bliss, General [Sir] Henry Rawlinson and General Bell [Major-General George Bell, Jr, commanding 33rd Division], and after them a host, including myself. About twenty officers and men of the 131st and 132nd Infantry stood at attention. The movie cameras clicked, the king pinned an English medal on each, the band played `God Save the King,' and then the `Star Spangled Banner'; the procession returned to the chateau, the band played `Illinois', and the little white-bellied donkey that wanders around our headquarters every day, stood nearby half asleep thru it all, ready to kick King George in the rear side as readily as a soldier of the ranks.*

Then the division left to join the American First Army in the east. On the same day, the King knighted John Monash.

ON WITH THE ADVANCE!

Foch was, as usual, all for pressing on, but German resistance was increasing on the Canadian and Australian front, and Haig decided to have Byng's Third Army push forward further north, towards Bapaume. The battlefield of July 1916, still strewn with the débris of that conflict, cut with old trenches and wrapped in rusting barbed wire, offered a foul place to fight; Haig planned to pass to the north of the Ancre. Foch advocated extending the attack both north and south while maintaining it in the centre, but was dissuaded by the men closer to the action. Allied indecision was matched by German hesitation. The reserves arriving to relieve the defeated divisions were shaken to be accused of needlessly prolonging the war by their demoralised comrades. Local commanders wanted to fall back once more to better positions, but Ludendorff demanded that they stood where they were. The German Army was starting to crack; this in spite of having forty-two divisions to the Allies' thirty-two on the Somme front.

Between Arras and Beaumont-Hamel, and rolling eastwards towards the Hindenburg Line, the country was still unscarred by war, giving, it was thought, an opportunity to use the remaining tanks. For the rest of August, however, the weather was very hot and tanks, noisy, smelly and oppressive enough at the best of times, became fume-filled ovens. The Whippets' Hotchkiss guns jammed and the crews passed out. The wonder-weapon showed its limitations once more, and the infantry's speed again set the pace. Byng attacked on 21 August and made some progress, but not enough to satisfy Haig. Rawlinson's men retook Albert the next day. The 18th (Eastern) Division, Fourth Army, entered the town and Major C. H. Lemmon of the Royal Field Artillery was ordered to take his battery there and find billets for them in the little town that had stood to the rear of the British lines before the 1916 battle. He recalled:

> Our maps showed that we were approaching Albert, but in the evening light no town could be seen at all... for all practical purposes there was no such place. A jumbled mass of stone and iron-work on our left was identified with difficulty as a cemetery, and then we entered a street, represented by two rows of brick heaps, in which there was hardly a cellar intact.

The names of terrible memory appeared on the reports once more, but with less cost and at shorter intervals. Thiepval, 24 August; Mametz Wood, 25 August; Delville Wood, 27 August. On 26 August the First Army opened the Battle of the Scarpe, east of Arras. It became clear to Ludendorff that another retreat to the Hindenburg Line was inevitable, and that troops would have to be transferred from Flanders, abandoning all hope of taking the Channel ports, to stiffen resistance further south.

Bapaume fell to the New Zealanders on 29 August, and the steady, bloody rolling-back of the German line continued. Although the prospect of losing the war was now apparent to them, their will to fight and to extract the maximum cost from the Allies for every gain remained formidable. To the west of Péronne, above the marshy Somme river valley, the German positions on Mont St-Quentin commanded the approaches to the town. The Australians facing this obstacle were now seriously depleted. Two battalions were available for the attack, but they were now at under half their usual strength. Something like 600 men had to eject a well-entrenched German force of greater numbers. Using their superiority in artillery and charging forward in the dawning light of 31 August, the Australians swarmed into the defences and harried the Germans from one strong-point to the next. By 0800 hours it was all over. The Australians took more prisoners than the total of their attacking force.

To the north, at Bouchavesnes, the 47th (London) Division attacked the next day. Three battalions of the London Regiment went in behind the creeping barrage. Lieutenant A. R. Armfield described the enemy defence positions, 'Forward of their front line were irregularly sited isolated machine-gun posts in shallow gun-pits protected by barbed-wire entanglements – veritable suicide positions from which to inflict heavy loss upon us before receiving their own coup-de-grâce.' If by-passed, these machine-gunners would open fire once more on the backs of the advancing troops, so thorough 'mopping-up' became a routine for experienced troops and it became wiser to shoot or bayonet a prone figure than risk his joining the action again. 'Soon after leaving the assembly trench and advancing over this open, gently rising ground, a runner came forward to tell me that a single enemy shell had wiped out the

Company Commander... and his entire headquarters party, and I was now in command.'

Armfield went on, revolver in hand. The other commanders were killed in turn, but the troops pressed on. He continues the story:

So that I might survey the forward position I had stopped in a very shallow depression about seven feet (2m) in diameter, the forward lip of which was then lined, in prone position, by my Lewis gun section of three men. After a few moments, I ordered the section to follow me forward. They did not stir, and when I turned towards them, my eyes looked through a gaping hole in a steel helmet, into a bloody mass that had been a human brain.

He pulled the Lewis gun from under the body and handed it to men who were coming up and on they went. Some men fired their rifles from the hip as they advanced. They reached the crest of the slope and their trench that was their objective. They jumped in to find the only things left there were the bodies of their enemies.

The Germans fell back once more to the fortified lines from which they had sprung forward in March, the Hindenburg Line and its various switch lines. The French and the Americans, with some help from the British, had dealt with the Soissons salient, and now the British Empire, with some help from the French and Americans, had flattened the great Amiens salient. It was time for the Americans to act on their own.

9

THE AMERICANS ACT ALONE

GENERAL PERSHING VISITED Field Marshal Haig on 12 August to seek the return of the five divisions training and serving under British command. Haig was not at all keen to comply, but could not deny the American command of his own men. Although Pershing's mission to create the American First Army and reduce the St Mihiel Salient had already been accepted, it seemed to Haig unwise to weaken a force that was rolling the enemy back in Picardy. Marshal Foch, as he now was, intervened, persuading Pershing to leave the 27th and 30th Divisions with the British, and the 33rd, 78th and 80th left for the build-up in the east.

Also in August, the AEF ceased training with the French and British entirely, taking full responsibility for raising their troops to combat readiness. It would soon be the case that virtually the only troops serving under French command would be the black regiments, the so-called 'colored troops', of the 93rd Division.

Pershing established the headquarters of the American First Army at Ligny-en-Barrois, 25 miles south-east of St Mihiel, on 29 August, and started work on the takeover of the Lorraine front. No sooner had this task been taken in hand, however, than the basic concept was changed. Foch revealed to Pershing his plan to reduce a larger salient than ever before – the entire German front line between Verdun and Ypres. This line was supported by the railway from Strasbourg that passed to the north of the River Meuse; if the Americans could strike up through the Argonne Forest, it could be severed in the region of Sedan and Mézières, leaving the Germans reliant on supply lines through Belgium alone. That the railway might have been more vulnerable further east was true, but it was also the case that alternatives through Luxembourg were available, and it must be said that the concept of the three great Allied armies advancing shoulder to shoulder had its attractions. If this chance to end the war in 1918 was to be seized, operations must start before the winter weather endangered their completion – that is, in early October. Before that Pershing wanted to wipe out the St Mihiel Salient with his independent army and he was not willing to abandon the idea. He would then have to move and assemble his forces to take up the battle miles away to the north-west. It was a very tall order indeed, but Pershing agreed.

ST MIHIEL

After the German invasion had been halted on the Marne in 1914, renewed attempts were made to outflank the French at Verdun by taking the Meuse Heights. The river runs south from Verdun and the heights lie to the east, terminating just south of St Mihiel, and east of them the plain of the Woevre stretches away to Metz. In the last days of September, the Germans seized the southern part of the heights and crossed the Meuse, only to be forced back to St Mihiel by the French XVI Corps, leaving a salient through Combres in the north, Chauvoncourt, across the river from St Mihiel, in the west, and through Apremont and Seicheprey and along the hills above the valley of the River Rupt de Mad in the south. James W. Block, a corporal of the 59th Infantry, 4th Division, described the view from the northern end of the salient on 7 September:

> Looking thru the powerful glasses out across No-man's land, I saw stretching before me a broad, rolling plain which rose gradually to the mountain in front of Metz. The visibility was excellent. Beginning at the foot of the hill below us, band after band of wire entanglements zig-zagged across our front and roughly parallel to it. There were miles and miles of it. Directly in front of the observation post and two kilometers distant on the Metz-Paris road, lay the powdered ruins of Manheulles. The extent of those ruins must be seen to be fully appreciated. Not a wall stood intact. About one kilometer directly south of Manheulles, was Bonzée-en-Woëvre, and about one and one-half kilometers east of Bonzée, lay Fresnes-en-Woëvre, both

reduced to heaps of mortar, brick and stone, with here and there a jagged fragment of a wall still standing. The outlines of entrenched positions could be seen. To the northwest of Manheulles, and directly in front of the left of our sector, was a dense forest. I asked the French Officer where the enemy front line was. He pointed towards No-man's land and said, `Out there somewhere, we don't know, but we think his lines run along the edge of that forest over to the left.' No movements of the enemy could be detected along any of the trenches at the edge of the woods, or in the towns mentioned. Adjusting the glasses, I looked over the region beyond. Scores of towns nestled among the low hills. Belching smoke stacks in the distance told of the industrial activity in the iron district of Lorraine, which we were facing. It was for the protection of this district and Metz, that the St. Mihiel salient had been pushed out by the Germans.

Raymond Austin of 6th Field Artillery, 1st Division, viewed the salient from the southern side, from which the main advance was to be made:

Beaumont is on a high but not extremely steep ridge which runs for miles from Pont-a-Mousson to Flirey, Beaumont, Rambeaucourt, etc. Seicheprey is at the foot of the slope just beneath Beaumont. From Seicheprey north there is a broad, rolling valley, dotted with towns formerly held by the Germans – St. Baussant, Lahayville, Richecourt, Nonsard, Pannes, etc. From almost any point along the Beaumont ridge a great Panorama is visible. The country is spread out before you like a map, beginning far to the left where the valley narrows noticeably toward Saint Mihiel, and opening wider and wider as the gaze passes to the right. Looming up high and commanding all the country for miles and miles in all directions is the great fort of Mont Sec which the French once took and held for seven hours with the loss of nearly one thousand men per hour. On the far side of the broad valley is a long ridge similar to the Beaumont ridge. Vigneulles is just at the base of this ridge, and Hattonville, near where our line

*now rests, is just at the top of the ridge. From the heights the valley
appears quite even and smooth, but it is really broken by many smaller valleys and hills, streams, woods, etc. At the time of our attack our
front lines ran just in front of Seicheprey, having been drawn in after
the fight there last April 7. Between Seicheprey, St. Baussant and
nearly to Nonsard there were many belts of barbed wire, machine-
gun emplacements, and other defenses.*

The presence of the Germans here was a constant threat to Verdun.
French efforts against the salient were directed, after a failed attack in
November 1914 at Chauvoncourt, against the northern flank. The eminence of Les Éparges was gained on 9 April 1915, but the line then
remained stable, if the constant raiding, mining and counter-mining
can be described as such, and out of the front line the Germans enjoyed
a measure of tranquillity.

Two ideas influenced the American approach to the reduction of the
salient: secrecy and efficiency. The gathering of the First Army was to
be concealed from the enemy as far as was possible. The operation was
to be the acid test of the abilities of that army – not of the fighting spirit of its men, for this was now beyond doubt, but of organization and
staff work. The staff were under the direction of Captain Hugh Drum,
First Army Chief of Staff and Colonel George C. Marshall, Jr, on loan
from AEF headquarters. They were responsible for the assembly of
550,000 American and 110,000 French soldiers, 3,010 guns, 40,000 tons
of ammunition, 267 tanks and 65 evacuation trains. In support, Colonel
Mitchell was gathering an air force of unprecedented size. He had 609
American aircraft at his disposal, of which 108 were US-built Liberty
DH4s, and with the contributions made by the French, British and
Italians, he assembled a force of 696 fighters, 366 reconnaissance aircraft, 323 day bombers and 91 night bombers. With 20 observation
balloons, the air fleet numbered 1,496 craft.

Private Francis of the 5th Marines, 2nd Division, wrote of his unit's
approach to the front:

We camped about ten miles back of the Front for about eight days, in dense woods. It rained every day... We finally received orders to move to the Front. Although it was raining, we hiked all night, and the morning found us in the front line waiting for Zero hour. We were standing in three feet of water.

The French were facing the tip of the salient at St Mihiel, while lined out along the southern side were the US 1st, 42nd, 89th, 2nd, 5th, 90th and 82nd Divisions. The eastern face of the salient was mainly the province of the French, with the exception of the American 26th Division. The 1st and 42nd Divisions from the south and the 26th from the west were to drive towards, and meet at, Vigneulles, trapping as many Germans as possible in the nose of the salient, while the rest of the attacking forces were to push towards the Michel Line, the fortified position which the Germans had built at the back of the salient. An assault on prepared positions like these, it was now known, required destruction of the barbed wire either by shellfire, Bangalore torpedoes (explosive charges contained in long tubes) or by tanks, which were also the key to overcoming the defenders' machine-guns. George Patton, by now a Lieutenant-Colonel and commander of the Tank Corps, was anxious to ensure that his tanks performed impeccably in the coming battle. He made a night reconnaissance with a French officer to inspect the tank route, for the light Renault tanks with which his corps was equipped had little weight of armour, relying more on speed (six miles an hour – 9.6kmph!) – than brute force to gain their objectives. Although he satisfied himself that the ground was firm, and having had the curious experience of hearing a German whistle to warn him off when he got too close, instead of shooting him, the plans were changed and another route was chosen, so that the job had to be done again, this time under shellfire. The last of Patton's tanks was detrained at 0300, with H hour only two hours off. He issued his orders, adding:

No tank is to be surrendered or abandoned to the enemy. If you are left alone in the midst of the enemy keep shooting. If your gun is dis-

abled use your pistols and squash the enemy with your tracks... [A tank's] presence will save the lives of hundreds of infantry and kill many Germans...

Corporal Rudolph A. Forderhase, 356th Infantry, 89th Division, was in the village of Flirey, preparing for battle:

We were ordered to make up combat packs (we rolled up our blankets, extra pair of shoes, tent pole and stakes, in our shelter half). Each man was issued with two extra bandoliers of ammunition. We hated these... [one] was slung over each shoulder... to bring so much pressure on both sides of the neck, that it was torture. We were checked and rechecked for not only ammunition, but grenades, intrenching tools, first aid kit and rations... I was aroused by the Platoon Sergeant, at midnight... a light rain was falling. It was so dark, and the rain made the footing so treacherous, that every man held on to the man ahead of him in order to avoid falling or straggling. We soon entered a communicating trench where the footing was no better. Suddenly the artillery began to shell the German positions we were about to attack.

It was 0100 hours on 12 September. The bombardment continued for four hours, and then the men moved forward. Raymond Austin wrote home:

The infantry went over at the appointed time, appearing as a line miles long moving slowly forward, followed at intervals by succeeding waves, the later waves being broken up into small squads instead of being in continuous long lines, as the telephone squads running wires, engineers, stretcher bearers, etc. advanced. It was a great sight, that broad expanse of country dotted everywhere with men and tanks, bursting shells, rockets rising and bursting into white, red, green stars, Mont Sec looming up dark and forbidding and showing here and there on its sides white puffs of smoke which told where our big 8-

inch guns were dropping their shells – all in the gray light of early morning under the broken storm clouds against which the fast, low-flying airplanes were sharply silhouetted.

Billy Mitchell's air war was going well. The night before the attack, massive British Handley Page O/400 bombers had hit Metz and Thionville, while the French bombers attacked targets within the salient. French squadrons and the American Second Pursuit Group flew strafing missions in support of the infantry, while 103rd Squadron of the Third Pursuit Group bombed transport and troop concentrations. Deeper into the salient, the French flew bombing missions alternately from north and south. The American First Pursuit Group swept down from the north, only 100 feet (30m) above the ground, to smash the German aircraft attempting to combat the total domination of the air which Mitchell had achieved. It was to be another two days before the Germans could gather themselves sufficiently to challenge the Americans and their allies in the sky. Corporal Forderhase was ready to go:

The order to advance came at full daylight. The rain had made the clay muddy and slick. The shorter men had some difficulty getting out of the trench that was about four feet deep, but the willing hands of the taller men were helpful. We formed squads, in single file, to start across no-mans-land. The enemy could not see us at first. When he did, we were greeted by both machine-gun and rifle fire. We dived into a large shell crater. I was unable to locate the gun. Almost instantly it stopped firing at us. I ordered the men to form, on either side of me, at intervals of twenty feet [6m] and we continued the advance. Evidently our advancing troops had overrun the gun that had fired on us. By the time we reached the main German trench their resistance had ceased.

Only one of Forderhase's men had been wounded, a slight flesh wound below the knee. He was sent to a dressing station, but never made it;

one of the few German shells fired that day killed him on the way.

The tanks of 304th Battalion, US Tank Corps, were operating in support of the 42nd Division and George Patton was following on foot. When he outran the length of the telephone line that had been laid, he went forward with a team of four runners to carry messages. Hearing that his tanks had halted in front of the village of Essey he hurried forward, striding along smoking his pipe as much, he said, to keep up his own courage as to give confidence to the men. An even more exposed position on a small hillock was occupied by an American officer. Climbing up, Patton found Brigadier-General Douglas MacArthur, Chief of Staff of the 42nd, viewing the battle. The tanks had stopped, it emerged, because they feared that the bridge into Essey was mined. Patton, 'in a catlike manner, expecting to be blown to heaven any moment', walked across it, and the tanks followed.

The Germans were fleeing or surrendering as fast as they could. The attack had clearly been a surprise, for the advancing Americans found food still on the tables of the houses the enemy had occupied, and clothing and equipment abandoned everywhere. By now the 304th's tanks had, except for a single vehicle, run out of fuel and Patton pushed on towards Pannes riding on the outside of the remaining Renault. Approaching the village of Beney, he noticed little chips of paint popping off the side of the tank and realised they were being shot at. He wrote to his wife, 'Here I was nervous.' First he rolled off and took cover, then sought help from the infantry some 100 yards (90m) to the rear. When they appeared to lack the enthusiasm to do much about it, he chased after the tank, knocked with his stick on the rear door and, when it opened, told the obviously disappointed sergeant, who had been enjoying the drive, to take him back.

Forderhase, to his surprise, found the advance equally easy, though confused. They came to a German dug-out where they found wine, brandy and 'some fancy-looking cigarettes that did not smell very good'. In the growing dark they went on until they came near a farm on the edge of a village. The exhausted men slumped to the ground while the buildings were reconnoitred, and were hard to rouse when their lieutenant came back. They bedded down thankfully in the hayloft of the farm. They had reached Xammes in a single day.

While the advance had been remarkable, the salient had not been closed. That night, part of the 26th Division marched along the Grande Tranchée de Calone from the north-west. Although it was entrenched in the war, it was originally the formal approach to a great château, bordered with rose bushes. The 26th struck along this ridgeway and had command of Vigneulles by 0200. The next morning the 1st Division pushed up from the south to join them by 1000 hours. By that evening almost all of the objectives had been secured. Attention was now turned to consolidating the American positions here and undertaking the second part of the operation – the mass transfer of the First Army to the new front between the Meuse and the Argonne.

The establishment of the new front line was more than a routine matter. Captain F. M. Wood, in command of D Company, 353rd Infantry, 89th Division, had established contact with the Marines of the 2nd Division on his right at the end of the first day's fighting. The next day he saw '...the Marines charge up the slope at Mon Plaisir Farm and be literally blown into the air by direct artillery fire. They formed again and again, only to meet with the same results.' The farm was a fortified strongpoint of the Hindenburg Line, and was to remain in German hands until the Armistice. Work now went ahead to create the new front line, out of what had been the St Mihiel Salient.

The Americans were delighted with their success. It was, however, not quite such a marvel as it appeared. The order to vacate the salient and withdraw to the Michel Line had been given by Ludendorff on 8 September and was conveyed to the German units on the ground two days later. The German artillery was already moving back when the attack took place. The American First Army was therefore fighting a force that had to turn a planned withdrawal into a fighting retreat. Even in these favourable circumstances their progress was marked by the confusion observed by the French, who remained sceptical about American staff abilities. In spite of these facts, the operation was vital to the Americans. They had captured 16,000 prisoners and 450 guns for the loss of only 7,000 killed, wounded and missing. Sooner or later their staff work had had to be tried in battle, and, more important, the morale of the newly-created, independent army of the United States needed to be raised to combat readiness by a clear victory.

The Germans were not very impressed. In an intelligence document dated 24 September, a Captain Weise commented, 'The advance of the infantry was meticulously scheduled, and resulted in considerable awkwardness in the movement on the terrain of the closely following waves of riflemen. The shock troops recoiled before the slightest resistance, giving the impression of uneasiness and helplessness. Neither officers or men understood how to utilise the terrain; on meeting resistance they did not seek cover but ran back.' The verdict was that, brave as he might be, the American infantryman was inexperienced and poorly-trained. In the use of machine-guns he was expert. The artillery was well handled and in good communication with the infantry, able to bring down fire on machine-guns nests quickly. The tanks were considered irrelevant as they trailed behind the infantry. 'Leadership is thoroughly weak and uncertain. The enemy obviously possesses a large number of officers, but they lack the quality of leadership. Their confusion was unmistakable after the attainment of the first objective.' Captain Weise was of the opinion that Frenchmen would have been readier to exploit any advantage and follow up a success. The high command was admired no more than the officers, the fact that the Germans had been able to disengage and establish a fresh line of defence being cited as evidence of their failure.

To what extent this report can be taken at face value is obviously open to question, given its source. It is clear, however, that the Battle of St Mihiel was no great victory, but it was a vital step in the learning process for the American army.

THE MEUSE-ARGONNE FRONT

The change from action on the eastern bank of the Meuse to the west, the other side of Verdun, did not command the support of, among others, Douglas MacArthur. He felt that continued advance across the

Woevre Plain towards Metz, the Moselle River and the heartland of Germany would bring the war to a swift end. Perhaps even more persuasive is the fact that the opportunity to cut the Germans' east-west railway between Metz and Verdun was not taken, although the lack of heavy tanks on this front made that difficult to contemplate. Lieutenant-General Hunter Liggett, commanding the American I Corps, took the view that such an operation would have been possible 'only on the supposition that our army was a well-oiled, fully co-ordinated machine, which it was not as yet.' Whatever their misgivings, however, the US forces threw themselves into the task of changing fronts.

The new American front lay across the south of the Argonne Forest eastwards to the River Meuse, where it flowed west of the heights above Verdun. Only three roads, and minor ones at that, could be used by the 600,000 troops, 93,000 horses and all their support and equipment making the sixty-mile (96km) journey from the St Mihiel Salient. Colonel Marshall therefore designated one road for motor vehicles and the other two for men on foot and animals. That the French had to withdraw from the Argonne sector at the same time as the Americans moved in was an added complication. Furthermore, the process could not start until the St Mihiel action was largely complete, on 14 September, and had to be finished in time for the new offensive to start on 26 September. There were delays, traffic jams and frustration, but a British observer, Colonel Charles Repington, the correspondent at the front for The Times, declared that it could not have been done better. The American First Army now held a front ninety-four miles (150km) long from the western edge of the Argonne Forest to the new positions forward of St Mihiel.

On the west of the area that the Americans faced, the River Aisne divided the high, open country of Champagne from the near-mountains of the Argonne Forest, which run due north. The little River Aire flows north on the eastern flank before turning west at St-Juvin and running past Grandpré to join the Aisne north of Binarville. East of the Aire the landscape is softer, with lines of rolling hills running east-west, punctuated by thick woods and more prominent hilltops, the whole area sloping eventually to the valley of the Meuse with its broad flood plain. Beyond that river, the land rises steeply to the Heights of the Meuse. In peacetime it is delightful; the fields, farms and villages have an air of enviable tranquillity. As a theatre for mobile warfare, however, it was deeply unpromising.

The area had been the scene of continuous fighting in the first year of the war as the armies of the German Crown Prince Wilhlem strove to break through the French lines. In the high woodland west of Varennes-en-Argonne countless bloody encounters took place amongst trenches and blockhouses that are still to be seen today. The front line passed eastwards, south of Varennes, through the height of Vauquois, once crowned with a healthy village. By September 1918 that village was not merely flattened, but where the houses once stood there gaped a hole sixty feet (18m) deep. Mining and counter-mining of incredible complexity had blown Vauquois entirely away, and over the months the French and Germans continued to torture one another from trenches fifty yards (45m) apart on the shattered lips of the crater. The front line then ran east to the north of Béthincourt to cross the Meuse some ten miles (16km) north of Verdun.

The second-line position built up by the Germans in the relatively quiet years since 1915 was based on the hill of Montfaucon which, while it seems modest enough in height, dominates the country for miles around. In the west the heights of the Argonne cover the flank here, as they do all the way north. In addition, through Apremont, Gesnes and on to Sivry on the Meuse, ran the Giselher Stellung, another of the Germans' carefully constructed defences of trench, pillbox and blockhouse, providing a supplementary line to the second position of resistance. Then came the third position, based on the hills at Romagne and running west to the north of Granpré, with a branch down to Exermont, and east to Brieulles and the Kriemhild Stellung, the Hindenburg Line proper. A fourth position, unfinished but still a serious obstacle, was centred on the Barricourt Heights and ran westwards to Buzancy and to Dun-sur-Meuse in the east. This is a simplified list, for many switch lines, intermediate trenches, belts of barbed wire, fortified farms, pillboxes and support trenches lay between the major works. Nowhere had the Germans constructed a more formidable system of defences. Now, his most experienced divisions in need of rest after the battle two weeks before, Pershing was to pit green troops against this barrier.

On the left, facing the Argonne Forest, was Hunter Liggett's I Corps with the 77th, 28th and 35th Divisions. To the east, from Vauquois, was Lieutenant-General George H. Cameron's V Corps with the 91st, 37th and 79th Divisions, and alongside the French was Lieutenant-General Robert L. Bullard's III Corps with the 4th, 80th and 33rd Divisions. The barrage began half an hour before midnight on 25 September, when the long range heavy artillery opened up on selected targets, the corps and divisional artillery joining in at 0230 hours on the 26th.

At 0530 the fifty-nine operational tanks of 354th Battalion, 1 Tank Brigade, US Tank Corps moved off with the 35th Division to join 137th and 138th Infantry Regiments in the assault to the west of Vauquois, towards Cheppy. There was very dense fog and progress was slow, although resistance was light. They had reached a hill just south of Cheppy by 0915 when, as the fog lifted, the German guns began to shell them. George Patton, not content to remain at headquarters, had taken command of 1 Brigade in the field and ordered the 354th to attack. Their way was blocked by two disabled French Schneider tanks, but the nimble Renaults set off left and right of the hill, coming under some fire from artillery near Varennes in their rear. That soon ceased, doubtless silenced by the 28th Division on their left, and part of the 354th and the 137th Infantry tackled the trenches south and west of Cheppy, while the rest of the tank battalion went to the aid of the 138th Infantry. The village was taken. Captain Ranulf Compton of the 354th writes in his report:

The infantry losses had been very heavy up to this time, both from shellfire and machine-guns. The machine-gun fire was silenced, but the shellfire continued. There was no counter-artillery fire apparently, and the Boche planes flew over constantly until the middle of

the afternoon, observing and directing artillery fire. Lieut.-Colonel
Patton had been wounded at about the time the 354th was ordered
into the attack.

The tanks were moved forward over the enemy trench in front of
Cheppy as a result of hurried digging by a crew of infantrymen Patton
bullied into the work, and by hitching one tank to another to heave it
over the obstacle. On foot, Patton then led the re-formed infantry forward until enemy fire pinned them down. Losing patience with
grovelling in the mud, he said to himself, 'It is time for another Patton
to die,' and called for further advance, during which he was hit. The bullet went in through his groin and exited through a buttock. His orderly,
Private Joseph Angelo, fixed a field dressing and relayed Patton's orders
until the position was taken. Patton's courage cannot be doubted, but
his wisdom may be called in question, for from this time on the liaison
between infantry and tanks became steadily less effective.

To the right of the 35th, the 91st Division pushed briskly forward
through Cheppy Wood virtually unopposed. As the fog lifted they, too,
came under fire from the Butte de Vauquois on the left, both from
artillery and from the numerous machine-gun nests in the woods. As
the divisional history points out, these machine-gun emplacements
were positioned to fire to the flank, covering the approaches to the
neighbouring gun, or gaps in the barbed wire. The source of flanking
fire is always hard to locate, and each nest has to be taken out by tanks
or artillery before further advance is possible. A frontal attack is suicide,
and an unsupported infantry flanking movement almost as dangerous.
The rest of the division hurried across the open ground and made the
cover of Cheppy Woods. On the northern side of the woods they were
held up for a while at La Neuve Grange Farm, but by noon they had
made it to the village of Véry. They dug in north of the village for the
night while, in their rear, the engineers laboured to rebuild roads to
move supplies forward into Cheppy Woods. They had advanced five
miles (8km) that day. On the extreme right the 80th and 33rd Divisions
had made a similar advance to establish a blocking line along the Meuse,

while on the extreme left the 77th had crossed the Varennes-Le Four de Paris road but stumbled at the salient made by the continued resistance of the bunkers around the Abri de Kronprinz, the concrete strongholds that stand in those woods today. In the valley of the Aire the 28th Division found the going harder, enduring flanking fire from the forest on their left, fire that would injure and slow all units advancing in the shadow of the forest in the coming weeks. It was the 79th Division that had the toughest time, making, as they were, for the commanding height of Montfaucon. From this perfect observation point the German artillery was directed onto pre-registered targets directly in the path of the Americans with fearful results. As a consequence the 4th Division on their right were held up, allowing the Germans to reinforce Nantillois and the Brieulles Woods.

In fact, Colonel Billy Mitchell's airmen were there, contrary to the complaints of the troops on the ground. The First Pursuit Group flew low-level missions, shooting down four balloons and eight aircraft, while the Second operated at a higher altitude, accounting for seven German machines. Mitchell himself flew over the battlefield and saw a severe traffic jam near Avocourt. He ordered First Day Bombardment Group to carry out a diversionary attack on Dun-sur-Meuse to draw the Germans away and to dislocate their supply lines. Lieutenant E. C. Leonard of 20th Aero Squadron was observer in the aircraft piloted by Merian C. Cooper:

> Our wheels left the ground at nine o'clock and we rose into the fog, straining our eyes for the sight of another plane above, below, on all sides. Our own motor made so much noise that we could hear nothing else. Consequently our eyes were the only guard against collision. The ground faded out of sight and we were swallowed up in the mist. It was like another world. It lasted but for a minute, thank goodness. The sun began to grow brighter and suddenly we burst into daylight and blue sky.

As they approached their target:

the observer in the leading machine fired a very light signal telling us to prepare to drop our bombs. I leaned over the side with my hand on the release, watching for the bombs to drop from the plane ahead. In a few moments, I saw them fall from the next plane and pulled the lever and marked up 448 pounds more of T N T for the Germans. At the release of weight, our plane gave a jump forward as if glad of the chance to hit the Hun.

They turned for home, hopeful that it would prove to be an uneventful mission. They were not so lucky:

I was beginning to think that is was only a joy ride after all, [wrote Leonard] *when I saw the Boche. There they were, tiny specks in the distance and yet, almost before we could think they were on us, five life size Fokkers, painted yellow and black. They slid around our heavier machines like yellowjackets, swerving up for an instant to let a stream of bullets go at us and then taking a new position. One of them got under our tail and hung there, sending a string of bullets at us. I couldn't shoot at him without shooting away part of our own machine. The tremendous noise from the engine and wind from the propeller made it impossible for me to tell the pilot, so I wiggled the controls from my seat to attract his attention and pointed out Mr. Boche to him. Promptly he turned, first to the right a little, then a little to the left. At every turn the Fokker under our tail came into plain view about seventy-five yards away. Each time we swung, I was waiting and let him have both guns. I could see the tracer bullets going right into his cockpit, and knew that one bullet at least must find the mark. And it did. At the third burst, my bullets reached home and Mr. Boche started down in a nose spin, out of control, dead, wounded or disabled.*

That was not the end of the affair, for soon another twelve little specks appeared and they were under attack once more. Leonard saw what he described as the beautiful, yet terrible, sight of one of their flight going down in flames:

I redoubled my efforts to shoot more Huns and took great care in aiming. We were still below the rest of our formation and it seemed as though all the lines of tracer bullets were coming in our direction. I worked faster and faster, but had not time to tell whether a Hun that slid away from my bullets was hit or not, for as fast as one moved away, a second took his place for a shot. I knew that couldn't last forever and was beginning to wonder how long it could last, when 'blam' I got it in the neck. The shot knocked me down on the seat with the sudden force of a pile driver. I thought my end had come, but it hadn't. The Fokker who had shot me, and seen my guns stop shooting, was coming up close beside us. I got on my feet, took good aim, shot at him with both guns from about fifty yards. The tracer bullets went right into his cockpit and he slid out of sight, `Coop' says that he went down in flames. Probably he did. I was too busy to watch him the instant his bullets stopped coming. I was conscious of only one thing – to get rid of three other Fokkers which had begun to close in on us from the other sides.

Suddenly our plane dropped into a nose spin. My first thought was that `Coop' had been shot and that in a very few seconds we would hit the ground and be through with everything. I slipped down on the seat unconscious, but only for an instant. When I regained my senses, we were still falling in a spin, but `Coop' had unfastened his safety belt and was standing up with one foot over the sides in the act of jumping overboard. And no wonder, for his cockpit was a mass of flames from the motor which was on fire. It was a question of dying an easy death by jumping overboard, or of burning to death. His first thought was to escape the terrible agony of the flames. He did not know whether I was dead or alive, but when he saw me open my eyes, he did not hesitate. Rather than desert a wounded and helpless comrade, he stepped back into what seemed, at the time, the certainty of burning to death.

We came out of the spin upside down ... By this time his hands were so badly burned that the stick slipped from his fingers and he had to use knees and elbows to work the controls. Finally by diving straight down ... the almost impossible was accomplished, and the flames put out.

We landed in a large field, barely missing some telephone wires as we came into the field. 'Coop' landed the machine with the control stick between his knees and elbows. Although we hit the ground with force enough to send the plane up on its nose and break the wings, neither of us was thrown out. The machine was pretty well shot up. The motor was a wreck. There were bullet holes all over the plane, sixty or more of them; little round ones and long gashes in the fabric. Surely a Divine providence must have guided the bullets from the vital parts.

The victorious Fokker landed alongside them and accepted their surrender before hastening to see that their wounds were treated. Merian Cooper became a Hollywood film producer and director after the war and included the film King Kong amongst his achievements. The raid on the German supply lines had assisted the American advance, but, despite these efforts, it is true that air support was, in the absence of the French and British reinforcement the Americans had enjoyed at St Mihiel, comparatively slender.

General Max von Gallwitz, commander of the Group comprising the German Third and Fifth Armies, was at first worried that the attack was a feint to covered a renewed onslaught in the Woevre, but swiftly appreciated that this thrust was the Americans' prime effort and transferred fresh troops to the sectors under attack. He was confident his series of defence lines could hold against such inexperienced troops. The days that followed appeared to justify his optimism.

The first line of the German defence had fallen easily, but the second, through Montfaucon, took another three days to conquer. American units flanked the pinnacle of Montfaucon on both sides before a costly assault reduced it on 27 September, the attackers thus gaining a viewpoint from which they could see the positions of the Kreimhild Line. In the Argonne Forest, the 77th Division clawed forward, often disorientated and sometimes ambushed in the thick woodlands. Where, in more open territory, swifter progress might have been expected, co-operation between tanks and infantry was lacking, exposing both to higher casualties than they would have taken operating in concert. On 28 September, Ranulf Compton reports, the western group of 354th Battalion's tanks advanced from Montblainville and entered Apremont at noon. They were unaccompanied by infantry and, despite clearing the Germans out, were not the appropriate force to hold the town. The men of the 28th Division, the Keystone Division from Pennsylvania, had taken Varennes-en-Argonne the day before, but now found themselves under the German guns on Le Chêne Tondu, the high bluffs overlooking Apremont. The 345th was summoned to help, but it was not until evening that they obtained the support of a small infantry unit to secure the town they had reached by midday.

The eastern group of the tank battalion got as far as Exermont on 29 September, but once again outran the infantry, the much-weakened 35th Division, and had to withdraw. The town would not be taken until 4 October. Artillery support was also poorly co-ordinated, depending too much on firing blind, although a notable exception was an action in support of the 35th Division. On 30 September a balloon observer reported to that division's 110th Field Signal Battalion that Germans were gathering to counter-attack a forward infantry unit. Paul Shaffer, lacking telephone lines to the artillery, had to run with the message to D Battery, 149th Field Artillery, and deliver the message to its commander, Captain Harry S. Truman – later to be President of the United States. Shaffer recounts:

...When he read my message he started runnin' and cussin' all at the same time, shouting for the guns to turn northwest. He ran about a hundred yards to a little knoll, and what he saw didn't need binoculars. I never heard a man cuss so well or so intelligently, and I'd shoed a million mules. He was shouting back ranges and giving bearings.

The battery didn't say a word. They must have figured the cap'n could do the cussin' for the whole outfit. It was a great sight... everything clockwork, setting fuses, cutting fuses, slapping shells into breeches and jerking lanyards [to fire the guns]...

Swept up in the spirit of the moment, Shaffer followed Truman up the little hill where, across the fields in front of them, they saw groups of Germans on the edge of some woods, creeping forward with weapons at the ready. Truman yelled fresh orders, and the next salvo scattered dismembered enemy soldiers in all directions.

Behind the front line there were more difficulties for the Americans. The few narrow roads that wound north into the area crossed what, for nearly four years, had been no-man's-land, terrain devastated by shell-fire. The engineers strove to make new roads, but their work was undone as fast as it was completed, either by enemy fire or by the attempts to move heavy guns and tanks forward. Although the first day of the offensive had been dry, rain had been falling ever since and the guns had to be moved forward with the help of infantrymen heaving on ropes. Pershing, disappointed with progress, went to visit his corps commanders; he makes no mention in his memoirs of the fact that it took him ninety minutes to travel two and a half miles (4km) when doing so. On Sunday, 29 September, the French Prime Minister, Clemenceau, attempted to visit Montfaucon. The chaos on the road prevented his reaching his destination at all.

It was clear to all that the divisions which had gone into the attack only three days earlier were at the end of their endurance. The 35th had been cut to ribbons and had lost all coherence. The 1st Division were sent to relieve them, while the 82nd were on their way to give the battered 28th a break. In the centre the 3rd and the 32nd assumed the ground of the 91st, 37th and 79th Divisions. 'It was a matter of keen regret,' Pershing was to write, 'that the veteran 2nd Division was not on hand at this time, but at Marshal Foch's earnest request it had been sent to General Gouraud to assist the French Fourth Army, which was held up at Somme-Py.' Pershing's great stride forward had come to a halt.

10

WITH THE FRENCH
IN CHAMPAGNE

THE ATTACK OF 26 September involved the French as well. To the west of the Argonne Forest the French 161st Division was also striking north and with them three regiments of the American 93rd Division, a unit that was never to operate as a division. These were the 369th, 371st and 372nd Infantry, drafted men and National Guard regiments comprised of African-American enlisted men with white officers. They had trained with the French, wore mainly French uniforms and fought with French equipment. Their abilities as soldiers in this war has been a matter of some discussion but it is enough to say that the use made of them in 1918 scarcely allowed them to do themselves justice. The French, however, did not share their American ally's doubts about these men, and their confidence was well rewarded.

On 26 September the 369th was in support of the attack to the west of Cernay-en-Dormois, but was soon brought forward to help overcome the resistance of the Germans at Rouvroy-Ripont on the River Dormoise. They took the town and, the next day, took Fontaine-en-Dormois and gained a hold on the slopes of Bellevue Signal Ridge to the north. On 28 September the 371st and 372nd came into the line on the 369th's right, on the other side of the French unit alongside them, and the drive continued, Ardeuil on the left and Séchault on the right falling the next day. The black soldiers' courage was high, but their casualties were heavy. The three regiments had 2,246 killed, wounded and missing by the time they were relieved, the last of them, the 372nd, on 7 October. By then they had won the admiration of one of the toughest of the French divisions, the 2nd Moroccan, which was fighting on their left.

The 92nd `Buffalo' Division, an African-American formation that did operate as a division in its own right, but also brigaded with the French, was on the left of the American First Army's 77th on 26 September. The 1st Battalion, 368th Infantry took part in the capture of Binarville four days later alongside the French 9th Cuirassiers, but their commanding officer was not enthused by their performance. He reported:

> *On the afternoon of the 30th of September we began an advance from the Turpitz Trench upon Binarville which we entered about 4 p.m. of the same day because every time the many halts under none too severe fire were made I personally and often at the point of the pistol literally drove forward the battalion... The cowardice shown by the men was abject. The officers when I was personally present did not run but carried out orders, but immediately the advance began it almost as soon stopped as soon as the officers and men were beyond the sound of my voice...*

Major J. N. Merrill specifically names eight officers who are absolved from this criticism. 'A few brave NCOs, a few brave spirits among the officers and a small group of men would follow, but the battalion, never.' Why this unit did so poorly and those more directly under French command so much better has yet to be adequately explained.

BLANC MONT RIDGE

Pershing's regret at the lack of the 2nd Division in the Argonne was understandable when their achievements in support of the French Fourth Army is considered. They were fighting northwards, to the west of the American First Army, hauling themselves forward over the repeatedly fiercely-contested ground of Champagne. From the height of the Ferme de Navarin, north of Suippes, the land slopes gently down to the valley in which lies Somme-Py (Sommepy-Tahure on modern maps) and just as gently rises again, the road today running through broad, neatly cultivated fields to the wooded ridge of Blanc Mont. Lieutenant John D. Clark, 15th Field Artillery, 2nd Division, described the land in his diary:

*A year ago it was Paris – today `No-man's land'. We are camped out
in the barbed wire in a picturesque grove of scarred stumps – devoid
of leaves and branches. `No-man's land' here fulfills all the expecta-
tions of one who has conned the illustrated magazines. It is desolation
indescribable. One cannot say the ground is merely pock-marked with
shell craters – it is nothing but holes. One steps from one into another. For miles stretch battered trenches, and the territory is thickly
strewn with `duds', unexploded grenades – solitary graves – the accu-
mulation of four years warfare. For we are on the Champagne front
between Rhiems and Verdun – directly north of Suippes.*

The American 2nd Division arrived on 1 October. The ridge held by the
Germans, the Blanc Mont Ridge, dominated the land as far as Reims to
the west and the Argonne Forest to the east, and nothing the French
had tried would remove them. General Gourard, helped by veiled sug-
gestions that the division was to be broken up and distributed amongst
his army, virtually dared Marine General John A. Lejeune to take Blanc
Mont. A complicated plan was put to him, but Lejeune countered with
a suggestion of a straightforward, head-on attack by the Marines combined with an attack on an angle by the 3rd Brigade of Infantry from
the right, by-passing the strongly-held Bois de la Vipère, Viper's Wood.
On the Marine's left was Essen Trench, another deep-dug, pillbox-pep-
pered complex, which the French were meant to secure as they came
up on that flank.

With a map laid out on the ground, the situation was described to
the platoon leaders and non-commissioned officers of the Marines.
The French failure to take these positions was stated, and that the
Marines would now do so was also stated as a fact. First the trenches,
then, by whoever was left, the ridge itself.

In the event, the Marines found the front line trench in the process
of being evacuated by the Germans as the Americans arrived in their
fire trench, and they thankfully occupied it themselves on 2 October.
Brigadier-General Wendell C. Neville's 4th Marine Brigade had the 5th
Marines on the left of the line with the 6th to their right, and beyond

them Brigadier-General Hanson E. Ely's 3rd Brigade was made up of the 9th and then the 23rd Infantry. The Marines were to attack the left flank of the Blanc Mont Ridge, while the infantry were to take the right, the centre of their start line, facing Viper Wood, being held by reserves. In front of the 3rd Brigade were the French, holding what were to be the jump-off trenches for the next day, but their 170th Division were driven out by the Germans, relieved by the French 167th, and fell back without communicating with their allies.

At dawn on 3 October, supported by artillery and forty-eight Renault light tanks, the 2nd Division began its task. The 5th Marines outflanked and took the Essen Hook, while the 6th made for the ridge through a hail of artillery and machine-gun fire. The Essen Trench was handed over to the French who lost it again the next day. Private Francis of the 5th Marines recalled, 'It was cold and we were wearing overcoats. I usually went over the top with a loaf of bread inside my blouse... I was always eating on it, not especially as I wanted it but because it took my mind off the fighting sometimes... We broke the German lines and gained our objective the first day.'

By noon the Marines were on the ridge. On the right, the infantry also made spectacular progress. By 0840 they were attacking Médéah Farm on the Mazagran road just beyond the ridge, but the French on their right and left flanks had fallen behind. As evening fell, the troops in both wings of the 2nd Division's front were holding salients, exposed on three sides to enemy fire. The next day, leaving men to cover the outside flanks, the Marines fought their way up Blanc Mont and succeeded in joining across the top of the ridge, where the monument to them now stands. Private Francis said:

> The French did not keep up with us, so that we were being fired upon from the front, each side and nearly from the rear. We were afraid that the Germans were going to close in together in the rear and cut us off from our lines. We fought desperately to keep the Germans from carrying out their plans. We were on a prairie with machine-gun bullets hitting all round. They were hitting only inches from me

on each side, and knocking dirt in my face. It seemed impossible for anyone to live through it... Later in the afternoon we took a German trench... That evening we stayed in a ravine and kept watch all night... About two o'clock in the morning someone was coming in, and we thought sure the Germans were attacking but it proved to be the French Chasseurs and they were surely welcomed.

The 2nd Division was holding a front about 500 yards (457m) wide projecting one and a half miles (2.4km) into German lines, which they held throughout 5 October, allowing the French to come up all along the line. 5 October was a long day, twenty-five hours to be exact, when the change from summer to winter time is taken into account. The next day, the men of the 2nd were again in the attack, Francis among them:

In the morning we started our drive again. We had only gone a little distance when we ran into the worst thing to face in the War – a three inch gun firing point blank at us, and just above 500 yards in front of us was a German 77 [77 millimetre gun]... It was awful, only a few yards in front men were blown to little bits, trees were knocked down; it didn't last long but it was surely terrible when it did.

By the night of 8 October, 71 Infantry Brigade, 36th Division, had come up to relieve them and was digging in at the place to which the 5th Marines had fought their way forward, St Étienne-à-Arnes, the German fourth line of resistance. Lieutenant Robert H. Sawyer was with the 36th's 132nd Machine-gun Battalion and was sent forward to establish what was going on:

As he [Colonel Brown] explained, I had arrived at a time I was badly needed. He said my company was in the line without water or food, that two officers had been killed and two wounded. He told me to go to Colonel Bloor and get him to get water to my men. I took a runner and started out for my company ammunition dump. It was then about four o'clock before I found it. There I found the first sergeant who had just returned from the line where he had carried water and food. He made a report to me and I found that no officers had been killed and only one wounded. I then took a fresh runner and started to the line which was about 1200 yards [1.1km] away. We got lost in the woods and ended up on the right flank of the American sector with the 141st Infantry instead of the left flank with the 142 where my outfit was. The Good Lord must have timed my journey, for the French started an attack on the right and machine-gun bullets were coming our way. My runner got in one shell hole and I in another. Then the big boys began to come over. Some went long and some went short but close enough to throw dirt on us and H.E, and gas enough to make us put on gas masks. Between the blinding flash and crack of the big shells there was the constant and methodical rat-tat-tat-tat of the Boche machine-guns and the thrashing machine retaliation of the French Hotchkiss. As I lay there in that shell hole waiting for the next one to hit I wondered if it was going to have my address. One of the big boys hit on my left in the woods and I heard a scream of agony – I knew that some poor devil had been hit. I could hear him groan and cry for a long time. I stayed awake as long as I could. I was about to freeze in that hole by myself. I called for my runner to come to me, and we arranged to keep just as warm as possible, one to remain awake for thirty minutes and watch for gas signs. The big shelling had just about stopped. By that means the both of us got about an hour of sleep. It was just about dawn that we crept out of our hole and started out again. We found Co.B. 132 M.G. about 200 yds from where we were and didn't know it. From them we oriented ourselves again and started out to find our outfit. We came to the spot where the fellow was hit during the night. He had one foot and leg blown off. We were now on the old battlefield, where on the morning of the 8th the 71st brigade had made a glorious page in history. The dead seemed to be in hundreds. Though I am quite sure it was my imagination, I saw some of my old comrades of border service who had made good, but had paid the great price. It brought home to me the thought of my own brother who had so willingly given his life. Never a word or a picture make one more conscious of the great truth, that this is truly our war...

My runner and I finally found our outfit the morning of the tenth. They were hungry and thirsty – I talked things over with Miller and found the situation pretty good. The Boche had retreated during the night towards the Aisne. Patrols reported [a] Machine-gun nest near an ammunition dump north of St Etienne, and the 72nd Brigade was going to leap frog us during the night. I formally took command of the Company. I wanted to send Miller back to the train to get G——— straight and get food and water up, but he thought I ought to go back as I knew where everything was. This was quite true. Our supply situation was serious, as Lt. G——– was taking no chances with his life. He had his train back between Souain and Somme-Py. Although some shells were dropping back in that area, it was entirely too far back for a ration dump. I ordered it moved forward. We had no rolling kitchen and were using the old field kits to cook with. After establishing a kitchen a hot meal was prepared and I sent G——— forward to the line in charge of the detail. The detail was caught in shell fire, but got through, excepting one man who was wounded and Lt. G———. This was the first act of cowardice I had seen. For an officer to desert a mission under shell fire is unpardonable. It was my duty to place him in arrest and prefer charges against him. But I didn't do it. The man had just married a young Ft North girl before we left and I could see that broken-hearted girl when she told him good-bye back in July. So I gave him another chance to make good. I am sorry to say that he never made good. He had lost the confidence of his men and he couldn't stand shell fire. So much for his case – it is only one of the distressing incidents that occur in the line.

This was the tenth of Oct. and I had everything setting pretty. Communication had been established with Bn Hdqrs. I left Lt. G——– with the kitchen and went forward. It was about dark when I got to the Company. The 72nd Brigade was to leap frog us during the night. As usual we again witnessed another of the successful pieces of spy work pulled off by the Boche. He knew the relief was to be made during the night and about good dark he began to put the big boys over.

About two thirds of these shells were gas. Patrol came in and report-
ed the Boche 'preparing a counter attack'. At this time we were over
half a kilometer in advance of the line. The French had not caught
up. We were in a bad way – our flanks being exposed. The Inf. Bn.
Commander decided to retire back to the main line. We retired and
consolidated. The 72nd didn't leap frog us and we held our position.

Having lost the ridge, and facing continued aggression from the
Americans and their French comrades, the Germans had fallen back.
The U.S 2nd Division had taken 4,973 casualties in this battle, 726
killed, 3,662 wounded and 585 missing, the heaviest they had ever
experienced, putting even Belleau Wood in second place. They now
needed rest, but some of them did not get it. Their 15th Field Artillery
and Second Lieutenant John D. Clark stayed with the 36th, the Lone
Star Division, all the way to the Aisne. They reached the river on 27
October, having baffled enemy tapping of their communication lines
by having the messages spoken in Choctaw.

BEYOND THE CHEMIN DES DAMES

While the French and the Americans had been driving forward into
the German lines in the east, the British had been making massive
inroads in the west. The German centre was thus compromised in the
south-western corner of their position on French soil, the Chemin des
Dames. In anticipation of being forced back further, fortification had
been started on a long defence line from the North Sea, south-west of
Ostend, and past Tournai, Le Cateau and Guise to turn east along the
northern bank of the River Aisne and across the Meuse-Argonne region
north of Verdun. These lines were named Wotan in Belgium, Hermann
in Northern France, Hunding north of Laon, Brunhild on the Aisne and
Kriemhild in the Argonne. Forward of this the Siegfried Line ran in
front of Cambrai and St Quentin, where it was breached by 28
September, and on to the Chemin des Dames.

General Mangin's Tenth Army had pushed forward from Soissons on
14 September to the western end of the ridge along which the legendary

Chemin runs, taking Allement and Luffaux Mill as well as Vailly. The Italians improved their position closer to Reims, but the Germans still held the Californie Plateau and the high ground around Caronne. This holding was supplied by the rail complex centred on Laon, itself sustained by the strategic rail link running west from Metz through Mézières and Hirson towards Lille. The Laon complex was defended from the crescent of high land south of the city on which the Chemin des Dames is built, and the French hope was to cut the Germans off here, as well as to retake Laon. The French Fifth and First armies were the pincers and Mangin's Tenth the pivot around which they would turn.

General von Böhn contrived, with great skill, to avoid being caught. The French were held off on the River Oise and at St Gobain while, on 11 October, the troops were pulled off the Chemin des Dames, with Mangin's men in pursuit both along the Soissons road and the valley of the Ardon and on the east from the Craonne heights. At the same time General Guillaumat's Fifth Army crossed the Aisne at Neufchâtel, north of Reims and rolled forward to Sissonne. North-west of that town the land falls away to the Marais St Boetien, a marshy area beyond which the Hunding Line had been constructed, and there the French were halted. On the same day, 12 October, Mangin advanced more than eleven miles (17.5km) to the very cliffs of Laon on its high bluffs.

The Germans managed a swift retreat, taking the Mayor of Laon and some 500 hostages with them but abandoning a great quantity of stores. They had not only their Hunding Line to shelter behind, but also the marshy country north-east of Laon and along the River Serre, to which Mangin pushed forward. Here the French advance, literally, bogged down. It would be to the north, on the British front, that Germany would suffer the fatal blow.

The Western Front, 1914–18

11

THE DEFEAT OF
THE GERMAN ARMY

The blows that rained down on the German forces followed one another so swiftly that the opportunity to reinforce one sector at the expense of another was denied to Ludendorff. As a result, the pressure exerted on him in Flanders, Artois and Picardy, principally by British and Empire forces, was to break the German army as a fighting force, obliging the German government to salvage what they could by means of an armistice.

THE CANADIANS ATTACK

The closing days of August saw the Canadians push forward along the road from Arras to Cambrai in what became known as the Battle of the Scarpe. The 3rd Canadian Division was north of the road with the 51st (Highland) Division, under Canadian Corps command, on its left, north of the River Scarpe. The 2nd Canadian Division was south of the road with XVII Corps of the 52nd (Lowland) Division to its right. The attack was planned for 26 August and was to start at 0300 hours, instead of the later hour of dawn, in order to surprise the enemy. The ruse was successful, and good progress was made until, as a result of action by the First and Third Armies further north, the axis of advance of the 2nd Division was turned to the south-east, across the Cojeul River. The 52nd Division had not moved forward with equal speed, so as the Canadians topped the ridge they were caught in heavy fire from the right flank and forced to dig in. On the left, the advance had been even more satisfactory and preparations were made for the renewal of the assault the next day. During the night it rained heavily, making the operations of 27 August late in starting and while the weather then improved, three days' hard fighting was needed to push the Germans back to their principal line, the Wotan position, which the Allies called the Drocourt-Quéant Switch, a system that connected with the Siegfried Line. These three days had cost the Canadians 254 officers and 5,547 men killed, wounded or missing while they had taken 3,300 prisoners, and now they faced the first of the truly substantial defence systems. The 2nd Division had been relieved by the 1st Canadian and the 3rd by the 4th British Division, under Canadian command until their own 4th Division could be transferred from the Amiens front.

Lieutenant-General Currie's purpose was to break the Switch on the Arras to Cambrai road, leaving the difficult terrain of the marshes along the Sensée River to the north alone. The first objective was the Red Line, through Dury north of the road and west of Gagnicourt to the south of it after which he intended to develop his position left and right. Six companies of Mark V tanks were allocated two each to the three attacking divisions. The artillery would give a three-lift barrage to support the attack. The Canadian Independent Force, 1st Canadian Motor Machine-Gun Brigade, 101st M. G. Battalion (less one company) and the Canadian Cyclist Battalion, under Brigadier General R. Brutinel was eventually, if possible, to thrust along the road and seize the crossings of the Canal du Nord. The improvement of the jumping-off positions required numerous small actions which were countered by German efforts to push their outer defences forward.

By 0730 hours on 2 September, the 1st Division had already taken part of the Drocourt-Quéant Switch and then moved on to take Cagnicourt and proceed to Buissy. On the right, the division's 16th Battalion had a tougher time, losing touch with the barrage and having to fight forward against heavy machine-gun defence. An American Lance-Corporal, W. H. Metcalf, guided a tank to destroy these strongpoints and the same unit's Commanding Officer, Lieutenant-Colonel W. Peck, did much the same soon after they had crossed the Switch and been stopped once more. Both men were awarded the Victoria Cross. The southern flank, the province of the British 52nd Division, was not made good until 1800 hours and the consequences for the Canadians were serious. In the centre, along the road, the ridge known as Mount

Dury was an exposed and dangerous place, and behind it a sunken road from Dury to the main road gave the Germans an excellent firing point. This was good terrain for tanks, however, and they came into their own, taking the position by mid-morning.

The next ridge stopped them. It ran at right angles across their route from Buissy to Saudemont, and the German artillery held it. Near the Roman road at Villers-les-Cagnicourt and at the factory on the Roman road itself nearby machine-gun posts were still in German hands. The armoured cars of the Independent Force tried to push through but failed. Currie's men prepared themselves for another hard battle on 3 September. It was not needed. The Germans pulled back beyond the Canal du Nord during the night.

IN FLANDERS FIELDS

To the north the Germans had abandoned the salient created by the Battle of the Lys in Operation Georgette, pulling off Mount Kemmel on 31 August. On 4 September the British were back at Ploegsteert. The Fourth Battle of Ypres opened on 28 September. The Allied Flanders Army Group consisted of twelve Belgian divisions, under King Albert and General Degoutte, in the northern sector, and ten British and six French, which stood broadly where the Allies had started in June 1917. In his diary Brigadier-General J. L. Jack, commanding 28 Brigade, wrote, 'How familiar the place-names of today were 14 months ago... The bones of most of my officers and many of the other ranks lie between here and Zonnebeke'.

The Belgians swept forward through the Houthulst Forest and on to Passchendaele on that first day. The British regained Wytschaete. The advance was four and a half miles at the least, and in some places as much as six miles. On 29 September, they leapt forward as far again, but rain, as usual, was making the going difficult, particularly in keeping the forward troops supplied. On 2 October the situation became severe; French and British troops had run out of food. Eighty aircraft were used to drop 15,000 rations to them, small sacks containing five or ten packs padded with earth to break their fall when slung out of the aeroplane. This first drop of rations to troops in the field constituted a load of thirteen tons. The ravaged countryside was clearly an obstacle to further progress, and the battle ceased on 2 October with the British just two miles short of Menin – their objective in the distant autumn of 1914. The British had lost 4,695 killed and wounded, the Belgians 4,500. Between them they had taken over 10,000 Germans prisoner, 300 guns and 600 machine-guns. In the Ypres Salient, the war was almost over.

BUILDING ATTACKING POSITIONS

Marshal Foch's massive pincer movement, attacking in the east and the west, required good footing for the jump-off and the British armies worked steadily to acquire it.

Lieutenant-Colonel Deneys Reitz was a South African. He had joined a commando at the age of seventeen to fight against the British in the war of 1899–1902, the conflict the English call the Second Boer War. He served under Jan Smuts, first on commando in Cape Colony and, second, in the suppression of the rebellion against the South African government in 1914. His service then extended to the East African campaign against the Germans before he came to Europe to fight, not for the British, as he explained, but with them against a common enemy. He was wounded in the defence of Arras on 29 March and evacuated to England. Recovered, he was ordered to France once more on 12 September and rejoined his battalion, the 1st Royal Scots Fusiliers, as second in command, at Hermies, near the Canal du Nord south-west of Cambrai, two or three days later. Some of their positions were the far side of the empty, unfinished canal and these were attacked shortly after Reitz's return. It began in the middle of the afternoon. A heavy barrage fell on a front from Moeuvres, west of Cambrai, to Havrincourt. Reitz had been at Morchies and managed to get back to the line when the barrage moved beyond him to the west, a clear signal that the infantry attack was coming in. By the time he arrived the battle was almost over with the few surviving attackers being made prisoner. The 1st Royal Scots lost ninety-nine men killed, wounded or missing that day and the British as a whole more than 6,000. It was the last aggressive act of the Germans on this front, and they had failed to shake the Allied hold on their start points for the taking of the Canal.

On 18 September, further south, General Monash was improving his position. He had had to do it without tanks, for they were few in number and needed to be conserved for larger operations. He had therefore doubled the machine-gun capability of the two attacking divisions by adding the guns of the units in reserve. The relationship of artillery barrage start line to the infantry's start line was tightly controlled so that the attackers would be safe from so-called friendly fire, while well-protected from the enemy. Finally, dummy tanks were built to scare the enemy. The attack went in at 0520 hours in rainy conditions. The barrage moved more quickly in some places than in others to allow for varying conditions and thus varying speed of the troops. It paused from time to time to permit mopping-up, the careful verification that no Germans remained active in ground taken, and the elimination of those that were. They were finished by 1000 hours. The terrain lost in March was now back in British hands and they overlooked the Hindenburg, or Siegfried, Line.

THE CANAL DU NORD

On 27 September, the day after the Germans received a mighty blow on the Champagne and Argonne fronts, the Canal du Nord was attacked. North of Cambrai, running east to west, the River Sensée and its associated canal pass through a marshy area, and artificial flooding had enhanced its usefulness as a barrier to the Allies by extending it southwards across the Arras to the Cambrai road as far as Sains-les-Marquion. Between that village and Moeuvres, further south, a 4,000-yard (3,660m) length of firm, dry ground existed and here the canal, its construction incomplete, was waterless. The eastern side was peppered with machine-gun posts and heavily protected with barbed wire, but the trenches did not appear to be particularly strong. Beyond that was the Marquion Line, a solid trench defence, and further east again the hill of Bourlon Wood overlooked the whole area. Between that and Cambrai was another line based on the Canal de l'Escaut, the Marcoing Line.

General Currie decided to use the dry area to cross the canal, take Bourlon Wood and then develop his attack north-eastwards to take the front left of Cambrai, while the British XVII Corps took the right. The range of the bombardment was too great to be provided by batteries in fixed positions and a series of artillery redeployments was worked out to permit extension of the barrage forward as the advance evolved.

It rained during the night of 26–27 September, but the day dawned dry. At 0520 hours the bombardment began with fearful efficiency. By 0945 the Canadians, supported by tanks of the 7th Tank Battalion and under the cover of a smoke screen, had crossed the canal and were in Bourlon village, advancing around the northern side of the wood. On the southern side there were problems. The British advance had been slower, leaving a Canadian flank exposed. On the left, the British 11th Division passed through the Canadians to press on to the north-east. By the end of the day the advance had taken them up to the Canal de l'Escaut defences.

Further south, 8th Brigade, 3rd Division, including Reitz's 1st Royal Scots, faced another part of the Hindenburg Line called, he says, the Whitehall and Ryder sections. He described the attack:

I speak only of our own immediate task that covered little more than three hundred yards of the German front, but all along the fourteen miles on which the offensive was to be launched similar measures were ready, whereby the leading battalions were to break into the first trench, followed by successive waves of other assaulting troops coming on behind. The battle plan was on so huge a scale that the fortunes of a single battalion should be multiplied nearly six hundred times to obtain an adequate conception of its entirety.

It was 3 a.m. by now. The men sat talking in undertones along the firestep, their bayoneted rifles in their hands, and some lay asleep on the duckboards... At 4 a.m. the enemy began to trench mortar us heavily, and a few men were wounded. Then a stillness fell over the line. A million men were facing each other on this battle front, but there was scarcely a sound, save for a rare shot loosed by some nerv-

ous sentry, and the tension became almost unendurable. As Zero hour approached, whispered orders were passed, and the men stood to, and then, punctually at 5.20, the British barrage came down upon the German line with one stupendous roar.

During the preliminary ten minutes the Fusiliers stood ready to vault the sandbags at the given word, and along the whole fourteen miles stood thousands upon thousands of other men ready to leap upon the enemy. At Zero plus ten minutes (5.30 a.m.) the barrage moved forward, and the moment had come. Bissett dropped his arm as a signal, and the men swarmed over the parapet straight for the German line.

Almost at once the German S.O.S. [defensive] barrage came down upon them, as they scrambled and stumbled over the wires and screwstakes and shell craters that obstructed every yard of the way. I have a confused memory of shells spurting and flashing, of men going down in great numbers, and almost before there was time to think, I saw the German soldiers rise from behind their breastworks to meet the attackers, and then the Scots Fusiliers were clubbing and bayoneting among them. The enemy gunners immediately drew in their fire to protect their next line of defence, and seeing that our men were on their objective, I rushed quickly across no-man's-land and dropped down into the great Hindenburg Trench. Flushed with victory, the men were rounding up prisoners and shouting down the dug-out staircases for others to come up, a process which they expedited in places by flinging Mills grenades into the shaft openings.

The trench was six feet wide by eight feet deep. Every few yards along the parapet stood a machine-gun, and there were many trench mortars and anti-tank rifles. The enemy soldiers had done their duty manfully, for on the floor of the trench their dead and wounded lay thick, and beside almost every machine-gun lay its crew, smitten down by the hurricane of the barrage.

Reitz then had a chance to look further afield and saw the evidence of the delay on the Canadians' right flank:

From here the battle situation as far as Bourlon Wood stretched clear before our eyes. I could see the British firing line half a mile away, and German infantry four hundred yards beyond. Both sides were in open country, and for the first time in four years of war they faced each other from behind such natural cover as they could turn to account, without trenches or entanglements between.

The English were slowly advancing, and on the crest of a long grassy slope were German soldiers and machine-gun crews. The British shell-fire was no longer a barrage, but it was not negligible, and the shrapnel was taking heavy toll from among the exposed enemy troops on the rise. About four miles back stood Cambrai. Through my glasses I could even see a group of German officers standing on the round tower of the brewery, and tall pillars of smoke were rising from among the houses, as though the city was being given to the flames. On the outskirts of Cambrai were black masses of German infantry in reserve, while their thinly held line was fighting a desperate rearguard action, chiefly with machine-guns.

Away to the left was the real trouble, for there the British advance was hung up before the village of Graincourt. It was being stubbornly defended, and the German garrison was inflicting heavy punishment on the British troops, whose dead lay thick before the ruins. Strong reinforcements of the Guards Brigade, however, were coming up, and I watched them attack afresh. They were well handled. The fire of several batteries was directed on the village, and the men went forward in artillery formation, until they had established a fire line, when they rose to their feet and charged. Many fell, but the attack was pushed home, and soon the men disappeared among the wrecked houses, after which the enemy machine-guns fell silent, and batches of prisoners were marched out.

THE SIEGFRIED LINE

Now it was the turn of the main Siegfried Position to receive the Allies' attentions. Here the German defences made use of the St Quentin canal which curves around the town from the east to Bellenglise. It then heads north to Riqueval to enter a tunnel under Bellicourt and Bony, before coming into the open once more at Le Catelet to make its way towards Cambrai. South of the tunnel it passes through a deep cutting and it was fortified with concrete pillboxes and barbed-wire entanglements on the banks and in the canal itself. By chance, plans of the fortifications in fine detail as they had been in 1917 were captured and were made available to General Monash on 10 September. While new works had, undoubtedly, been carried out since, at least the majority of the German positions became known. Closer to St Quentin the canal was almost waterless, but still full of mud in which a man could drown. Evidently the open country over the tunnel was the only place tanks could be of use, but here the depth of the defences was greatest and here the Allies were still well to the west, too far off to mount an attack.

Once more Monash and the Australians were given the tough assignment of breaking the German line above the tunnel, but by now they were deeply fatigued and short of men. The Australian 1st and 4th Divisions were withdrawn from the line and replaced by the fresh, though inexperienced, American 27th and 30th Divisions under General George W. Read. They, with eighty-six tanks, were to overcome the German forward positions and the Australians, with seventy-six tanks, would pass through them to smash through the main line. An attempt was made to compensate for the lack of American combat knowledge by seconding 200 Australian officers and NCOs to them, but it was a dangerously optimistic arrangement. An additional proposal was submitted to Rawlinson by Lieutenant-General Sir Walter Braithwaite for an assault further south by the 46th (North Midland) Division with the 32nd Division in support and this was added to the battle plan. Before this main assault, on 29 September, could be undertaken the jump-off point had to be secured, and the Americans were tasked with taking it.

At 0530 on 27 September, the 106th Regiment of the American 27th Division went into action. The confusion of the battle is matched by the confusion of the historians; exactly what happened is uncertain. The Americans pressed forward, and took at least the most advanced of the enemy positions. Individual acts of bravery such as Lieutenant William Bradford Turner's taking of two machine-gun posts and leading his men in the crossing of four trenches were not enough. Turner lost his life and gained the Congressional Medal of Honor. German counter-attacks regained many of the strongpoints that had been lost and by the end of the day the Americans had sustained 1,540 casualties. Monash wrote of the day:

> There remained no doubt that some enemy were still left in occupation of trenches on our side of the objective for that day, and such American troops as may have gained their objective could not therefore be reached. It appeared afterwards that small parties of Americans had reached the vicinity of their objectives and had very gallantly maintained themselves there, although surrounded on all sides, until relieved by the Australians on September 29th.

The next attack, two days later, now faced a ghastly problem. With an unknown number of their own troops out in front, should the attack have the support of a bombardment that might fall on their comrades? In purely technical terms, the American start line was not secured. It skewed back to the north-west, leaving the forward German trenches still to be overcome and the artillery were briefed in detail to lay down a bombardment from the planned start line, a thousand yards (900m) ahead of the actual one. Monash sought a postponement of the operation to re-plan the bombardment, but in the scale of the planned attacks up and down the line this was a small detail. The postponement was denied, but additional tanks were granted. On 29 September the 27th went in once more, but without a creeping barrage in front of their first objective.

In the dense fog confusion reigned again. When the Australians came up they found the Americans still valiantly fighting to take their objectives. The tanks failed to provide the answer; faced now with more flexible use of field artillery, anti-tank rifles and, a new development, land mines, more than half of them were immobilized. Private

Walter J. Strauss, 102nd Engineers, 27th Division remembered 29 September clearly:

Up at 3 a.m. Pack up. Big push started. I was detailed with my squad to go ahead of British tanks to hunt for tank mines and all we had were bayonets on our rifles to dig in the ground to try and find the mines. They were round, about 10" [25cm] with a short fuse sticking in one side, the tip of which was even with the ground level so that when the tank rolled over it, the fuse would ignite the mine, it would blow, and all 12 men in each tank would be blown and burned to death – and they all were! I will never forget some of the tank men trying to crawl out of the tanks with their clothes burning, after they had hit a mine! So barrage! 10,000 guns and machine-guns. Noise! Full pack up to Ronsoy. Men dead and wounded. Across no-man's-land. Sheltered in shell holes. Machine-gun bullet in Bible in pack as I was diving into shell hole when machine-guns opened fire on me. Refuge in trenches. Saw many dead on road and tanks in action. Returned to St. Emilie at night to deep dug-outs with British Red Cross men.

Other parts of Strauss's recollections suggest that this experience was all within the area that the 27th had been unable to secure two days before.

The American 30th Division was in action also, and was equally mauled. As noon approached the attack seemed stalled, and Monash himself went forward to appraise the situation. It was clear that no quick breakthrough could be achieved and he made the decision to abandon the carefully crafted plans he had made; they were now irrelevant. The first task was to secure what had been taken and then, over the next few days, work to regain the initiative. By the afternoon the Australians pushing forward found themselves accompanied by Americans unwilling to give up and rejoin their own units, so they went on together, but still had not reached their final objectives when darkness fell. Private Willard M. Newton, 105th Engineers, 30th Division, wrote:

Soon we are moving again, going further this time than we did before. When halted again the lieutenant signals `take cover' — in other words, find a shell-hole and get in it, and lose no time in doing so. One man out of each shell-hole must look up every few moments and see if the lieutenant is signalling. The corporal of the squad I am in is in a shell-hole with others of us and to him falls this pleasant duty of watching the lieutenant.

Shortly after we have found a shell-hole, a score or more machine-gun bullets whizz over us. We hug the bottom of the hole. Rifle bullets also find their way over our hole at intervals. Getting in a cramped position, I take a chance and look up a few seconds. The infantry we were following has also taken cover and hardly a soul can be seen. Ahead of us the doughboys are struggling with the Huns.

Looking up again, I see a few yards ahead of us four German prisoners bringing back a wounded man on a stretcher, who also is a German. An Aussie, belonging to the medical corps, stops and motions them to set the wounded man down. He then makes the four prisoners take off their blouses and lay them on the wounded. This leaves the backs of the four almost bare, having only sleeveless undershirts to protect them from the chilly weather. The Aussie points to the rear and away they go with their less able comrade, happy of the opportunity to get off of the battlefield and out of danger.

Something happens that causes us all to take special notice of. (We are in a small shell-hole a few feet from the Aussie and need not run any risk of being hit by machine-gun or rifle bullets in order to see him.) An American sergeant, with one of his arms shot off above the elbow and wounded in the face, walks up to the Australian and asks for a drink of water and a cigarette. `Sure, Yank,' says the Aussie, and in a few moments the American is drinking from the Aussie's canteen. Getting a cigarette lit, the sergeant starts for a dressing station, thanking the Australian for his kindness. While we are still in this shell-hole the Huns begin sending over high shrapnel... thus making it pretty `windy' for us fellows in the hole.

In thirty minutes we are moving forward again. We pass the first and second platoons, who are busy filling newly made shell-holes and moving destroyed wagons and other wrecked vehicles so the artillery could pass on. Scores of dead Americans, Australians and Germans can be seen lying here and there, some covered with rain-coats and overcoats and others lying just as they fell. Walking wounded are going back in twos and threes, while those unable to walk are being carried off of the field as rapidly as possible under the circumstances. Men with arms shot off, with slight shrapnel wounds and gassed victims are being helped to the rear by German prisoners and by other men similarly wounded." The 30th Division took 1,881 casualties, and by the time the battle waned three days later the Australians had suffered 1,500.

The German ability to mount counter-attacks on the stalled advance was limited by what was happening further south, in the attack added at the last minute as a diversionary exercise. The attempt to break the Hindenburg Line at Bony and Bellicourt had failed perhaps, but on 29 September that was not the only attack in progress. Formidable though the obstacle might be, extensive plans had been made to master the St Quentin canal.

The Royal Engineers devised a series of gadgets. Mud mats of canvas and reeds were to provide footing over the mire, ladders would be available to scale the steep canal banks and collapsible boats would ferry troops across. The cross-Channel steamers were plundered of their life-belts. Experiment showed that a fully-armed man could rely on a life-belt to keep him afloat and that the boats could be unfolded and on the water in twenty seconds. This was not only prudent and practical but excellent for morale.

As the Americans launched themselves against the line to the north, the 1st/6th South Staffordshires rose behind a creeping barrage from the positions secured by the 138th Brigade two days earlier. In the fog, and organized into small groups, they worked their way up to the enemy positions then rushed in with the bayonet. The west bank was soon in their hands and they waded across to overwhelm the allegedly impregnable positions opposite. By 0830 Bellenglise was in their hands. On their left the 1st/5th South Staffords made use of the boats to cross the waterway, also exploiting the advantage of the poor visibility.

Close to the southern end of the tunnel the Riqueval bridge crosses over the canal opposite the junction with the Le Cateau road to give the local farmers access to the fields on the western bank. It was, of course, in a state of readiness to be blown up in case of attack. In the fog of the morning of 29 September, Captain A H Charlton had to navigate by compass to find the bridge at all. As his company of the 1st/6th North Staffords emerged from the mist they came under fire from a machine-gun sited in a trench on the western side. A bayonet charge put an end to that. Alerted by the firing, the demolition party of four men appeared from the German bunker beyond the bridge and ran to blow the charges fixed to the structure. Charlton and his men beat them to it, killing all four and cutting the wires to the explosives. The rest of the company dashed over the bridge and cleared the trenches and bunkers to secure passage for the Brigade.

The supporting troops moved up and through the successful assault force to continue the advance. To the rear the fog persisted, causing confusion amongst units attempting to move up and great difficulties for those wounded seeking the dressing stations behind the line. The tanks became targets as the fog dispersed in front, but the progress continued and great columns of prisoners started their journeys to the cages. By the time, early in the afternoon, that the commanders could see clearly they were rewarded with the most heartening sight of this long war, a genuine breakthrough.

The 46th Division took 4,200 prisoners that day, eighty per cent of the total to fall into Allied hands on this front. They had done this at the cost of fewer than 800 casualties. But most remarkable of all, against the strongest defensive system the Germans had been able to construct, they had advanced nearly three and a half miles.

In the days following the momentum was maintained. The 49th Division and the Australian 2nd Division took Ramicourt and Montbrehain, to the right of the Le Cateau road, to complete the conquest of the Siegfried Position and by 5 October the entire Hindenburg Line had been broken. The capture of Montbrehain was the last action in which the Australians took part, for the exhausted corps was relieved and sent to the rear for a deserved rest. The war was to be over before they were ready for further service. Ahead lay green fields and unblemished countryside, and an enemy now doomed to defeat.

On 28 September Ludendorff told Hindenburg that it was necessary to seek an armistice with the Allies. Not only had the Germans suffered defeat on the St Quentin to Cambrai front, but their allies, the Bulgarians and the Turks, were abandoning the fight. The next day at a crown council held at Spa, Kaiser William, Von Hintze, the Foreign Minister, and the two military leaders decided to approach President Woodrow Wilson of the USA to initiate negotiations. The German government was reorganized, with the moderate Prince Max of Baden at the head of a parliament. For the next six weeks, the life expectancy of thousands of men would depend on the balance between warfare and diplomacy.

In the Fourth Army there were, to General Rawlinson's eyes, subversive hopes of peace. He issued an order on 7 October in which he said that the enemy was trying to:

divert the attention of officers and men from their single task of defeating the enemy. All ranks are warned against the disturbing influence of dangerous peace talk.

The Field-Marshal Commanding-in-Chief wishes it to be understood clearly that at no time has there been a greater need of relentless effort... and orders the Army to concentrate its entire energy on bringing the operations in the field to a successful and decisive issue...

BREAKTHROUGH IN THE ARGONNE

The American advance in the Argonne sector had been slow. The German resistance was determined and the terrain was on the defenders' side. On the hills and in the woods on the west, the Americans clawed forward while, down in the Aire valley on their right, the men of the 1st Division were overlooked. The raw, inexperienced soldiers of springtime were much changed. Private Donald D. Kyler, 16th Infantry, 1st Division, described his mental attitude:

I was seventeen and one half years old. It was over one year since I had first entered combat. During that time I had seen many men, my friends, my acquaintances, and others, maimed and killed. At no time, either at the front or behind the lines, was I ever away from the sound of battle. Sometimes it was faint and far away, but always there. At first, I had been very much afraid. Then gradually, insensitiveness to danger, so far as fear was concerned, came. I realized danger with my mind, and could take measures to counteract it, but the emotions, life or death, were sort of blocked out. It seemed to me then as though the dead were luckier than I was. I could see no end to the war, and did not expect to survive it. It did not seem probable at the time.

I was tired physically and mentally. I had seen mercy killings, both of our hopelessly wounded, and those of the enemy. I had seen the murder of prisoners of war, singly and as many as several at one time. I had seen men rob the dead of money and valuables, and had seen men cut off the fingers of corpses to get rings. Those things I had seen, but they did not effect me much. I was too numb. To me, corpses were nothing but carrion. I had the determination to go on performing as I had been trained to do – to be a good soldier.

The 1st Division were, in the first week of October, fighting their way forward to take the Kriemhild Line, the last of the great defence fortifications. The Germans resisted strongly but not always wisely. Kyler continues:

Early in the morning, our scouts observed enemy troops in and around Fléville and beyond getting ready for what looked like a frontal attack on our position. They probably intended to overrun us and advance down the river valley and attack the troops then making a river crossing. Their intent was tactically sound. They were desperately trying to delay or halt our offensive by whatever means. Hence, their decision to make a frontal attack without artillery support. But their execution of it was at fault in several respects.

They would have been a perfect target for our artillery. But our artillery was busy elsewhere, and were helping the 82nd Division make their attack across the river, and our other regiments in their effort to take the difficult ground on our right. Realizing that our group could not deliver effective fire from the sheltered position just above the ravine, Captain Wildish decided to man the rifle pits to the front, but abandon the ravine and put the rest of the men echeloned along both flanks rearward. In that way, in case the enemy made a frontal attack, our men would be less bunched up and would be able to deliver enfilading fire on them as they advanced. Corporal Sanders was told to pick the best marksmen and post them in the rifle pits up the bank. He proceeded to do so and included me in the group. I do not know exactly what the captain told him, but in general we were to hold off the enemy as long as possible.

We expected a mortar and machine-gun barrage, but it did not occur. Instead, they began advancing straight toward us from their positions around Fléville. Perhaps they had no mortars or machineguns available, or perhaps they thought us so weak that resistance would be minimal. They soon found out differently, however. We had a perfect field of fire, with good dug in positions in our individual rifle pits. We had narrow slots cut in the bank from which to fire. We had no rifle grenades, but did have hundreds of rounds of rifle cartridges at each pit. The enemy left their shelters in small groups and advanced on a broad front, from beyond Fléville almost to the high ground to our right front. We did not fire until they were at about 400 yards [365m] range. Then we began firing with carefully aimed deliberate shots. At that range, most of us were able to hit a man with every shot. The first volley threw the enemy into confusion. They deployed, hit the ground, and began an ineffective fire in our direction. *They kept advancing by crawling a short way and then firing again. I was approximately in the center of our line. I could see enemy soldiers, who by their actions evidently were leaders, and I directed my fire on them when they were opposite my place in line. We fired steadily, but not hastily. The enemy kept coming, several hundred of them at least. As they got closer I directed my fire on those who had worked their way nearest to us. We did not want them to get within grenade throwing range. Also, we thought that they might charge us.*

I do not understand why they did not. That would have been their best way of taking our position. If they had done so, we could not have fired fast enough to hold them. They had no mortar or artillery support. Among them, they did have several of their light machine-guns, which I would class as about half way between an automatic rifle and a machine-gun. Their fire was not accurate. Their bullets kept hitting the bank in front of us and many going overhead. We presented only a few square inches of exposure. By contrast, our fire was deadly. We were able to drop them almost as fast as they moved forward. As they got closer, we increased our rate of fire. My rifle got so hot that I could barely hold it. As the range lessened, we did not need to take so careful aim, and we pumped bullets as fast as we could. And then their line stopped. The survivors fell back. Some carried or dragged wounded with them. Others just fled. We continued firing.

All over that open ground to the front of us there were wounded and dying men. Some slowly tried to move out of our field of fire. Many did not move at all. When we could see no more movement we ceased firing. Several of our men had been hit. Others had retreated when they thought the enemy were getting too close. Five of us remained firing to the last. I was nearly exhausted. My right hand was bleeding from having raked against rocks in working the rifle bolt; my right shoulder was bruised from having absorbed the recoil of my rifle so many times, my left hand was burned, my right eye, cheek and chin were bruised by being bumped by my rifle in firing. I stayed in the rifle pit a little while. Soon men came up to relieve us, and our company reoccupied the position.

*That night, when we were trying to rest in our holes, we kept hear-
ing wounded Germans to the front of our position crying out in their
misery. A young soldier from Montana, whom I had known for almost
a year, sprang up and said that he would make them shut up. He
took his bayonet and silently crept forward between our outposts. In
a little while the cries ceased and he came back. Our attitude was
that they were better off than we were. Their misery was over.*

For all their bravery and determination, the Americans still failed to
get through. On 16 October Major-General Hunter Liggett took over
command of the American First Army in the Argonne while Major
General Robert L. Bullard became commander of the American Second
Army, newly formed, and tasked to operate in Lorraine. Two days earlier another great effort had started and the 32nd and 42nd Divisions
at last, after three days of heavy conflict, achieved the breakthrough.
The price had been high. The 42nd Division alone had taken 2,895
casualties in the operation. Liggett paused to regroup, resupply and
prepare for a final onslaught.

THE ADVANCE TO BELGIUM

While the British thrust round the south, the Canadians pushed forward north of Cambrai on 8 October, forcing the Germans to abandon
the city which they left in flames. Deneys Reitz, who had temporarily
been placed in command of 7th King's Shropshire Light Infantry on 27
September, did not take part in the action, for the battalion had suffered
thirty-two killed, four died of wounds, four gassed, twelve missing and
123 wounded by 7 October. They, and both of the Royal Scots Fusilier
battalions, were relieved and Reitz was restored to his original unit,
now in command as a result of the death from wounds of his colonel.

With the taking of Cambrai the Canadians were given a chance to
rest. They were relieved by XXII Corps. In the period from 22 August
to 11 October they had casualties totalling 1,544 officers and 29,262
men and had taken 18,585 prisoners, 371 guns and close on 2,000
machine-guns.

To the east, General Rawlinson's Fourth Army was coming up the Roman road from the St Quentin canal at Riqueval to Le Cateau, site of the 1914 battle. The morning of 9 October was once again a foggy one. At Maretz, the British 66th Division came under machine-gun fire from the village of Clary, north of the road, and the woods, the Bois de Gattigny, between the road and the distant village. The 3rd Cavalry Division under Major General A. E. W. Harman moved forward to deal with the trouble. The 6th Cavalry Brigade was placed on the right of the Roman road and the Canadian Brigade on the left. At 0930 hours they advanced, and the Germans opened up again. Lord Strathcona's Horse charged and silenced the fire from Clary before wheeling right around the woodland. The Fort Garry Horse, with a battery of the Royal Canadian Horse Artillery, tackled the wood and, supported by the infantry of the South African Brigade, cleared it by 1100 hours.

On the right the 6th Brigade were unable to make progress, so the Canadians were asked to conduct two further flanking movements on the left to keep the progress north-eastwards in being. The Royal Canadian Dragoons cut off the village of Reumont which the Fort Garrys were then able to take and by nightfall the Lord Strathcona's Horse and the Dragoons had crossed the Le Cateau to Cambrai road, completing an advance of eight miles (13km) in the day to a point north of the old battlefield. With the penetration beyond the trench lines, mobile warfare was once more a possibility and the cavalry again a force to be reckoned with.

Deneys Reitz had enjoyed his leave, once the grief over the death of his former commanding officer had dulled. He visited the towns of Albert and Doullens in search of familiar places, but found them in ruins. Now he was back in the advance. In the approach to Le Quesnoy, through which walled town the Germans were said to be preparing a new line of resistance, they were charged with the capture of the towns of Vertain and Escarmain on 23 October. They went forward through Solesmes to make a reconnaissance:

We rode through the streets, with dead German soldiers still lying where they had fallen, and then up the road to the shrine this side of Pigeon Blanc Farm, where we left our horses and proceeded on foot. The Germans were briskly shelling all this area, and in the porchway of the farmhouse lay a number of British dead, who had been killed in the forward rifle pits. We hurried on to a rise beyond Pigeon Blanc, from where we could see the villages of Vertain and Romeries, two thousand yards away, with Escarmain lying further back. The Germans were in possession of these villages, and they had numerous machine-guns and rifle posts in the open country. As the shell-fire was heavy, and the air humming with bullets from the German rifle pits, we made a quick examination of the ground lying before us, and inspected the sunken road in which we were to assemble our companies during the night.

At 0230 Reitz assembled his men in the dark. Almost immediately a gas shell fell amongst C Company, killing a lieutenant.

At 3.30 the British barrage came down. It was not the solid wall of flame of the old days, but it was heavy enough, and the Royal Scots went off behind it. In the dark we could see the figures of the advancing men outlined against the barrage with the light playing upon their bayonets. German machine-guns and rifles were spitting away, but they went on until they were swallowed up in the dark. As we were to follow fifteen hundred yards behind, we watched until we could no longer distinguish them, then when I judged that they would be nearing Vertain, I started my men off.

We advanced in open order across the level plain, passing many Royal Scots lying dead or wounded. They had caught the brunt of the enemy fire, which already was slackening down, and we lost only four men killed, and five or six wounded, even though shells dropped freely among us. It was getting light by now, and we could see the dim shadow of Vertain before us. The Royal Scots were not in sight, but as the small-arms fire had ceased, I knew that they had entered the village.

To our immediate right, at Romeries, heavy fighting was in progress, and further south too the battle was thundering away. We now came to a small stream, the Georges, through which we waded knee deep, and beyond that we were among the houses and gardens of Vertain.

Almost immediately, heavy shelling came pounding down. Reitz recognized the tactic; once a village had been abandoned the Germans smashed it with shellfire. He got his men out of there and sheltered behind a field embankment, coughing and weeping because of the gas. There they waited for the next British barrage, for they had yet to undertake their task, the capture of Escarmain:

At 8.30 the men were in the assembly line, ready for zero hour. It is always a trying time waiting for the final moment, but I had no fear of the outcome. From what I had seen of German army orders and newspapers, and of their infantry of late, I knew that their spirits were low, and that we were not so much fighting an army as hustling demoralised men.

At 8.40 to the second, the barrage came roaring down. A British 6-inch howitzer shell dropped between our front and rear waves, and killed three men, and all the way to Escarmain this infernal gun dropped shorts among us, causing eight or nine further casualties. The rest of the barrage worked smoothly, and we followed behind it at a walk. The German infantry in the rifle pits opened fire on us, but they they were rattled by the shells, and their firing was wild, whilst their batteries were too thin to do much damage. The moment the barrage reached their rifle pits the infantry crouched down while it swept over them, and as soon as they saw the curtain of bursting shells move on beyond, they came running towards us, hands in air, and our role was practically confined to following in the wake of the barrage and receiving the prisoners in batches as they came to meet us. Including the losses caused by the 6-inch howitzer, we had under fifty men hit in crossing from Vertain to Escarmain, and we took over two hundred prisoners on the way.

And now we reached and entered the village, the elated men rushing down the streets, and fetching out more prisoners from houses and cellars. They speedily cleaned up the place of such Germans as were still lurking about, and we then waded the stream that runs through Escarmain and climbed the slope beyond to the Chapelle de la Rosaire, from which we had an extensive view across another open plain sloping down towards the Ecaillon, a small river two miles away. German infantry were streaming back, and we sped their passage with rifle-fire. Many gun teams too were galloping in the distance, and it was clear that the enemy was retiring on a wide front. Our instructions were to reach the red line on the battle map, and no further, so we made no attempt to pursue, and I had the satisfaction of sending a runner back to Brigade with a note to say that the 1st R.S.F. [Royal Scots Fusiliers] had reached its objective according to orders.

The New Zealanders came up on Reitz's right, and the 2nd Royal Scots and the 7th Shropshires were on his left as they took position facing the Le Quesnoy-Valenciennes railway. Here, at Ruesnes, they held their ground for some days as intelligence reports suggested the forces facing them were abundant. From the medieval walls of Le Quesnoy the Germans kept up intermittent rifle fire.

On 28 October Reitz was included in the circulation of a captured German document. It was an exhortation from Ludendorff to his troops to stand firm. 'Still stands it in your power to stave off disaster. Hold but for a few weeks more and a peace such as you desire we shall wring from the enemy... Stand, or the Fatherland is doomed, and you with her.' Reitz's battalion was relieved the next day with only a couple of hundred of men left fit to fight. The New Zealanders took Le Quesnoy in true medieval style, using scaling ladders.

The advance continued. On 26 October the 51st (Highland) Division had advanced to Famars, south of Valenciennes, but came under fire from the high ground of Mount Houy to the north-west. They fought on to take the hill, but could not do so, in part because counter-battery fire was inhibited by the fear of killing civilians still in Valenciennes. The industrial area of Marly was thought to be full of Germans, and was shelled accordingly. Careful plans were made and with the involvement of the 4th Canadian Division the hill was stormed on 1 November. With the fall of Valenciennes, the Hermann Line was turned and the way to Mons was clear.

FORWARD IN FLANDERS

The American 91st Division was switched from the Meuse-Argonne campaign to Belgium in October 1918 to serve, as did the US 37th Division, under the command of the King of the Belgians. The Americans were attached to the French Army of Belgium under Major General de Boissoudy in the centre of the line, with the Belgian Army on the left and the British Second Army on the right. Their task was made clear in the field order of 30 October: 'The French Army of Belgium will attack the enemy and drive him east of the Scheldt River.'

For the attack of 31 October, the 91st was given the objective of the wood known as Spitaals Bosschen from a front between Waereghem and Steenbrugge, west of Audenarde (Oudenaarde). The 182nd Brigade of the 91st (363rd and 364th Infantry Regiments and 348th Machine-gun Battalion) was assigned the northern sector and the 181st (361st and 362nd Infantry and 347th Machine-gun) the southern, while a battalion of 364th Infantry and two machine-gun companies were detached to mop up the wood. A significant problem was that civilians were still in the area, farmers and their families sheltering in their cellars from the fighting.

At 0530 on 31 October, the attack began. The infantry tackling the northern side of the wood, 363rd, made quite good progress against determined resistance, and had gained some 3,000 yards (2,750m) in three hours, but shelling from Anseghem (Anzegem) slowed the 362nd on the south considerably. The mopping up force set out as ordered at 0650 but, instead of gathering prisoners amongst positions already gained, found itself in front-line fighting. It was only at great cost that, by the end of the day, the wood was taken, but as the Germans still held Anseghem it was necessary to pull back on the right and consolidate for the night. The Germans, however, had been outflanked to their south by the British, so the French 41st Division might, it was hoped, be able to overcome them next day. In the meantime the 361st Infantry was switched to the northern side of the wood to take part in the continuing advance.

At 0630 on 1 November, the attack resumed, but the 361st did not get to the start line until 0800 and had to race to make contact with their comrades. By 1000 they had caught up and swept forward, with only artillery fire from east of the river to delay them. By evening it was learnt that the three bridges in Audenarde had been blown up and the ruins had partially blocked the waterway, flooding the western side. The outskirts of the city had been reached by 361st Infantry and one of the canals had been crossed, but the prospects for a further advance were not clear.

That night, an officer from Utah, Captain John H. Leavell of the 316th Engineers, took a party of four men forward to see what conditions were. He confirmed that the bridges had indeed been destroyed, and reported the locations of machine-gun posts covering them. Leavell tried again before morning to see if there was a way to make use of the wreckage in fashioning some kind of crossing, but ran into a group of Germans leaving a cellar near the Cathedral, Sint Walburgakerk. Five of the Germans were killed in the subsequent fire-fight and a Belgian helping them escape from the city was captured. Leavell was awarded the D.S.C. and the Croix de Guerre for these feats.

Downstream, between Eyne and Heurne, the American 37th Division found they could get over on fallen trees and makeshift footbridges and they established a foothold on the eastern bank on 2 November. By daylight the next morning, the 364th Infantry, which had been waiting impatiently to get clearance to enter the 37th Division's sector, arrived on the bank of the Scheldt and was ready to begin bridging operations soon after dark. To their surprise, they were withdrawn, and remained in reserve for six days. Orders came to renew the assault, attacking on the evening of 10 November, but as they moved up on 9 November, intelligence came that the Germans were pulling back from the Scheldt. The timing was brought forward, and at 0630 on 10 November over they went, both here and in Audenarde itself, where improvised bridges had been completed on the remains of the peacetime crossings. The Americans prepared themselves for what they anticipated would be the toughest phase of the action, the attack of 11 November.

ON THE MEUSE

On 1 November General Liggett resumed his advance in the Argonne. The incomplete Freya Line was still to be overcome, and against it he sent the veteran 2nd Division and the less experienced but equally eager 89th. The attack had been prepared with a care that now matched that of their allies, and by the end of the day the 2nd had taken Bayonville, the 89th held Barricourt, and both were moving beyond the fixed defence lines into open country.

On 7 November rumour swept the lines – an armistice had been signed! It proved false, but it was not a frivolous invention, for the Germans had cabled to Marshal Foch the names of their envoys to armistice talks to obtain safe passage for them. The meeting took place on the 8th, and though the German representatives were shaken by the Allied terms they had no alternative but to accept. Meanwhile the war went on.

On the Meuse, the 89th Division were now on the hills overlooking Pouilly and seeking a way across the river. Due to the difficulties the 89th had had in bringing up their artillery at the same brisk pace at which their infantry advanced, the Germans had managed to get most of their equipment back over the river. They had also taken or destroyed all the boats and raft-making materials. The bridges at Pouilly, hopping across the islands of firm ground in the marshy flood plain, appeared to be intact, and were so reported. In this report, however, Captain Arthur Y. Wear, 3rd Battalion, 356th Infantry, was mistaken, for the last arch of the bridge closest to the town was badly damaged and the bridge over the canal was gone. They had to find a way across the river.

Accounts of what followed vary. Sergeant Forderhase tells it this way:

> *Captain Arthur Y. Wear was now in command of the battalion. He*
> *had orders to get men across the river. He now called for men to vol-*
> *unteer to swim across the river and attempt to get information as to*
> *the strength and disposition of the German troops. The stream was*
> *near bankful... the water was cold and deep. Only about half of those*
> *who volunteered were selected. Of these, only a few succeeded in get-*
> *ting across. About half were killed by the enemy or drowned in the*
> *cold water. Only about half of those who got back were able to give*
> *information of any value. The Battalion moved to the top of the hill*
> *to wait for daylight... When the surviving swimmers returned and*
> *informed Captain Wear of what had been accomplished, he walked*
> *a short distance into the dark and somber woods and shot himself in*
> *the head with his service pistol.*

On 10 November the engineers produced the answer to the river-cross-
ing problem. They had managed to bring up pontoons and float them
in a little tributary to the Meuse. That night the 356th Infantry were
ferried over. Cautiously, Forderhase's squad advanced through the fog:

> *Captain Ernsberger did not see the two young Germans, with their*
> *light machine-gun, until he was close up to them. They were standing*
> *in a shallow pit they had dug, with their hands held high in surrender.*
> *I could not see the incident, but the Captain called me to come. I was*
> *quite surprised to see them. The Captain knew I could speak a bit of*
> *German and told me to ask them why they had not fired on us. They*
> *informed me that all fighting was to end at eleven o'clock that morn-*
> *ing and they saw no reason to sacrifice their lives, or ours, needlessly.*
> *Neither the Captain, nor I, knew whether to believe them or not.*

Far to the left of the 89th, outside Sedan, a chaotic situation had just
been resolved. Shortly after noon on 6 November General Summerall,
commanding V Corps, had arrived at 1st Division headquarters and

handed Brigadier General Frank Parker a message purporting to be from General Liggett, the First Army commander. It was addressed to the commanding generals, I and V Corps and stated that General Pershing 'desires the honour of entering Sedan should fall to the First American Army'. It went on to say that the C-in-C was confident that I Corps, assisted by V Corps on their right, would enable him to realize this desire, and concluded with the words, 'Boundaries will not be considered binding.' It was a formula for confusion. The 1st Division was then set in motion to turn left and head for Sedan, seven miles from its own sector, passing through the I Corps area, across the fronts of the 77th and 42nd Divisions. Parker sent liaison officers to I Corps HQ (arriving 2100 hours) and to the 6th Division (arriving 1830) which has been said was to the 1st Division's immediate left. Other sources put the 77th there. Five columns moved off between 1900 and 2000 hours to make a night march on, perforce, the roads.

THE ARMISTICE

At 0510 hours on 11 November the Germans signed the terms for an armistice to come into force at 1100 hours that same day. The British Fourth Army sent a message to the headquarters of the 2nd American Corps at 0735 hours:

> *Hostilities will cease at 1100 hours today November 11. Troops will stand fast on line reached at that hour which will be reported by wire to adv. Army Hdqrs. as soon as possible. Defensive precautions will be maintained. There will be no intercourse of any description with the enemy until receipt of instructions from Army Hdqrs. Further instructions follow.*

On 10 November, at about 2300 hours, the Canadians had begun their quiet entry into Mons. The 5th Lancers, who had fought here in the famous battle of 1914, took St Denis. The 2nd Division circled south of St Denis and pushed north-east to Havré and cleared the Bois du Rapois. One of the 2nd's battalions, the 28th North West, went beyond

Havré to Ville-sur-Haine. There, at 1058 hours, a Canadian soldier was talking to excited villagers outside 71 rue de Mons when a shot rang out. Private George L. Price fell dead.

The Scots Fusiliers, Reitz reported, remained comparatively unmoved by the news of the armistice. 'A few cheers were raised, and there was a solemn handshaking and slapping of backs, but otherwise they received the great event with calm.'

The telegram informing the parents of Second Lieutenant Wilfred Owen of their son's death in the Battle of the Sambre on 4 November was delivered to their home that morning. The air was full of the sounds of church bells welcoming the end of the war.

A year or so later General Monash recorded his views on the ending of the war:

It must never be forgotten that whatever claims may be made to the contrary, Germany's surrender was precipitated by reason of her military defeat in the field. Her submarine campaign, disappointing to her expectations as it had been, was still a potent weapon. Her fleet was yet intact. Our blockade was grievous, but she did in fact survive it, even though it continued in force for a full eight months after her surrender. The defection of Bulgaria and the collapse of Turkey might conceivably be a source of increased military strength, even if one of political weakness. Had she been able to hold us at bay in France and Belgium for but another month or six weeks, she could have been assured of a respite of three months of winter in which to organize a levy en masse. Who can say that the stress of another winter and the prospect of another year of war might not have destroyed the Entente combination against her? On these grounds I believe that the real and immediate reason for the precipitate surrender of Germany on October 5th [sic], 1918, was the defeat of her Army in the field.

FURTHER READING

For the human aspect of war Malcolm Brown's *Imperial War Museum Book of 1918* is rewarding, and the strategic aspect is well covered by John Terraine's *To Win a War*. The most coherent overall history is, in my view, David Trask's *The AEF and Coalition Warmaking* which, while obviously addressing itself to the American involvement, offers a clarity of narrative rarely found. The final days of the war are fascinatingly described in Stanley Weintraub's *A Stillness Heard Around the World* and both German and French views of events and plans can be obtained from Martin Kitchen's *The German Offensives of 1918*.

SOURCES

In addition to the sources listed below, material has been quoted from unpublished papers held in the World War I Survey archives at the United States Army Military History Institute, Carlisle, PA for access to which the author is deeply grateful. Certain first-hand accounts have been requoted from the works of Malcolm Brown, Paul Greenwood, Lyn Macdonald, Sir John Monash, Laurence Stallings and John Terraine. The unpublished memoirs of Dr Maurice Burton have been made available by Robert Burton whose kindness is acknowledged with equal gratitude. Mr Jan Deneys Reitz has been generous in permitting quotation from his father's work.

BIBLIOGRAPHY

American Battle Monuments Commission, *American Armies and Battlefields in Europe*, Washington, DC, US Government Printing Office, 1938; Center of Military History 1992.

Banks, Arthur, *A Military Atlas of the First World War*, London, Heinemann Educational Books, 1975; Leo Cooper, 1989.

Brown, Malcolm, *The Imperial War Museum Book of 1918, the Year of Victory*, London, Sidgwick & Jackson, 1998; Pan Books, 1999.

Coombs, Rose E. B., *Before Endeavours Fade*, London, Battle of Britain Prints International, 1994.

Goddard, Calvin H., *Relations between AEF Forces and British Expeditionary Forces 1917–1920*, unpublished paper, 1942, US Army Military History Institute, Carlisle, PA.

Goddard, Calvin H., *Franco-American Relations*, unpublished paper, 1942, US Army Military History Institute, Carlisle, PA.

Gray, Randal, with Argyll, Christopher, *Chronicle of the First World War*, 2 vols, Facts on File, New York, Oxford and Sydney, 1990.

Gray, Randal, *Kaiserschlacht 1918*, London, Osprey, 1991.

Greenwood, Paul, *The Second Battle of the Marne*, Shrewsbury, Airlife, 1998.

Griffith, Paddy, *Battle Tactics of the Western Front: The British Army's Art of Attack 1916–18*, New Haven & London, Yale University Press, 1994.

Griffiths, William R., *The Great War*, West Point Military History Series, Wayne, NJ, Avery, 1986.

Hammerton, J. A., *A Popular History of the Great War, Volume 5: The Year of Victory*, London, The Fleetway House, 1934.

Henry, Mark, 'A Place Just Built for Calamities', *Osprey Military Journal*, Vol. 1, Issue 1.

Johnson, Douglas V., II, and Rolfe L. Hillman, Jr, *Soissons 1918*, College Station, Texas A&M University Press, 1999.

Keegan, John, *The First World War*, London, Hutchinson, 1998.

Kitchen, Martin, *The German Offensives of 1918*, Stroud, Tempus, 2001.

Linnenkohl, Hans, *Vom Einzelschuss zur Feuerwalze*, Bonn, Bernard & Graefe, 1996.

Livesey, Anthony, *The Viking Atlas of World War I*, London and New York, Viking, 1994.

Macdonald, Lyn, *To the Last Man, Spring 1918*, London, Viking, 1998.

Marix Evans, Martin (ed.), *American Voices of World War I – Primary Source Documents*, London and Chicago, Fitzroy Dearborn, 2001.

Marix Evans, Martin, *The Battles of the Somme*, London, Weidenfeld & Nicolson, 1996.

Marix Evans, Martin, 'Oudenaarde Revisited', *Battlefields Review*, Issue 17, Barnsley, 2002.

Marix Evans, Martin, *Passchendaele and the Battles of Ypres*, London, Osprey, 1997.

Marix Evans, Martin, *Retreat Hell! We Just Got Here! The AEF in France, 1917–1918*, Oxford, Osprey, 1998.

Middlebrook, Martin, *The Kaiser's Battle*, London, Allen Lane, 1978 and Penguin 1983.

Monash, John, *The Australian Victories in France in 1918*, London, Angus

& Robertson, 1936 and London and Nashville, Imperial War Museum and Battery Press, 1993.

Nicholson, G. W. L., *Canadian Expeditionary Force 1914–1918*, Ottawa, Queen's Printer, 1962.

Pershing, John J., *My Experiences in the World War*, New York, Frederick A. Stokes, and London, Hodder & Stoughton, 1931.

Reitz, Deneys, *Trekking On*, London, Faber, 1933; Prescott, Arizona, Wolfe Publishing, 1994.

Reports from Mounted Infantry in South Africa, 1899–1900: Machine Guns, 57 Cape 8122, National Army Museum, London, 7805-26.

Schmidt, Capt., *The Battle in the Intermediate Zone*, Supplement to *Summary of Information* No. 140, GHQAEF, 1918.

Sheffield, Gary, *Forgotten Victory. The First World War: Myths and Realities*, London, Headline, 2001.

Spaulding, Oliver L., and Wright, John W., *The Second Division American Expeditionary Force in France 1917–1919*, New York, Hillman Press, 1937.

Stallings, Laurence, The Doughboys: *The Story of the AEF 1917–1918*, New York, Harper & Row, 1963.

Terraine, John, *The Smoke and the Fire, Myths and Anti-Myths of War 1861–1945*, London, Sidgwick & Jackson, 1980.

Terraine, John, *To Win a War. 1918, The Year of Victory*, London, Sidgwick & Jackson, 1978.

Trask, David F., *The AEF and Coalition Warmaking 1917–1918*, University Press of Kansas, Lawrence KS, 1993.

Weintraub, Stanley, *A Stillness Heard Around the World. The End of the Great War, November 1918*, New York, E. P. Dutton and London, Allen & Unwin, 1985.

Zabecki, David T., 'Colonel Georg Bruchmüller and the Birth of Modern Artillery Tactics' in *Stand To!*, No.53, September 1998.

INDEX OF ARMIES, BATTLES & COMMANDERS

ARMIES: ALLIED

AMERICAN

American Expeditionary
Force (AEF) *passim*
First Army 21, 112, 172,
176–7, 180, 185, 187, 196,
198, 224, 232
Second Army 224, 236
I Corps 187, 189, 234
II Corps 130, 235
III Corps 189
V Corps 189, 234
Tank Corps 181, 184, 189
US Marine Corps 98–9, 100,
101, 104–5, 137, 180, 185,
199, 200

BRITISH &
COMMONWEALTH

British Expeditionary Force
(BEF) *passim*
First Army 45, 172, 206
Second Army 230
Third Army 35, 39, 43–4,
52–6, 172, 206
Fourth Army 156, 158, 173,
220, 224, 234
Fifth Army 38–9, 43–52, 56,
59, 128
Reserve Army (see Fifth
Army)
Cavalry Corps 44
Machine-gun Corps 32
Royal Flying Corps 49, 57
Royal Air Force 78, 134
Tank Corps 79, 131, 164
III Corps 43, 49, 50–2, 156,
159, 160, 168
IV Corps 43, 45, 55
V Corps 43, 53, 56, 233
VI Corps 43, 45
VII Corps 43, 45, 46, 53–5,
59
IX Corps 88
XVII Corps 43, 207, 212
XVIII Corps 43–4, 47, 50, 52,
54–8
XIX Corps 43, 47, 52, 54–6,
59, 60, 61
XXII Corps 119, 145, 225
Australian and New Zealand
Army Corps (ANZAC) 45
Australian Corps 129, 130,
156
New Zealand Cycle Corps

146
Canadian Corps 156, 171,
207

FRENCH

First Army 156, 205
Third Army 51, 106
Fourth Army 114,118, 196,
198
Fifth Army 76, 91, 112, 115,
145, 202
Sixth Army 88, 115
Tenth Army 76, 88, 109, 136,
204–5
Detachement d'Armee du
Nord (DAN) 79
II Cavalry Corps 56, 80
I Colonial Corps 112
II Colonial Corps 236
V Corps 56
XX Corps 144
XVI Corps 178
XXI Corps 99

ARMIES: GERMAN

First Army 88–9, 114
Second Army 18, 39, 53, 60,
135, 156, 160, 194
Third Army 51, 112
Fourth Army 72, 74
Fifth Army 51, 194
Sixth Army 72
Seventh Army 89, 106, 114
Seventeenth Army 19, 39,
45, 53
Eighteenth Army 107, 156
Alpine Corps 80
Bavarian II Corps 79
VII Corps 89
VIII Corps 112
XI Corps 61–2
XVIII Corps 80
XXXIX Corps 55
LIV Corps 89
LXV Corps 89
IV Reserve Corps 89, 90, 112
VII Reserve Corps 89
X Reserve Corps 80
XXIII Reserve Corps 53
XXV Reserve Corps 89

BATTLES

Aisne, Second Battle of 83,
87, 88–92
Amiens 154–170

Cambrai, First Battle of
(1917) 18–19, 26, 38, 43
Cambrai, Second Battle of
204, 211–213
Caporetto 14, 57
Belleau Wood 99–105, 112,
202
Flesquieres 38, 51, 53
Hamel 61, 128, 135, 139, 158
Kaiserschlacht 19, 44, 81,
129, 155
Langemarck 37
Lys 63, 73–5, 80, 89, 209
Matz, the 108–110
Menin Road, the 74
Messines 29, 75
Passchendaele, *see* Third
Battle of Ypres
St Mihiel Salient, 175,
178–186
Verdun 11, 18, 106
Villers-Bretonneux 61–3
Ypres, First Battle of 79
Third Battle of 12, 29, 37, 74,
Fourth Battle of 209
Scarpe, the 207, 174
Somme, the 36, 51, 131

COMMANDERS: ALLIED

AMERICAN

Baker, Newton D., US
Secretary of War 21, 112
Bliss, Gen. Tasker 57, 112,
172
Dickman, Maj-Gen. Joseph T.
92, 115
Liggett, Lt-Gen. Hunter 187,
189, 225, 232, 234–5
MacArthur, Brig-Gen.
Douglas 184, 186
Marshall, Col. George C. 180
Patton, Lt-Col. George S. 181,
184, 189, 190
Pershing, Gen. John J. 21, 58,
81–2, 92, 111, 112, 133
Wilson, Woodrow, US
President 221

BRITISH &
COMMONWEALTH

Bell, Maj-Gen. George 172
Birdwood, Gen. Sir William
130
Butler, Gen. Sir Richard 43,
49, 50–2, 54

Byng, Gen. The Hon. Sir Julian 34–5, 39, 43–4, 51–5, 59, 172–3
Cameron, Lt-Gen. George H. 189
Campbell, Maj-Gen. D.G.M. 46
Churchill, Winston S. 63
Congreve, Lt-Gen. Sir Walter 43, 46, 55, 59, 60
Crozier, Brig-Gen. F.P. 74
Currie, Lt-Gen. Arthur 157, 208–9, 212
Fanshawe, Lt-Gen E.A. 43
Fergusson, Lt-Gen. Sir Charles 43
Gough, Lt-Gen. Sir Hubert 38–9, 43, 45, 47, 51–60
Haldane, Lt-Gen. Sir Aylmer 43
Jackson, Maj-Gen. Henry 88
Maxse, Lt-Gen. Sir Ivor 43, 47, 50–58
Milner, Lord, British Minister of War 56–7
Monash, Lt-Gen. John 129–134, 156–9, 162, 165, 169, 170–2, 211, 215–17, 237
Plumer, Gen. Sir Herbert 54, 75, 78, 80
Rawlinson, Gen. Sir Henry 60, 131, 133, 156, 172–3, 215, 221, 226
Salmond, Maj-Gen. Sir John 57
Watts, Lt-Gen. Sir Herbert 43, 47, 52, 54, 56, 60, 61

Wilson, Gen. Sir Henry 56–7
FRENCH
Berthelot, Gen. Henri 115, 119, 145
Clemenceau, Prime Minister Georges 57, 196
Degoutte, Gen. Jean 99, 115, 119, 209
Duchêne, Gen. Denis 88, 89
Fayolle, Gen. Marie 54, 56, 60, 108–9
Foch, Gen. Ferdinand 38, 57–60, 63, 76, 81, 91, 108–12, 114, 119, 136, 156, 172–5, 196, 210, 232
Gouraud, Gen. Henri 115, 119, 120, 196, 199
Humbert, Gen. Georges 51–2, 56, 60, 108
Maistre, Gen. Paul 76
Mangin, Gen. Charles 109, 114, 119, 136, 138, 143, 145, 204–5
Micheler, Gen. Joseph 76
Nivelle, Gen. Robert 87, 109
Pellè, Gen. 56
Pètain, Gen. Henri 21, 38, 52, 54
Poincarè, President Raymond 57
Robillot, Gen. 56, 80

COMMANDERS: GERMAN
Arnim, Gen. Sixt von 72
Below, Gen. Otto von 19, 39
Below, Gen. Fritz von 89, 114
Böhn, Gen. Hans von 89, 114, 205

Brauchitsch, Gen. von 60
Conta, Gen. 89
Eben, Gen. von 109
Einem, Gen. Karl von 115
François, Gen. Hermann von 89, 91
Guderian, Gen. Heinz 37
Hindenburg, Field Marshal Paul von 19, 155, 221
Hutier, Gen. Oskar von 19, 39, 49, 50–54, 107–8, 156
Kuhl, Gen. Hermann von 18
Larich, Gen. 89
Ludendorff, Gen. Erich von 15–21, 45, 51, 53, 61, 63, 68, 71–2, 81, 87–9, 92, 105, 107, 110, 125, 152, 155, 170, 173–4, 185,
Marwitz, Gen. Georg von der 19, 39, 156
Quast, Gen. Ferdinand von 72
Rupprecht, Crown Prince, 18, 79
Schmettow, Gen. 89, 91–2
Stäbs, Gen. von 55
Wetzell, Col. Georg 19, 72, 87
Wichura, Gen. 89, 91
Winkler, Gen. 89, 91